Roland Allen

The Ministry of the Spirit
Selected Writings

with an introductory essay by
Lamin Sanneh

with a memoir by
Alexander McLeish

edited by
David M. Paton

The Lutterworth Press

The Lutterworth Press
P.O. Box 60
Cambridge
CB1 2NT

www.lutterworth.com
publishing@lutterworth.com

This edition 2006

ISBN (10): 0 7188 9173 2
ISBN (13): 978 0 7188 9173 2

British Library Cataloguing in Publication Data
A catalogue record is available from the British Library

Copyright © The Lutterworth Press, 1960, 2006

Introductory Essay

BY LAMIN SANNEH

The writings of Roland Allen (1868-1947), an English missionary who served in China from 1895 under the auspices of the Society for the Propagation of the Gospel (SPG), suffer from a fault that would be the envy of most writers: they are a casualty of their own farsighted brilliance. In a deeply ironic way Allen was the unruly child of a post-Christian West and the thwarted voice of a post-Western Christianity. His career in China effectively cut short, he served briefly as a parish priest; but (for reasons he gives in Chapter 7 of this book) he resigned, and spent the rest of his working life writing about the Church and its mission. In the 1930s he retired to East Africa, where his son and daughter were working. He died in Kenya in June, 1947.

Allen wrote fluently on missionary methods and principles as well as on the philosophy of cross-cultural mission. He offered critical reflections on the role of civilization and the enlightenment in Christianity in general, and in missions in particular. Without realizing it, Allen had set out to delineate the course of post-Western Christianity at a time when the church and his contemporaries thought almost exclusively in Christendom terms. That he did so with such undeviating consistency and unflagging commitment is testimony to his unique talents and Christian gifts. He was a voice crying in the wilderness, a prophet without honour in his own country. And yet the future which he shaped by his ideas, one to which he by right belonged for having so keenly discerned it and so eloquently given it expression arrived too late to claim him and to be claimed by him. It should not be that way if the church is the one unbroken continuous stream of witnesses that the apostles bequeathed. It was to the church that Allen looked for the work of the Holy Spirit, and at its door that he laid his rare gifts of indomitable faith and toughness of mind. Or, then again, perhaps it should, for nothing can separate the faithful in the love of Christ.

When he criticized the nature of Europe's engagement with the Gospel Allen meant no dishonour to his country or to the Western heritage whose greatness he never minimized or misrepresented. He was restless about the glaring gap he saw between the church's stated objectives and the conflicting means used to reach those objectives. He was all too aware, and deeply troubled, too, by the easy assumption that mission and colonial rule were ordained co-partners in a joint enterprise, and he turned that restlessness into a searching critique of that association. For him mission was the work of the spirit, not just in the flaky sense of bustling excitement and uncontrolled enthusiasm but in the sense of openness to the mind of Christ and to the witness of the apostles, especially to that of Paul. Europe's chronological ascendancy in the expansion of Christianity held little weight for Allen because for him New Testament eschatology was not beholden to such rules of historical preference.

That root theological conviction enabled Allen to transcend his own cultural limitations and, equally momentously, enabled him to see a natural bridge between New Testament Christianity and the missionary enterprise in China and elsewhere beyond the West. The fundamental basis of human identity for Allen was not cultural but theological. Human beings are first and last subjects of God's redemptive work in Christ, and their cultural state carries no prior moral entitlement or disqualification.

It was that radical religious anthropology that made Allen uneasy with what he called the cultural righteousness of the West. It was a righteousness that was in scandalous breach of apostolic faith and practice but also in political conflict with the rights of access to the Gospel of non-Western populations. Allen said the situation was eerily evocative of the Gentile controversy in the early church. He said it was extraordinary that the Gentile breakthrough should be reconstructed by Western missions to say that just as the Gentiles were broken off bits of the synagogue, so should Third World churches be seen as broken off bits of Christian Europe. It was that deliberate distortion of the New Testament that led missions to fixate on giving a European rather than a Christian justification for their work. When Europeans went abroad as missionaries they thought of themselves in the first place as going to people they regarded as heathen. The question for missionaries was how they should relate to the heathen social order, and that cultural question took precedence over any religious or theological questions.

Missionaries, for instance, decided that it was impossible for them to dwell among the people and to share their life. It would have seemed like sharing the sinful life of unredeemed heathen even if it was physically feasible to do so. Europeans could not be nomads, wandering teachers, passing from village to village, pausing here a while, and there a while, to instruct any who cared to listen to them. Instead, missionaries settled permanently, acquired land, built houses, and established mission stations somewhat removed from the people. To these quarantined stations missionaries brought their wives and established their families.

Conversion to Christianity was conceived in similar terms. To educate and to civilize local people meant to inculcate in them the taste for European cultural habits and the skill to make European style houses and other artifacts. Technical ability and the accompanying economic affluence would lead to the proliferation of modern houses, which in turn would lead to the multiplication of Christian families wishing to live in those houses. The existence of the house was far more important than anything that happened in the native village. Before any converts arrived, the house was there. The success of Christian mission would thereby be assured, and easy to measure and count. One could plan for it on the basis of precise, rational projections.

Converts or Clients?

This concentration on missionary life as the model Christian life required converts to be dislodged from their cultural system and to be cast on the goodwill of missionaries. Converts suffered a double jeopardy. They were uprooted from their culture only to be cast adrift on the fringes of the missionary community as adopted clients. Suddenly and unexpectedly, converts found themselves bogged down in an untenable contradiction, for the very qualifications missionaries established for them undermined their credibility in society.

Utterly deaf to local voices, missionaries persisted with the old certitudes by assembling an experimental community by artificial selection. The brightest and fittest students would rise to the top in mission schools, to be creamed off for recruitment into various branches of missionary service. The cycle would be self-generating and self-sustaining, except that it would not be self-supporting or self-reliant.

Evidence of Western obstruction and local resistance could be had from examples of converts who were rejected, driven from their homes or villages, and otherwise stigmatized. Cut adrift in the cross-currents of an assertive European political order and a rising local reaction, converts became marginal. Persons cannot live without some social order, and converts were stripped of their roots in their own society. They once had a home. Now, thanks to Christianity, they had none. Their communities disgorged them, and missionaries received them with tongue firmly in cheek. Christianity dispossessed them of their natural ties without giving them a real stake in missionary culture. The new civilization centered on the mission compound had no root, and when converts flocked to these compounds they were as driftwood. The missionaries taught them standards of cleanliness and hygiene, imbued them with polite manners and mild sentiments, and put them in European clothes, but instead of feeling honored and appreciated they felt violated and mocked. After all, that was not their culture, and they could ill afford to claim it on any other ground. European civilization became the religion's trap, and their's, too. In China, for example, an idea took root and quickly spread that to become a Christian involved submission to foreign domination. That belief had a powerful effect in deterring people from approaching the missionary or from receiving missionary teaching with open minds. (Allen, *Missionary Methods*, 1912, 78.)

In time an earthquake rocked Christianity's cultural foundations when predictably the nationalist reaction arose and threatened to overwhelm it. The prohibitions and impositions of Christendom only pinned down the religion sufficiently to allow local reaction to assail it with unrelenting accuracy. Local converts turned upon their foreign teachers: "It is you who hold us down: it is your insistence upon your Western creeds which has crippled our thought: it is you who will not put us into positions of authority: it is you who will not trust us with the money which you have taught us is necessary for any religious expansion." (*Ministry of the Spirit*, 180.)

Allen said missionaries believed that they were training their converts for freedom and found they had only exasperated them, and driven them into revolt. The true domination of the foreign missionaries was not so much a lust to keep power in their own hands as an incapacity to see that to nurse converts in the beginning, and to act as their patrons, was to become lords over them, and that to stifle their first unrecognized, unspoken instinct for self-expression was to make certain first of sterility and then of sterile revolt. If Christianity survived that shock it would be by reason of a post-Western cultural euthanasia, by virtue of a radical redrawing of the boundary. Allen had shown why.

Cultural Osmosis

Allen asked the question about what might be wrong with the picture missionaries created of their work, and he suggested that it was the Western cultural captivity of the Gospel. Missionaries assumed that it was their responsibility to set and maintain the Christian standard of morality when in fact that was not their business or in their power. Insofar as the moral life had its seat in the unfettered conscience of the person, missionaries could not go there to maintain it. All they could do was to enforce external law, such as colonial administrators enforced, but that was not the remit of missions. When missionaries assumed the role of enforcer, they defeated the very purpose of their announced vocation. They became like the Judaizers in the early church, the people against whom Paul railed for being obstacles to the church's mission! Mission as European cultural righteousness contradicted the Gospel as God's irrevocable gift to all people. Apostolic faithfulness, not to say anything of the gospel's vernacular genius, demanded repudiation of mission as the transmission of Western civilization.

Allen drew briefly on the Islamic comparison to describe where and how Western missions went wrong. Islam, he said, had a fixed, established code of morals and ethics. Muslims operated by a deliberate external code. Yet Muslims admitted converts before they had learnt the code or had even advanced in their understanding of it. Muslims did so in the conviction that in time converts would acquire the habits and knowledge requisite to correct belief and to canonical practice. Once converts had attained to such a standard, they acquired a permanent status within Islam, Allen argued. Christianity, he urged, could not behave like Islam and expect to retain its moral authority. Only disaster lay on that path. Yet, ironically, mission seemed set on that path, which made Christianity appear like Islam but without the intrinsic advantage Islam enjoyed as *Dár al-Islám*, as worldly domain. Earthly dominion succeeded in projecting Islam's power and ideals, as was the case in Moghul India, but it ruined the church's reputation, as was the case in New Spain. The Kingdom of God in Christianity could not share a common fence with the Kingdom of Mammon without cross-contamination in which God became the covenant of national glory, and Mammon the norm of cultural righteousness. What tempted missions into invoking the wraith of Islam, Allen warned, could not be the spirit of the Christ of apostolic teaching. Missions had to all intents and purposes slipped from that apostolic benchmark, Allen charged. It was safe to assume that those converts who, upon entering the church, received a new moral law by virtue of external imposition would sooner or later recognize no moral necessity for it or take personal responsibility for it. Missionaries could not ask converts to place their social relations on the chopping block in exchange for Christianity as a mere token in their idiom and expect lasting results. It would be like letting missions stew in their own juice.

The Failure of Success

Allen noted that the civilization mandate saddled missions with a distracting message and a crushing burden. The distraction was by way of split of priorities as missionaries spoke variously of the gospel of enlightenment, the gospel of healing, the social gospel, and the gospel of sex equality. Missions stretched their resources to cover medical, educational, and social work as forms of preaching the Gospel. Social uplift became the goal and nature of the gospel itself. The work of Christ was interpreted as lifting people out of poverty and backwardness. Accordingly, "missionary work was preparing for the day when races and tribes and peoples instructed in Christian ethics, strengthened by Christian science, enriched by Christian sociology, would recognize the source of all this blessing, and would be able to worship and serve Christ duly as Christians ought to do." (Allen, *Spontaneous Expansion,* 1927, 110.) Yet, insisted Allen, Paul deliberately rejected any means of propagating the faith that might distract people in any way from the truth that the Christian faith was founded not in a human philosophy but in the power of God. Salvation was not by cultural osmosis.

The crushing burden on missions was because of the shifting social contours they riveted on their high calling. Large institutions, guilds, clubs, halls and structures were created and staffed with an army of expensive recruits. Heavy machinery was purchased, transported, and maintained at great cost by skilled expatriate specialists who were parachuted into remote areas which had scarcely the means to inherit or to perpetuate such top-heavy elaborate infrastructure. Missions were consumed in the creation of offices and departments, with directors, clerks, accountants, divided and sub-divided. Organization was an end in itself by overshadowing the end for which it existed. Samuel Butler painted a disturbing picture of the power of machines over people when he showed people destroying their machines because they were afraid that they might become their slaves, tending and feeding them for their lives. "May not man himself become a sort of parasite upon the machines; an affectionate, machine-tickling aphid? The servant glides by imperceptible approaches into a master; and we have come to such a pass that, even now, man must suffer terribly on ceasing to benefit the machines." (Cited in Allen, *Spontaneous Expansion,* 1927, 134-135.)

Missionaries' love of organization led them to repose complete trust in organization and to expect spiritual results from it. The effectiveness and continuity of missionary work depended on the strength and continuity of organization. Organization was the vehicle for globalizing Christian mission, and missionaries looked to it to produce ends it was ill-designed for. The organization network created its own momentum and rationale. The large output of tracts and leaflets designed for missionary intercession, with their emphasis on appeals for gifts of money, might lead an unsuspecting observer to conclude that the authors of these leaflets and tracts had discovered, not the power of intercession, but a silver mine. Technical gear for fund-raising was mounted to facilitate appeals for money, and that became a cause in its own right. It fostered an environment of unhealthy competition. English missionary bishops, for example, urged the Church of England not to allow itself to be outmatched in funds and numbers by American Presbyterians and Wesleyans. The day would come when the West would continue to hold the purse strings of the church but when Christianity would cease to be the monopoly of the West. Allen foresaw that time to be one of no small strife. That is part of the culture clash that has now erupted between a post-Christian West and a post-Western Christianity. Can the wealth of the churches in the West purchase the agreement or acquiescence of Third World Christian leaders in the West's radical social agenda?

Bequeathing the heavy baggage of a professional institutional missionary organization into local hands seemed an impossible and a foolhardy proposition. In the meantime, the machinery of mission appeared as a formidable obstacle to conversion on the ground. It was the first and last barrier local people must cross to make it into the church. Yet the fact that many crossed it without seeing the need at the same time of joining the church stripped civilization of its religious mystique and challenged converts to drop the Christian requirement, in other words to rebel. Civilization just kept compounding the problem of missions, which explains Roland Allen's impassioned and urgent plea for separating the two.

Allen attacked the deleterious consequences of Western materialism and its drag on missionary impetus. With words he placed in the mouth of an imaginary Muslim interlocutor, he articulated those sentiments, of which a paraphrase might be as follows. The Muslim muses to himself about Christian missionaries who pour out their money and who establish all this extravagant machinery. In spite of it all they make only a few converts. Their work will do Muslims more good than harm. They know not the power of a true religion. Whilst the missionaries labor at these material things, Muslims advance by their own spiritual power. Missionaries organize and build, they toil and sweat to convert by material methods; Islam grows with much less toil and sweat. With all their money and their talents missionaries purchase a few converts only, and then they must begin all over again in the same costly way to make a few more. One convert to Islam is the sure first fruits of a great harvest. Islam advances automatically. God works without material aid by outsiders (Allen, *Spontaneous Expansion,* 1927, 142). Allen's picture, it has to be observed, was created for effect. The picture might succeed in rallying the troops to whom it was directed, but it scarcely reflects the complex character of the mission of Islam. Allen took a certain editorial liberty with his account, justifiably, perhaps, in light of the object he had in view.

The material question was not whether separating civilization and Christianity should be undertaken, but whether an alternative boundary was at all conceivable for Christianity in its post-Western phase. Was Christianity conceivable without Western civilization or without globalization, which is the same thing? The cumulative weight of practice and the distractions of the call to social action were against the idea. Post-Western Christianity in numerous subtle and obvious ways carries the purebred genes of its European origins. Yet the cost of persisting with mission on that basis was too high to be sustainable in the long-term. The impasse shows the inevitable fate of missions as Western civilization, and it suggests that however well endowed, missions could not be salvaged in their foreign character but only in their vernacular roots as locally-led churches. Allen hinted at that shift as a question of methods, and thus failed to lift it up as a matter fundamentally of vernacular appropriation. But it seems the only way to slip the civilizational trap he identified and to establish local priority for Christianity.

Technically, Allen was correct in his diagnosis of the problem. Missions subordinated Christ to the social preconditions they set for the Gospel, conditions that favored stationary centers built under European direction. Those conditions became the preoccupation of missions; they crowded out the gospel. The logic of requiring intellectual, moral, and social advance before faith in Christ, Allen confessed, assumed that intellectual enlightenment and moral and social advance were based on a foundation other than trust in Christ. When missionaries assumed that enlightenment and improvement would issue in acceptance of faith in Christ, they made it reasonable to conclude that faith in Christ was not the foundation but the coping stone of social and moral progress. They put the cart before the horse. Other well-intentioned people had also made that strategic mistake.

The procedure was flawed from the start. Enlightened and socially advanced local groups could and did cling to their newly acquired cultural status without feeling the least need or inclination to pay any regard to Christianity except to demand that cultural advantage should be firmly disentangled from the need to profess the Christian faith. Of a piece with that is the fact that enlightened and socially advanced ideas could be and were used to deleterious ends, which left Christians having to fight, or at the least to disown, the very thing their own agency created. Nothing demonstrated the futility of Christian teaching better than the indifference or hostility of the class of cultured despisers it raised. The fact that missionaries were blind to that shows how complete was their own cultural captivity. Complacency is a more deadly foe of the gospel than persecution.

Allen recalled that Roman slaves who lived in social conditions deeply repugnant to what the West called the Christian life still converted to Christianity before any ameliorative social remedies were available to them. The Christian life embraced slaves and concubines without bashfulness or reservation while they were slaves and concubines because the Christian life did not make social disadvantage a disqualification of membership. While the Gospel acted to dissolve social stigma and to empower the cause of equality and justice, the offer of salvation was not made conditional on that. The tail did not wag the dog there.

Redrawing the Boundary

Roland Allen asked for critical honesty from his missionary colleagues. When they spoke of 'Christian civilization,' they had in mind frankly the civilization of Christian England, Western civilization. Allen objected that this was not Christian civilization. To a life devoid of Christian faith missionaries more willingly gave the name of Christian than to a life devoted to Christ and inspired by Christ under conditions the missionaries regarded as uncivilized. Allen protested the notion of the church as cultural establishment, declaring: "Ignorant men speak as if

Christ and His Church had nothing to offer which is not the natural inheritance of every Englishman, nor any right to lay down rules and conditions on which those gifts may be obtained; because they see every man, whatever his belief or his character, admitted without question to the highest privileges which the Church can bestow." (*Ministry of the Spirit*, 194.)

It was mistaken to believe that it was possible to introduce Christian social conditions apart from the Christian faith, Allen pointed out. Educational work, medical work, agricultural work, and social work have been called Christian work only because Christians happened to do them. But they are work that non-Christians have done too, and often with distinction. Not to see that was to be blinded by the force of the ideological gospel. Allen quoted a writer from Japan who noted that Japan had to all intents and purposes adopted the accoutrements of modern civilization without any sign that it paid, or needed to pay, any heed to Christianity. Japan did not confound civilization with Christianity, it was clear, and so why did missionaries?

When he turned from missionaries to local populations, Allen expressed serious doubts about the value of the work of civilization missionaries put their hands to. Organization, for example, looked very different from the ground. The erection of buildings, the management of property, and the maintenance of a vast corps of professional preachers, were all made necessary by missions' civilizational mandate, but were absurd in frontier cultures. You did not want an elaborate system of structures and institutions to propagate faith and values. You needed faith and values. Monetary rewards subverted the religious motive. Naturally, missionaries seemed like cultural mercenaries. The stationary mission station as the model structure for establishing Christianity in foreign lands was misconceived. It was the diocesan structure transferred root and branch to conditions unlike anything in Europe. In a nominally Christian society, such as Europe, synods, church councils, committees, schools, halls, and bureaucratic organization were what you needed to shepherd a flock largely anonymous and largely occasional in its religious habits. In the mission field that was historically non-Christian, totally different needs had to be addressed by totally different ideas and practices. Missionaries seemed unequipped for that task.

Such a verdict points firmly to the need for a fresh, radical overhaul of Christianity's characteristic missionary enterprise, and in a 1912 work, *Missionary Methods*, Allen devoted some general thoughts to that issue. The missionary he had in mind did not go out to persuade others that the religion in which they were brought up was a bad one and that the missionary's religion was to be preferred. The question, he said, was not one of cultural innocence, namely, that Eastern nations had religions appropriate to their cultural needs just as the West had a religion equally appropriate for it. Some people objected to mission because they felt non-Western societies were too far behind on the scale of civilization to be able to comprehend Christianity's sophisticated system of ethics and theology. It was wrong to force Christianity on such people before they were ready for it. In any case, the simple religions of non-Western populations were far more effective for their equally simple needs, and missionaries should not interfere with what God had seen fit to leave in place. Allen rejected that understanding of Christian mission, calling on Paul for support.

Unusual for his time and among his missionary colleagues, Roland Allen was unflinching in his criticism of what he saw as wrong with mission and with the Western cultural captivity of Christianity. Repeatedly he made the point that undertaking mission in colonized societies should be carefully dissociated from colonial ideas of power and the superiority of Western civilization. Allen was writing in an era of high nationalist agitation when notions of Europe's unquestioned mastery over all spheres of life, including missionary societies, was under attack. Allen was, accordingly, unrelenting in his attack on the folly and hazard of Christian missions promoting civilization. He remained a man of his time in speaking almost by reflex of indigenous people as heathen and primitive, but he roiled the complacency of those who felt entitled to rule the heathen and primitive world unchecked and unquestioned. Even though he was a child of his culture, historical circumstances compelled Allen to undertake a searching critique of the European order and its shortcomings in a world of rising and shifting expectations. His thought moved very much in the currents of Christianity's local promise, though it was a later generation of people who grasped fully the challenge of context for Christian life and thought.

It happened that Roland Allen never had the opportunity to create a plan to carry out his well thought-out ideas and deep convictions in any mission field. He developed his ideas and opinions specifically with China in mind, though the model of mission he put up for emulation was that of the Apostle Paul. And Paul's model of mission, Allen argued, "was not peculiarly St. Paul's. The method in its broad outlines was followed by his disciples, and they were not all men of exceptional genius. [The method] is indeed universal, and outside the Christian Church has been followed by reformers, religious, political, social, in every age and under most diverse conditions." (Allen, *Missionary Methods*, 1912, 5.)

Yet we may point to something else possibly as being more crucial in Paul's missionary approach than the fact that reformers of every stripe copied it, and that was Paul's uncompromising insistence that embracing the Gentiles as full and unqualified members of the fellowship was the *sine qua non* of the church's mission. The church could not be the church without equal access for those previously considered to be ritually impure. It does not require any special exegesis to appreciate how Paul staked his reputation, and even his life, on that. An important implication for missionary practice of the kind Allen criticized is whether the requirements of civilization conflicted with that Pauline standard, at the heart of which is the weighty matter of the completeness of salvation for Gentiles without permanent Mosaic vetting or oversight.

Allen said the Gentile boundary had been a formidable one for the early Christians to breach, but breach it they did. The Mosaic code seemed an insuperable obstacle. Jesus appeared in the world within the Mosaic system and upheld its impeccable authority. He appointed his apostles within the terms of the covenant. Though in one rare case he commended a Gentile for his faith, saying he had "not found so great a faith, no, not in Israel" (Luke 7: 9), he appointed no Gentile to preach the gospel to Gentiles. The thought of preaching Christ without the law was inconceivable. How could the disciples of Jesus, then, go outside the covenant, outside the Mosaic system, and admit or recognize as servants of Christ those who were not within the covenant? The answer was that the witness of the Holy Spirit to the redemptive work of Jesus made that move necessary and inescapable. To deny that or to undo it was a blatant contravention of practice and principle.

The covenant was accordingly expanded to make room for Gentiles who "desired communion with the apostles. The apostles acknowledged that they had the Spirit. Being led themselves by the Spirit, they put aside all the countless and crushing objections which could be raised, they put aside all the serious disabilities under which these new converts laboured, they recognized the fact and accepted the consequence. God gave the Holy Spirit; they admitted at once that nothing more was needed for salvation, nothing else was needful for communion." (*Ministry of the Spirit*, 57.)

That is the fact that the enforcers of civilization evaded or defied but which Allen demanded they heeded. "For thirty years he pleaded that the Church (overseas) be placed on its own feet, that is, for an indigenous Christianity. This, he held, could not be imposed from outside[,] for an indigenous Church is not simply a Church that is master in its own house, but a Church that had the gift of the Holy Spirit and knew what this gift meant for its own life." (*Ministry of the Spirit*, xvi.)

For more than just personal reasons, I am most delighted that this book is being reprinted, a judicious collection of some of Roland Allen's seminal writings, and that the public will thereby once again be introduced to his ideas. The book is as sparkling today as when it was first published nearly half a century ago. It is in fact hard to believe that Allen first broached these ideas nearly a hundred years ago, for they are so resonant with contemporary meaning. Allen's argument of cultural righteousness as an unacceptable barrier to the Gospel is vindicated by the current post-Western Christian resurgence.

LAMIN SANNEH,
*Professor of World Christianity and of History,
Yale University, New Haven, CT*

Editorial Foreword

TO THE FIRST (1960) EDITION

The present selection from the writings of Roland Allen is designed as a companion volume to *Missionary Methods: St Paul's or Ours?* (first published 1912) and *The Spontaneous Expansion of the Church and the Causes which Hinder it* (first published 1927), both published by the World Dominion Press. It contains full or abbreviated texts of those of his other writings which, after careful study and discussion, seemed likely to be most useful. They have all been long out of print, and most of them are now unobtainable even to persistent advertisers. Some editing has been necessary; but we have distinguished carefully between our work and Allen's. We have also followed modern usage in the matter of capitalization, and occasionally broken up an overlong sentence.

Roland Allen is perhaps now at last coming into his own, and is indeed acquiring an interested public of astonishing ecumenical width. We have tried to include in this volume those parts of his work which on the one hand will, when taken together with the other two books still in print, afford the student access to all his teaching, and also enable Allen himself to make his contribution to the solution of some of our contemporary dilemmas. We hope that the book (which it has been both pleasant and interesting to put together) will prove to be of value not only to those concerned with the mission of the church in Africa and Asia but also to those in older churches. Since Roland Allen was in danger of becoming an almost legendary figure, we have printed a memoir kindly written by Alexander McLeish with some help from others; the discerning reader will notice in it the unity of theory and experience. We have also provided as complete a bibliography as we have been able to assemble.

Our thanks are due to the many friends who have helped by advice and suggestion, recollection and research; and in particular to the Reverend Alexander McLeish and other members of the Survey Application Trust; to Mr John Allen, the son of Roland Allen; to the Society for the Propagation of the Gospel, and to the Reverend Dewi Morgan, its Editorial Secretary, and Miss Carolyn Merron, its Archivist.

The name of Sir Kenneth Grubb might very properly have appeared above my own; I have been able to rely gratefully upon his experience and judgement at every stage of the work; but neither he nor the others named should be held responsible for any errors that remain.

DAVID M. PATON

Biographical Memoir

I first met Roland Allen in 1921 when on my third furlough from India. On that occasion I had been asked to stay over in London for talks with Sydney Clark and Thomas Cochrane. I found Roland Allen daily present and he joined in our conversations. He was helping Sydney Clark in the writing of several pamphlets of which he was a severe yet helpful critic. These men formed a unique group and had very different backgrounds. Sydney Clark had been a successful businessman and was a Congregationalist. He was the founder of the Survey Application Trust. Dr Cochrane had been a missionary of the London Missionary Society in Mongolia and was a Presbyterian. For a time he was a secretary of the of the London Missionary Society. Roland Allen was an Anglican and had been a missionary for the Society for the Propagation of the Gospel (SPG) in China. All were united in the conviction that a revolution was overdue in missionary work, not only in methods and principles but also in the objective itself. The was no doubt as to the bond which united such different men, who formed a good cross-section of the churches in the United Kingdom. As a group they were in advance of their time; they have had to wait for recognition generally until the Ecumenical Movement had taught us not merely to cooperate but to welcome the cross-fertilisation of ideas between different Christian traditions; and until under the stimulus of what is called Biblical Theology we have begun to learn again to subject customary church and missionary practice to the scrutiny of the New Testament. Roland Allen had an inkling of all this; he prophesied to his son that his writings would come into their own about 1960.

Roland Allen was born on December 29th 1868. He went up to Oxford from Bristol Grammar School with a scholarship to St. John's College, and got a second in Classical Honour Moderations, a second in Modern History, and the Lothian Prize.

F. E. Brightman, the great liturgist at Pusey House, was to him at that time, 'my dear Father in God'. After Oxford he went on to the Leeds Clergy Training School to prepare for Holy Orders. The Principal, Winfred Burrows, later Bishop of Chichester, described him as a 'refined' intellectual man, small not vigorous, in no way burly or muscular. 'He is not the sort of man to impress settlers or savages by his physique. And I should think he is academic and fastidious rather - though I have no doubt he will bravely accept whatever comes. I only mean that learning and civilisation are more to him than to most men.' This was written to the SPG in support of Allen's application to the Society in 1892, in the course of which Allen himself wrote:

> I am simply thirsting to go to the Foreign Mission Field, and I am ready to go wherever and whenever the Society has a vacancy.
>
> These I call my qualifications for the duties which I perhaps over boldly propose to undertake. Unfortunately there are two disqualifications which may mitigate against me. Firstly, I have *no* money. Secondly, I have a weak heart. It is this which has prevented me from applying to you before. From my earliest years I was as firmly convinced of my vocation as I was of my existence. Then six years ago I had occasion to get a medical certificate and it was refused. I then fell into a very bad state of health, and almost gave up hope of going abroad. I went to Oxford and thence here (Leeds). The other day I was telling our Principal of my desire and he suggested that perhaps after all I should not find my health an insuperable barrier. For two years ago I saw Dr Berkart of 71 Wimpole Street, who, instead of denying me exercise, encouraged it, and since that time I have been growing continually stronger, so that I am now in very fair health except that I cannot bear sudden exertion.

We need not perhaps take either of these descriptions of Allen as a young man au pied de la lettre. It is true that he was invalided home from China in 1903; but his 'weak heart' served him well till he was over 70; he travelled widely; and he wrote a large number of books and articles of the combative sort that can easily exhaust an author. Nor was it true, at all events in his later years, that he had 'no money'- these things are after all relative; he would not however have been able to finance his later travels from his own resources, and they were financed by Sydney Clark as part of the common enterprise. Above all, it was not yet evident - or perhaps the Principal did not see - that Allen was in a relatively short time to become a somewhat formidable person with a creative mission; in later years, indeed, he came to seem, without intending it, somewhat frightening to a younger man who might find it difficult to get close to him.

It seems that Kaffraria, Saskatchewan and Burma were all considered and rejected as being unsuitable on medical or other grounds. In the event, Allen was ordained at Advent 1892 in Durham to a curacy at Darlington, and went to the North China Mission of the SPG in 1895. Writing to the society very early in 1896 Bishop C. P. Scott says that Allen is acting as Legation Chaplain and engaged in language study in Peking, and 'steadily preparing himself to train men for a native ministry'; by July 1897 he was already lecturing in the school for native clergy. He continued in this work until the Boxer Rising and the Seige of the Legation (of which his first published book was an account). He seems to have been well regarded by Bishop C. P. Scott, whose Chaplain he was from 1898 to 1903, and by F. L. Norris, later Bishop, who was some years senior to him in the Mission. He was on furlough in 1901-2, during which time he got married. On his return to China he was sent to a country station at Yungching, from which it is evident that he had already arrived at some of the conclusions which were to dominate the rest of his working life:

> The existence of lapsed Christians is a disgrace to the Church and a condition which cannot be tolerated. The church must pray for and wrestle with them individually, and then if any will not repent he should be cut off. Because tho' people may persist in refusing to have anything to do with us, yet any ill-doing of which they may be guilty is laid to our door.
> But here I must say that the continued presence of a foreigner seems to produce an evil effect. The native genius is cramped by his presence, and cannot work with him. The Christians tend to sit still and let him do everything for them and to deny all responsibility . . . A visit of two or

three months stirs up the Church, long continued residence stifles it. All the Churches here pay their own expenses. I feel sure that in a short time they can and will provide their own schools. At any rate I see no reason whatever for suggesting that I or any other should do these things for them. I hold my hand.[1]

In 1903 his health broke down, and he returned to England with his wife and young child. In 1904 he became Vicar of Chalfont St. Peter in Buckinghamshire, and was there until 1907 until he resigned on the issue of what would now be called 'baptismal rigorism'. He wrote to his parishioners:

> One form of protest, and only one, remains open to me, and that is to decline to hold an office in which I am liable to be called upon to do what I feel to be wrong. I have chosen that. I have resigned.

His name was included in Crockford's Clerical Directory until he died, forty years later; but the entry ends with Chalfont St. Peter. He never again held any formal ecclesiastical office, but became a voluntary priest, earning his living in other ways. But Peking, Yungching and Chalfont St. Peter were decisive experiences. In the preface to his last major work - *The Case for Voluntary Clergy* published in 1903 - he wrote:

> I have been a stipendiary missionary in China where I tried to prepare young men for the work of catechists with a view to Holy Orders; and there I first learned that we cannot establish the Church widely by that method. Then I was in charge of a country district of China: and there I learned that the guidance of old experienced men in the Church, even if they were illiterate, was of immense value. I held a benefice in England; and there I learnt the waste of spiritual power which our restrictions involve at home.

Thereafter he exercised his priesthood only as a 'voluntary clergyman'; and for many years his principle friends and colleagues, particularly in the Survey Application Trust, were not only not High Churchman but not Anglicans. Allen's

[1]This and the previous quotation are from letters and papers in the archives of the SPG and are quoted by permission.

ecclesiastical outlook hardly came into our discussions. We were not interested in the ministry and the sacraments in the way in which he was; he joined us in a deep concern for the place and the pre-eminence of the Holy Spirit in all the work of the Church everywhere, and in the practical activities that this conviction involved. Allen regarded himself as a faithful disciple of the Anglican tradition with a leaning towards the Catholic content, though he differed in important - some would have said, crucial - particulars from the majority of those in that tradition at that time.

Roland Allen had first met Sydney Clark in 1914, and they had found much in common. Roland Allen gave some help in the preparation of an immense tome called *The Christian Occupation of China*. (This title gave great offence to nationalist-minded Chinese, suggesting to them a design of 'missionary imperialism', to use a phrase, coined later, of which much has since been heard.) This was a detailed survey of the occupation by Church and Mission with a view to discovering the extent of the unfinished task. It was by far the most detailed and comprehensive review of missionary occupation of any survey done up to that time anywhere. It was done in China and printed at Sydney Clark's expense. But even then it was clear that Roland Allen could never get up any enthusiasm for the survey of unoccupied fields. His attitude was, 'What are you doing where you are? Till you have set that on the right lines what is the use of discovering and entering new fields to make the old mistakes?' By this time Roland Allen had published several books which had greatly attracted Sydney Clark's interest, and their association was carried on in London. It was there that I met him in 1921 and had many long talks with him. I learned then of the work he had been doing in China until the Boxer Rising and then illness had put an end to it.

I did not know until late that Mr Clark has asked him to become a Trustee of what was then a new Trust called the Survey Application Trust. Allen refused. This led Clark to ask me to become a Trustee, to which I agree provided I had some time on my furlough in 1926 to attend the office and find out about the nature of the opportunity it presented. The Survey Application Trust was founded in 1924 very largely to carry out Allen's own ideas of the revolution needed in missionary methods and even its objectives, so far as he elaborated them in The Spontaneous Expansion of the Church and the Causes which Hinder it. Sydney Clark whole-heartedly enforced Allen's arguments and added to them in his own pamphlets - the Trustees were in fact instructed to look for guidance to the writing of Clark and Allen. The trust was designed to be a perpetual challenge to the tendency of Missions to get into a rut and to follow conventional methods and principles. It was further designed to draw ever new attention to New Testament teaching on the whole enterprise of the Gospel in the world.

Roland Allen had gone to East Africa by this time and I had no chance to consult him. After this he made only a few short visits to England on private business. He never had any doubts about what he felt it right to do. Money he refused to handle and would not act as a trustee even on a minor Trust to which Sydney Clark appointed him. He was at this time full of enthusiasm for voluntary clergy in the Anglican dioceses overseas. With the object of discovering the facts and promoting the plan he visited bishops in Canada, Assam, Kenya and Southern Rhodesia, and often undertook short tours for them. Thomas Cochrane tried to interest him in doing missionary surveys in the areas he visited. He generally reported that he felt unable to do any such work.

One comes across remarks such as the following in the letters to Cochrane. 'I gravely doubt whether mission sent out by Christian societies are not really doing in Africa destructive work . . . their message is more intellectual than religious if they have any message at all. How many I ask have definitely in view the building up of a "Christian Church"?' He visited Rusapi, Umatata, Salisbury, Kimberley and Kenya and reported that 'mission methods are the main obstacle, and the message is too negative. Finance seems to dominate most situations.'

In 1930 he spent some time in Thetford, Norfolk, acting for his brother who was ill, and returned to his home at Blackheath in 1931. In 1932 he set off to Kenya again, but returned the same year to act temporarily in a church at High Wycombe and again returned to his home. He said he did not feel there was any place for him in England. He disposed of his house about this time and decided to live permanently in Kenya where his son and daughter had settled.

His main reason, I think, was the desire to be near them; but other factors were involved. Much of the resources of the Survey Application Trust in the period between the wars was devoted to compiling surveys of the actual state and progress of missionary work, Thomas Cochrane and others feeling that the making and publishing of these surveys was very necessary, and indeed the only way in which at that time the extent of the unfinished task could be revealed. Allen, however, was quite uninterested in these surveys and wished the whole resources of the Trust to be devoted to the direct study and propagation of thought on the indigenous church. I do not recall that this divergence of judgement about the right *methods* with which to pursue our common *ends* ever came to a head in a concrete form, but it undoubtedly influenced Allen's actions at this time.

In 1932 he wrote from Kenya after some travelling about East Africa:

It is impossible to say what the effect of my being in these parts is having. The idea (voluntary clergy) is spreading. I never ask anyone to do anything, and consequently I do not get a 'yes' or 'no'. I say what seems to be obviously true, but they do not know what to do about it. One day someone will see what action is demanded, and perhaps screw up their courage to take it. If I were out to organise and lead that would be different, but as you well know I long ago determined that that was not the way of the Spirit for me. It is the popular way, but it is not mine. I hold that truth must win its own way, and I stand aside when I have pointed to the truth. To me, 'He must increase and I must decrease' is a lively word. All I can say is that 'This is the way of Christ and his Apostles'. If any man answers, 'That is out of date', or 'Times have changed', which as a reply is the same thing, or anything of that sort, I can only repeat 'This is the way of Christ and his Apostles', and leave him to face that issue. How long shall I go on? One day I shall know that I have nothing more to do here, no word to say more, and then I shall withdraw, as I came, silently. Whether I have done anything at all , or shall do anything at all is known only to God. The day will declare it.

He did not, therefore, fit well into the accepted scheme of things, and was always a rebel in spirit. His efforts to help the various bishops he visited were not very successful. To Dr Cochrane's various requests for his opinions and judgement he almost invariably returned the answer, ' I have nothing to say'. In answer to repeated requests for help in survey work we have one memorable reply (1932):

> As well ask the Apostle Stephen to write a survey of Judaism in the Roman Empire as ask me to write a survey.

Or again:

> For me to sum up things as a survey requires, as I see it, would not help you, for I seem to be trying to do the opposite of what you are doing. You would not understand what I am really after, any more than I could understand you if you tried to tell me what you were doing. Meanwhile you feel you have my sympathy, as I feel I have yours.
>
> . . . . You like tales of success which I cannot give you. These stories you send me to pronounce on are hopeful, but I do not trust spectacular things; give me the seed growing secretly every time.

His later letters tell of declining physical strength borne most patiently. His mind remained clear and he was always interested to know how his books were going. He died on June 9th 1947 in Kenya.

As Dr. H. R. Boer pointed out in an appreciation of Allen's life and work in World Dominion (January 1948, vol.XXVI), Roland Allen was a man of singularly clear vision and prophetic outlook. He is principally known for the only two of his books which have had a long life, Missionary Methods: St Paul's or Ours? (5th edition, 1960) and The Spontaneous Expansion of the Church and the Causes which Hinder it (4th edition, 1960). Many other books very quickly sold out and not reprinted. But his main concern and interest was in usual sense in the place of the Holy Spirit. For this reason his small book on the Pentecost and the World is given prominent place in this anthology. To him 'the Spirit of life and of witness is the source and power of the Church's address to the world.' This view of the Holy Spirit's place dominated his whole thinking: 'to him, the Acts of the Apostles was the story of the faith of the Early Church in the power of the Holy Spirit'.

'For thirty years he pleaded that the Church (overseas) be placed on its own feet, that is, for an indigenous Christianity. This, he held, could not be imposed from the outside for an indigenous Church is not simply a Church that is master in its own house, but a Church that had the gift of the Holy Spirit and knew what this gift meant for its own life.'

It was this conviction of the need of the presence and activity of the Holy Spirit in the Church everywhere which dominated his whole thinking; and now that Allen is dead, Christians of many traditions and in many places who seek the unity and renewal of the Church in the Spirit are finding that Roland Allen being dead yet speaketh with a force which in his lifetime most men failed to appreciate.

ALEXANDER MCLEISH
from the first (1960) edition

Contents

7. TO THE PARISHIONERS OF CHALFONT
   ST PETER

I

Pentecost and the World
The Revelation of the Holy Spirit in the 'Acts of the Apostles'

B

Editorial Note

The whole text of Pentecost and the World *is printed apart from the Preface and the elaborate analysis of the contents.*

The Gift of the Holy Spirit

The Acts of the Apostles is the record of the fulfilment of a
promise made by Christ to His disciples and of the consequences
which followed. It is not merely the story of the words and deeds of
the apostles after the Resurrection and Ascension of Christ, telling
us how they established the Church in the world: it is the story of the
coming, and of the results of the coming, of the Holy Spirit. So clear
is this that the book has been called the 'Acts of the Holy Spirit'.

This description of the book is indeed one-sided. To entitle the
book the 'Acts of the Holy Spirit' rather than the 'Acts of the
Apostles' obscures the human element. The apostles were men.
Their acts were their own acts. They were not mere will-less instru-
ments in the hands of another. Nevertheless, the fact that it was
possible to call the Acts of the Apostles the 'Acts of the Holy Spirit'
reveals at once the truth that men have found in this book not merely
the record of the acts of men, but the revelation of a Spirit governing,
guiding, controlling, directing men in the acts here recorded. And
this is no delusion. In this book it is the guidance and government of
the Spirit which is constantly recalled to mind. That the men of
whom St Luke writes were men liable to the errors and passions of
men is clear enough; what is insisted upon is that they were the
recipients of a gift of the Holy Spirit sent upon them by Christ, and
that all the labours and successes of their lives were due to the influence of that Spirit. In this degree the title 'The Acts of the Holy
Spirit' is true and useful, and should save us from the error of reading the book merely as the Acts of the Apostles.

To do this is indeed a serious mistake. It blinds us to the great
revelation made to us in Acts of the nature and purpose of the gift
of the Holy Spirit. We cannot fail to observe that constant reference
is made to the Holy Spirit in this book; but, if we read it simply as
the Acts of the Apostles alone, we tend to fix our attention upon the
apostles as men, we think of their growth in learning and experience,
we think of them as actuated by common motives such as zeal,
loyalty, devotion; then we imagine such common natural motives

sufficiently strong to produce the effects here spoken of, we ascribe the labours and triumphs of the truth to these motives; and finally we end by thinking of the Holy Spirit as a term to sum up these motives. Thus we interpret the Holy Spirit by the common human motives with which we are familiar; and consequently any revelation of the Holy Spirit is obscured, or lost altogether.

In the book the emphasis is all the other way. The Holy Spirit is first given, then all the acts are described as consequences of His descent upon human beings. If we read the book in this way, then we see not the consequences of familiar human instincts and qualities, but the consequences which follow the giving of the Holy Spirit to men already possessed of these instincts and qualities. We see what happens when the Holy Spirit descends upon men of like passions with ourselves. Loyalty to Christ did not drive the apostles to abandon the religious privileges of their race and the traditions of their fathers in order to embrace heathen Gentiles within the fold of the Church. Zeal for Christ's honour did not teach them how to approach those heathen and to establish the Church. It was the Holy Spirit, the Spirit of the Redeemer, which did this. From this point of view their words and acts become a wonderful revelation of the Holy Spirit.

That St Luke intended to tell the story not so much of the labours of men as of the effects of the coming of the Spirit is revealed at the very opening of his work. St Matthew ended his Gospel with a command given by Christ to His apostles to 'go and make disciples of all the nations': if St Luke had begun this book with a similar statement it would have been easy to suppose that his story was the story of men who, having received such a command, set out to obey it. But that is not what we find. Never in this book does he suggest such a thought. Once only in Acts is any reference made to a command of Christ to preach the gospel, and that is an incidental reference in St Peter's address to the household of Cornelius (10.42). There St Peter is reported to have said that Christ 'charged us to preach unto the people.' But St Luke does not so begin Acts: nor did he so end his Gospel. He begins Acts, as he ended his Gospel, not with a command, but with a promise of the Spirit.[1] In the Gospel he wrote, 'He said

---

[1] Many interpret the saying in Acts. 2.2, 'After that he through the Holy Ghost had given commandment unto the apostles,' as a direct reference to this command (St Matt. 28.19), but it seems more natural to interpret St Luke by St Luke than by St Matthew. Then the commandment here spoken of is the commandment given

unto them, Thus it is written and thus it behoved Christ to suffer and to rise from the dead the third day; and that repentance and remission of sins should be preached in his name among all nations, beginning at Jerusalem. And ye are witnesses of these things. And, behold, I send the promise of my Father upon you: but tarry ye in the city of Jerusalem until ye be endued with power from on high' (St Luke 24.46-49). In Acts he says, 'The former treatise have I made of all that Jesus began both to do and to teach, until the day that he was taken up, after that he through the Holy Ghost had given commandment (RV) unto the apostles whom He had chosen' (1.2), and he proceeds to say that Jesus 'charged them that they should not depart from Jerusalem, but wait for the promise of the Father' (1.4). Of this promise, he adds that Christ said, 'Ye shall receive power after that the Holy Ghost is come upon you: and ye shall be my witnesses both in Jerusalem, and in all Judaea, and in Samaria, and unto the uttermost part of the earth' (1.8) It is with this promise and its fulfilment that he deals in Acts.

These words are, indeed, often quoted as a version of the command given in St Matthew, and I am far from wishing to deny that they imply a command; but the significance of the form must not be overlooked. Acts does not begin with 'The Lord Jesus said, Go'; but with 'Ye shall receive power, and ye shall be witnesses.' St Luke fixes our attention, not upon an external voice, but upon an internal Spirit. This manner of command is peculiar to the Gospel. Others direct from without, Christ directs within; others order, Christ inspires; others speak external words, Christ gives the Spirit which desires and strives for that which He commands; others administer a dead letter, Christ imparts life. This is the manner of the command in St Luke's writings. He speaks not of men who, being what they were, strove to obey the last orders of a beloved Master, but of men who, receiving a Spirit, were driven by that Spirit to act in accordance with the nature of that Spirit.

This spiritual unity links the work of the apostles with the work of Jesus Christ. In the preface to Acts, St Luke says that his Gospel contains an account of all that Jesus began to do and teach, ending

---

in v. 4 of this chapter, which is itself a repetition of the command given in the Gospel (24.19): 'Tarry ye in the city of Jerusalem until ye be endued with power from on high.'

with a commandment which He gave to His apostles through the Holy Spirit. He suggests that the work which Jesus began on earth was being fulfilled after His departure through the same Spirit, in the story which he is now about to relate; for immediately after saying that Jesus gave the commandment through the Holy Spirit, he adds that the commandment was, that they should wait in Jerusalem for the promise of the Father. He then introduces the promise, 'Ye shall be baptized with the Holy Spirit not many days hence,' with the apparently irrelevant note that 'John baptized with water.' This note does more than contrast the baptism of water ministered by John with the baptism of the Holy Spirit. It suggests more than a controversial answer to those who were preaching John and his baptism (19. 3, 4). It recalls the baptism by John not only of the multitude who received the baptism of water only, but the baptism of Jesus Himself, when the Holy Ghost descended upon Him, and John, recognizing the sign, proclaimed, 'This is he which baptizeth with the Holy Ghost' (St John 1.35; St Matt. 3.11). Jesus was baptized with the Holy Spirit for His ministry: the apostles were to be baptized with the Holy Spirit for theirs. The same Holy Spirit which descended upon Christ was to descend upon them. The same Spirit which in Jesus fulfilled the commandment of the Father to come into the world was in the apostles to fulfil the commandment to 'Go into all the world.' Thus the work of the apostles with which this book is concerned is linked with the work of Jesus Christ as the carrying on of that which He began on earth under the impulse of the same Spirit through whom He acted and spoke.

This note links the work of the apostles as described in Acts with the work of Jesus Christ: it also separates their work from the work of John the Baptist. It suggests a contrast between the work of John and the work of those who were to be baptized with the Holy Spirit. It asserts a definite contrast between those who were baptized with water and those who were baptized with the Holy Spirit. The work of the disciples of Christ was to be in the power of His Spirit, not in the power of the Spirit given to John the Baptist, though of him the promise was made that he should be filled with the Holy Ghost from his mother's womb (St Luke 1.15). There is here a sharp distinction drawn between the prophets and forerunners of Christ inspired by the Holy Spirit, and the apostles and followers of Christ baptized with His Spirit.

This should make us very careful how we interpret the Acts of the Apostles; because it is easy to think of the inspiration of the apostles as identical with the inspiration of the prophets and of John the Baptist himself, as though the apostles carried on after Christ's Ascension the work which the prophets began before His Incarnation. There is, of course, a truth in this; but the introduction to Acts certainly directs our attention not to this truth, but away from it, rather separating the work of the apostles from the work of the forerunners of Christ, and directing our attention to the unity of the work of the apostles with the work of Jesus Christ, and to the unity of the Spirit which inspired them with the Spirit which dwelt in Him.

There is a danger in interpreting the New Testament by the Old. We have seen it in attempts to found our ideas of the sacraments instituted by Jesus Christ, especially the Sacrament of the Lord's Supper, upon our reading of the Old Testament. We read the accounts of Old Testament sacrifices, and then interpreted the sacrifice of Christ by those Old Testament sacrifices. We studied the Old Testament sacrifices, and then read into the accounts of the Lord's Supper the ideas derived from that study. We have often been warned against this. The sacrifice of Christ cannot be interpreted by the Old Testament conceptions of sacrifice: it surpasses them far too highly. The sacraments of Christ cannot be interpreted by Old Testament rites: they are of a different order. It is possible to read the Old Testament in the light of the New, and to find in Jewish rites singular and beautiful types and anticipations of the glory of the New Testament sacrifice and its sacraments; but to read the New Testament by the light of the Old is like studying sunlight by the light of a gas-jet, and transferring to sunlight ideas derived from gas. This is also true of the New Testament gift of the Holy Spirit. In the light of that gift we can understand the references to God's Spirit in the Old Testament better than those who have read only the Old Testament; but to transfer the ideas of God's Spirit revealed in the Old Testament to the New Testament, and to interpret the gift of the Holy Spirit to Christians by these, is to endanger the larger revelation, and to run the risk of blinding our eyes to its true significance and character. Men have studied the New Testament in the light of the Old, and have ended by describing the Spirit given at Pentecost as the Spirit which inspired the prophets, only given in 'larger measure,' or as 'given to all' whereas before He was given to few. But this is far from satisfying the conditions. The essential character of the Spirit in the New Testament is revealed in the fact that the Spirit given at Pentecost was peculiarly Christian, depending upon a relation to Jesus Christ. To know the Spirit revealed in the New Testament it is necessary to begin with the New Testament, and to believe in Jesus the Christ, and to receive the gift mediated by Him. Then, knowing that Spirit, we can read the Old Testament and perceive more than the Old Testament could ever have taught, realizing that the light which we now see is not derived from the teaching of the Old Testament, but from the radiance of Jesus Christ.

The result of seeking to interpret the New Testament revelation of the Spirit by the light of the Old Testament is seen in the common ideas of our people concerning the Holy Spirit and missionary work. They have been taught about the Holy Spirit as 'the spirit of wisdom and understanding, the spirit of counsel and might, the spirit of knowledge and of the fear of the Lord' spoken of in Isaiah (11.2). Some of them can distinguish 'wisdom' from 'understanding.' But they have not realized that the Spirit given to them is the Spirit of the Son, the Spirit of the mission of the Son, the Spirit of the Incarnation, the Spirit of redeeming love. They think of the gift of the Holy Spirit given to Christians as the Spirit which inspired Bezaleel and Aholiab for the adornment of the Tabernacle (Exod. 31.2, 6); they do not so often think of Him as the source and inspirer of self-sacrificing efforts to bring the souls of men to God in Jesus Christ. But that is what we see in Acts.

The account given to the second chapter of the event which took place on the day of Pentecost is in perfect accord with St Luke's introduction. The story there told by St Luke is obviously designed to bring home to his readers a sense of the definiteness, reality, and certainty of the fulfilment of the promise made in the first chapter.

The gift was given at a definite time, in a definite place, with definite signs which the apostles could recognize. The time, the day (v. 1), the hour of the day (v. 15), the place, the city (v. 5), the house (v. 2), the signs, the wind (v. 2), the tongues of fire (v. 3), are all specified. The symbols were sufficiently clear and familiar. The apostles were instantly aware that the promise of Christ had been fulfilled.

The gift was a definite gift. Not only were the circumstances definite and clear; the gift itself was a definite gift. St Peter said that it was a fulfilment of the prophecy of Joel (v. 16), but he said also that it was sent by Jesus (v. 33). It was the Spirit of God (v. 17), but it was a Spirit which could be received only upon repentance and baptism in 'the name of Jesus Christ' (v. 38). The apostles did not confound the gift which they received with the manifestation of the grace and power of the Holy Spirit in the Old Testament. They did not for a moment question the truth that 'men of old spake as they were moved by the Holy Ghost,' but they did not for a moment suppose that the men of old had received the gift of the Holy Ghost which they had received. The gift which they had received was quite distinct from that inspiration granted to the prophets of former days. It was so different that St John could write that before the Ascension of Christ 'the Holy Ghost was not yet because that Jesus was not yet glorified' (John 7.39). This gift was intimately connected with Jesus Christ glorified. It could only be received by those who believed in Jesus. It was unknown outside the Church. The Holy Spirit of God might, and did, inspire prophets and good men outside the Church, but only Christians had this gift, because this gift was Christ's gift. The Holy Spirit received at Pentecost and given universally to Christians was peculiarly 'the Spirit of his Son.'

The gift which the apostles received was a definite gift received at a definite time. It was not the experience of a vague influence which they felt more or less markedly at different times: it was a definite fact concerning which they could name the time and place. Later the Holy Spirit was given to many others, but always this peculiar definiteness marked the coming of the gift. There was always a time and a place at which each convert received the gift. It was perfectly natural for St Paul to ask certain men at Ephesus of whom he stood in some doubt, 'Did ye receive the Holy Spirit when ye believed?' (19.2, RV). He asked a definite question expecting an equally definite answer, as a matter of course. He expected Christians to know the Holy Spirit, to know whether they had received Him, and to know when they received Him. It is true that St Paul did not put this question to people who had been baptized as infants and had grown up in the faith. He did not necessarily expect such to know and to be able to state a definite moment when they first consciously received the Holy Spirit; but he did expect them, too, to know the Spirit and to know that they had received Him. In this the gift of the Holy

Spirit to all the later disciples partook of the same character as the first gift on the day of Pentecost.

We do not find it easy to understand this. We commonly think of the Holy Spirit as a Spirit of God which is the life-giving principle in the world and in men. All men live because they partake in some degree of this Spirit. Some men partake of it more than others, or are more conscious of its influence than others. These are the more religious men and the moral men of all ages and races. A few who have manifested peculiar religious power in their age and place, becoming prophets and religious leaders and founders of great schools of thought, seem to us peculiarly endowed with this Spirit; but we all share in it more or less. Consequently we are quite unconscious of having received any special gift. We do not think of the gift given to us as in any way distinct.

Since it is the same spirit of life in all religious people, and indeed in all men everywhere, it is rather a vague influence: it has few definite, clear characteristics; it is not essentially Christian at all. It is just an influence which makes for righteousness. We hear that nearly all men have an idea of righteousness, and a feeling that they ought to try to act righteously, and a tendency to feel remorse when they have broken the code of righteousness with which they are familiar. We are conscious ourselves of something of the sort, and we call that the Holy Spirit. But for Christians to claim any monopoly of that Holy Spirit is absurd.

Viewed in this light the Holy Spirit is often confounded with conscience. Ask our young people if the Holy Spirit does not urge them to such and such a course of action, or seek to restrain them from such and such vices, and many of them will say, 'Oh! you mean my conscience.' Conscience may approve or disapprove an action; but does conscience inspire, guide, lead us to communion with God, or fill us with desire for the salvation of men's souls? Yet our common speech about the Holy Spirit as known to us renders us liable to such a confusion. It is one thing to talk of the Holy Spirit speaking through conscience; it is quite another to confound the Holy Spirit with conscience. To do that is to end by losing sight of the Holy Spirit altogether. Conscience is common to man; and is certainly not the gift of Pentecost.

There is a way of thinking and speaking of the Holy Spirit which banishes this vagueness and makes it perfectly clear why the apostles

spoke of the gift of the Holy Spirit as being given only to Christians.
If we think of this gift as the gift of the Spirit which dwelt in Jesus
Christ, in the man Christ Jesus of whom the Gospels speak, instantly
the title becomes clear and definite. We cannot confound the Spirit
which inspired Jesus Christ with the Spirit which dwelt in Confucius
or the Buddha. We have only to compare Jesus Christ with Confucius or with the Buddha to see the difference. We know quite well
what sort of person Jesus was. We know quite well what sort of Spirit
animated Him. We can read and see. If I say that by the gift of the
Holy Spirit I mean *that* Spirit, no one doubts my meaning who is
familiar with the Gospels. The Spirit revealed in Jesus Christ, that is
what we men need; that is what we see given to the apostles. Their
enemies noted it. 'They marvelled at them and took knowledge of
them that they had been with Jesus' (4.13). This Spirit could only be
given to Christians. He could be received only by those who knew
Jesus. How could any who did not believe in Jesus receive Him? To receive the Spirit was to receive Jesus, to have Jesus indwelling. But this
gift was a new and definite gift. The story of Cornelius is conclusive
on this point. Cornelius was a devout man whose prayers and alms
were acceptable to God. By what spirit was he moved to give alms
and pray? Undoubtedly by the Spirit of God. Yet the gift of the Holy
Spirit, the Pentecostal gift, was a new gift to him, a gift which he had
not before St Peter taught him to believe in Jesus Christ.

Secondly, the gift was a real gift. There was a day when the apostles
had it not, in spite of the fact that Jesus had breathed on them (St
John 20.22). There was a day when it came; from that day forward
it was theirs. On that day something did really happen. I find it impossible to read these chapters and to suppose that the event here
described was simply the climax of a gradual growth in the minds of
the apostles of a new conception of their relationship to the Master
whom they had known on earth, and of their duty to Him, these
ideas, gradually, half consciously, or unconsciously, growing stronger
and deeper till at last they broke forth into consciousness with the
force of an illumination. I find it impossible to suppose that the
event here described is the sudden realization of the possession of
spiritual powers, which, in fact, the apostles actually possessed before
the day of Pentecost, the sense of their possession half consciously
ripening within them till it broke upon them with the force of an
illumination, and they knew that they possessed them. The account

given in these chapters is essentially the account of the reception of a real gift, of a new gift. Realization of its meaning and its power followed afterwards.

It is equally impossible for me to read these chapters and to suppose that I am reading the description in poetic language of the result which followed the study of the Old Testament promises in the light of the life of Christ, with some assurance given by Him that these promises were about to be fulfilled. Surely it is clear in the whole history of the Gospel and the Acts that the disciples did not discover the fulfilment of any promise made in the Old Testament until some event had taken place which satisfied, and more than satisfied, the requirements of the promise made in the Old Testament. They saw the event first, and then saw that it was a fulfilment of the promise. They did not discover the promise first, and then perceive something which they thought was adequate fulfilment. This is certainly true of the great facts of the Incarnation, of the Passion, and of the Resurrection on the third day. It is equally true of the events of the day of Pentecost. No reading of the Old Testament could have suggested such an event as is here described. Such an event as this when it really happened might well recall the prophecy of Joel, as indeed it naturally did. Obeying the command of Christ, they waited at Jerusalem; the day came; the gift was given; then they understood the Old Testament.

Thirdly, the gift was sure. St Luke writes as one who is quite certain of his facts. The apostles in his pages speak and act as men who are quite certain that they have received a gift. Both his own words and those which he ascribes to the apostles, if we accept them at all, bring home to us a like certainty.

We must, then, read Acts as men who believe in the gift of the Holy Ghost. If we are willing to do that, then it is plain that in the acts of the apostles we shall find a revelation of the Holy Ghost; for we shall certainly learn something of the Spirit in studying words and deeds which were the direct results of His coming into the hearts of those who so spake and acted.

II

The Spirit Revealed as the Inspirer of Missionary Work

A cts is the record of the events which followed the gift of the Holy Spirit. From that record we are to seek a revelation of the nature of the Spirit. What, then, is the character of the story here revealed?

1. The book is a volume of Christian biography. In it we find accounts of the deeds and words of prominent men in the early church. But there is a careful selection made: only some of the leaders of the church are mentioned, and those mentioned belong to a special class. They are not mentioned because they were specially chosen and ordained by Christ to be His apostles; of most of the apostles we read nothing, whilst many of whom we read much were not apostles in that sense. They are not mentioned because they were leaders of many diverse forms of active life in the church; they are all leaders of one form of activity. Of James of Jerusalem, though he was certainly a most important leader of the church in Jerusalem, we read very little; of the men who organized the churches in Syria and Asia Minor, and Greece and Rome, we hear scarcely the names. St Luke tells us nothing of settled bishops and pastors, in spite of the importance of their work. Those of whom we are told much are all missionaries actively engaged in preaching the gospel to those outside the Christian Church: St Peter, and St John, Stephen, Philip the Evangelist, Barnabas, St Paul with Barnabas, and John Mark, and Silas, and Timothy.

And further, of the lives of those men of whom the most is recorded only certain events are told us. These events also are carefully selected, and they all have some important bearing upon the preaching of the gospel to those outside the Church. The appointment of Matthias (1.15 ff.) is one apparent exception, the punishment of Ananias and Sapphira (5.1-11) is another; but, for the rest, the incidents in the lives of these missionaries recorded by St Luke are all missionary incidents. St Peter is mentioned as preaching at Pente-

cost (2.); as using with St John the miracle of healing at the Beautiful
Gate as the subject of a missionary sermon (3.); as defending before
the Council the preaching of the gospel to the people (4.); as healing
the sick in Jerusalem, with the other apostles, whereby 'believers
were the more added to the church' (5.12-16); as being released
with other apostles from prison by an angel who told them to go and
speak to the people (5.20); and as proclaiming in the Council the
paramount duty of so preaching (5.29-32). Indeed, his life at this
period and that of the other apostles is summed up in the words,
'Daily in the Temple, and in every house, they ceased not to teach
and preach Jesus as the Christ' (5.42). Later St Peter reappears in
the narrative as going with St John to Samaria to confirm the
disciples converted by the preaching of Philip, encountering Simon
Magus, and using the opportunity afforded by their journey back to
Jerusalem to preach the gospel in many villages of the Samaritans
(8.25). Thereafter he is mentioned as passing throughout all quarters,
visiting Lydda and Saron and Joppa and healing Aeneas and Dorcas,
miracles which resulted in many turning to the Lord (9.35) and
believing in the Lord (9.42). Finally, at Joppa he received his vision
and was prepared for the call to preach to Cornelius in Caesarea,
and so to open the door to the Gentiles (10., 11.).

Omitting incidental references, we are told nothing of St Stephen
except the fervour of his preaching, the boldness of his defence, and
his glorious martyrdom (6., 7.). The case of Stephen is remarkable.
He was specially ordained with others for a particular work. The
others presumably did the work for which they were ordained. He,
too, presumably did it; but he did something else. St Luke neglects
to tell us anything of the work for which he was ordained, or of the
result of that work. He narrates only how he did the work for which
he was not specially ordained, and the result of that work. And that
work was missionary work.

One other of the seven is mentioned by St Luke, and in his case
too the same remarkable fact appears. Philip is mentioned, not as
doing the work which the seven were appointed to do, but as preaching the gospel to the Samaritans (8.5-13), and to the Ethiopian
eunuch (8.26-40). The rest of the seven disappear from St Luke's
pages altogether.

Of Barnabas we are told very little except his missionary labours.
He is said to have introduced St Paul to the Apostles (9.27), he is

said to have sought out St Paul and brought him to Antioch (11.26), and with him to have carried alms to Jerusalem (11.30, 12.25); but, for the rest, he is a preacher of the gospel in Antioch and engaged in missionary journeys with St Paul and John Mark.

John Mark is mentioned only when he is engaged in missionary work (13.5,13; 15.37,39). Silas also (15.40) and Timothy (16.1) are mentioned only as fellow missionaries with St Paul. Apollos appears in the Acts only as a mighty evangelist (18.24 ff).

With St Paul himself half the book is concerned; but it is with St Paul the missionary to the Gentiles rather than with St Paul the theologian, or the church organizer. When we think of the close attachment between St Luke and St Paul, and of the very large place which St Paul occupies in Acts, it is surely remarkable that St Luke should have told us nothing of his early life (except the incidental references in the speeches of St Paul which he reports) before his conversion; nor anything of his later life except his missionary labours. St Paul was a great organizer, a great reader and thinker and writer; but on these matters St Luke is absolutely silent. He does not mention the writing of any epistle. St Paul stayed at different times for comparatively long periods in certain cities, and there were intervals between his missionary journeys. St Luke passes over these periods in a brief sentence. He tells us scarcely anything of the work of St Paul at these times. This can only be because his attention was wholly fixed on one thing: the preaching of the gospel in ever wider fields, the progress of his hero towards the capital of the world.

Thus it is plain that, if we consider Acts as a book of Christian biography, we must consider it as a work of missionary biography.

2. Similarly, Acts is a book of church history; it tells us of the growth of the church. But it is the missionary history, not the internal history, that is here set forth. Of the organization of the church, of its order, ministry, councils, of its character, of the formulation of its doctrine, of its observances and its festivals, St Luke says very little. On these matters we can gather from his writings only a few hints from which to draw precarious conclusions. Of the internal history of settled churches he scarcely tells us anything. He had, for instance, an intimate acquaintance with the early history of the church in Philippi; but the account which he gives of the church there is not a sufficient introduction to the Epistle to the Philippians. Still less is

the Acts a good introduction to the Epistles to the Corinthians, or to the Galatians, or to the Ephesians. It is not a satisfactory introduction to any of the Pauline epistles: but a good church history should certainly have prepared us for these epistles. St Luke is concerned almost entirely with the spreading of the gospel; when he has told us how the first converts were won, how they faced persecution and were established, he passes rapidly on. Even when he does stay to describe some important event, or to sketch the internal condition of a church, he nearly always adds a note to point out its influence on the evangelization of the world.

Take, for example, his account of the church in Jerusalem. When he draws a picture of the church, 'And all that believed were together and had all things common; and they sold their possessions and goods, and parted them to all, according as any man had need. And day by day, continuing stedfastly with one accord in the Temple, and breaking bread at home, they did take their food with gladness and singleness of heart, praising God, and having favour with all the people,' he adds, 'And the Lord added to them day by day those that were being saved' (2.44-47).

When he has to deal with a strictly internal difficulty, such as the dispute which led to the appointment of the seven, he treats it in a most strange way—strange, I mean, if his concern were not almost wholly with evangelization. He tells us how the dispute arose, he tells us what steps the apostles took to meet it; but then, instead of telling us what was the consequence of their action upon the Christian society, he says, 'the word of God increased; and the number of the disciples multiplied in Jerusalem greatly'; and then he proceeds to fix our whole attention upon the one of the seven who was a mighty preacher of the gospel.

Of the persecutions which befell the church he speaks at some length; but he tells us little indeed of their effect upon individual Christians or upon the society generally. He speaks of them solely as opportunities for revealing the missionary zeal of the apostles (4.; 5.27-32, 41-42; 6.9-60); or as examples of the deliverance of missionaries from peril (5.17-23; 12); or as occasions which drove the Christians to preach in wider fields (8.4; 11.9).

There was in Jerusalem a great Church Council. St Luke mentions it four times. It met to decide how to silence the murmurs of the Grecians against the Hebrews (6.); it met to satisfy the doubts of those who were ready to condemn St Peter for going to the house of Cornelius (11.); it met to discuss the admission of Gentiles into the Church (15.)[1]; it met, again, to deliberate with St Paul, and to advise how to silence the murmurings of the Jewish Christians against his conduct of his missions (20.). I have already pointed out how St Luke treats its decision on the first of these occasions to ordain the seven. For the rest, the meetings mentioned are all concerned with missionary questions of the first importance. Doubtless the Council met frequently to settle questions affecting the internal life of the church in Jerusalem. Of any such meetings St Luke takes no note, because he is concerned, not with the internal politics of individual churches, but with the propagation of the gospel.

Similarly, he tells us something of the church in Antioch (11.22 ff.; 13.1 ff.). He tells us of the first preaching in that city, of the conversion of the Greeks, of the work of Barnabas, of the arrival of Saul, of the dispute which arose there over the relations between Jewish and Gentile Christians; but here, again, his interest is mainly in the missionary zeal of the church in Antioch. It is the admission of a new class into the church, it is the sending forth of Paul and Barnabas, it is the conversion of the Gentiles, on which his mind is fixed. He does not deal with the relations between Jew and Gentile in the church as a point of local interest, as it affected the church of Antioch: he speaks of it rather as a step towards the general propagation of the gospel throughout the Gentile world.

These considerations are surely sufficient to convince us that the book of the Acts is strictly a missionary book. But we have seen that it is the record of the acts of men moved by a Spirit given to them. The conclusion is irresistible, that the Spirit given was, in St Luke's view, a Spirit which impelled to missionary work, in fact a missionary Spirit. Unless we fully accept this conclusion Acts appears unintelligible: the opening chapters do not agree with the main portion of the book, and the events narrated in the book have no proper foundation laid for them. But if the Spirit given as recorded in the earlier chapters was indeed a missionary Spirit, then all the rest is in strict harmony with that beginning.

This becomes still more clear if we consider the passages in which St Luke makes special mention of the Holy Spirit.

---

[1] Some would distinguish the Council mentioned in ch. 15 from the others. This does not affect the argument. It was still a strictly missionary Council.

1. The promise of the gift of the Holy Spirit is connected with world-wide witness (1.8): the descent of the Holy Spirit on the day of Pentecost was with the appearance of tongues like as of fire (2.3), and the apostles immediately began to speak with other tongues (2.4), and to preach to the people (2.5-13). The gift of the Holy Spirit and the preaching of the gospel to those outside the Church are thus intimately connected. And this same note is repeated later. When the apostles were threatened, they returned to their own company and prayed. Then 'the place was shaken where they were gathered together: and they were all filled with the Holy Ghost,' and, adds St Luke, 'they spake the word of God with boldness' (4.31).

2. When St Peter and St John were brought before the Council to make their defence concerning the miracle wrought upon the lame man, and St Peter proclaimed the name of Jesus with the great declaration, 'In none other is there salvation,' he is said to have been 'filled with the Holy Ghost' (4.4).

3. In speaking of the seven, St Luke specially mentions Stephen as being a man 'full of the Holy Ghost' (7.5). It is Stephen who is the great preacher of the gospel unto death.

4. Philip is said to have been sent to meet the eunuch on the road from Jerusalem to Gaza by 'an angel of the Lord,' and, when his work was accomplished, to have been caught away by 'the Spirit of the Lord' (8.26, 40).

5. The conversion of Saul is ascribed to the special intervention of Christ Himself, but no sooner was he converted than Ananias was sent to lay his hands upon him that 'he might receive his sight and be filled with the Holy Ghost (9.17), 'for he is a chosen vessel unto me to bear my name before the Gentiles and Kings and the children of Israel' (v. 15), and 'straightway,' says St Luke, 'he preached Christ in the synagogue' (v. 20).

6. In the same chapter (v. 31), a little note on the effect of the cessation of persecution upon the churches in Palestine is interesting. 'Walking in the fear of the Lord and in the comfort of the Holy Ghost,' they were 'multiplied.' St Luke's peculiar eagerness to note the spread of the gospel could not find a better illustration. After a severe persecution we think of 'refreshment,' 'recovery,' 'illumination,' 'reconstruction,' 'intellectual and social progress.' St Luke notes only 'multiplication.'

7. The special intervention of the Spirit in preparing and directing St Peter for his interview with Cornelius is manifest (10.). The importance of that event in the missionary history of the Church is also manifest.

8. When St Luke recounts the next step towards the wider preaching of the gospel to the Gentiles, namely, the events which occurred at Antioch, he says: 'Some of them spake unto the Greeks also, preaching the Lord Jesus,' adding: 'the hand of the Lord was with them' (11.20, 21). Then he tells of the arrival of Barnabas, and he says 'he was a good man and full of the Holy Ghost and of faith: and much people was added to the Lord' (v. 24).

9. The sending forth of Paul and Barnabas on their first missionary journey is definitely ascribed to the direction of the Holy Spirit. 'The Holy Ghost said, Separate me Barnabas and Saul for the work whereunto I have called them' (13.2). So they, being sent forth by the Holy Ghost, departed (13.4). 'Filled with the Holy Ghost,' Saul at Paphos refuted Elymas when that sorcerer tried to turn away the proconsul from the faith, and so made yet a further step towards the general preaching to the Gentiles (13.9). When he made the final decision at Antioch in Pisidia it is true that no definite assertion is made that he took that step at that moment under the direct influence of the Holy Spirit, but the whole course of the history has implied and asserted the guidance of the Holy Spirit, and the actual words 'they waxed bold' or, 'they spake out boldly' (13.46), imply it, and the chapter ends with a note of quiet thankfulness, 'the disciples were filled with joy and with the Holy Ghost' (13.52).

10. The decision of the Council of Jerusalem to deliver the Gentile converts from the yoke of the law is recognized as the voice of the Holy Spirit: 'it seemed good to the Holy Ghost' (15.28).

11. The guidance of the Holy Spirit in the direction of St Paul's missionary journeys is asserted definitely only once: it is in leading him to Macedonia. 'They were forbidden of the Holy Ghost to preach the word in Asia' (16.6). 'They assayed to go into Bithynia; but the Spirit suffered them not' (v. 7). So they came to Troas, and there the man of Macedonia called St Paul to preach in Europe (vv. 8, 9).

12. Finally, at Rome St Paul appeals to the witness of the Holy Ghost, speaking through Isaiah to justify his preaching to the Gentiles; and with this the history closes.

There are other references to the Holy Spirit: Agabus prophesied the famine by the Holy Spirit (11.28); on his last journey to Jerusalem, St Paul was warned of danger by the Holy Spirit, through the disciples at Tyre (21.4), and at Caesarea through Agabus (21.11). What is perhaps more important, St Paul appealed to the elders of Ephesus by reminding them that 'the Holy Ghost had made them overseers' (20.28). But the many passages quoted above show that St Luke in the Acts is speaking most of the spread of the gospel in the world, and therefore points out how the Holy Spirit, at crucial moments, directed the minds and the actions of the apostles to that end. He is writing of the Holy Spirit primarily as the dictator and inspirer of missionary work.[1]

Now the Spirit which inspires and directs a certain action must necessarily be a Spirit whose nature is such that this action is agreeable to Him and expresses His mind. The history of the spread of the gospel must, then, be a revelation of the mind of the Spirit; the zeal of the apostles must be a revelation of the nature of the Spirit which inspired them to such action.

In our day this revelation of the Holy Spirit in Acts has been strangely overlooked. We have been content to read Acts as the external history of the Church: we have used it as a happy hunting-ground for arguments on behalf of different theories of church government. For each of these theories we have sometimes claimed the authority of the Holy Spirit on the strength of one or two isolated sentences, or even of a single word introduced incidentally by St Luke. No doubt we are compelled to this by the failure of our author to give us any full and definite information. But in tithing the mint and the rue of the Acts we have passed over mercy and the love of God. The great fundamental, unmistakable teaching of the book has been lost. Our best writers on the Holy Spirit have been singularly blind to it. Neither Prof. Swete, nor Bishop Welldon, nor Bishop Moberly, nor Bishop Webb, nor Mr Hutchings, nor Bishop Moule,

---

[1] Additional references to 'the Spirit' in the Western Text strengthen the argument.

17. 15.   After 'Ἀθηνῶν D adds παρῆλθεν δὲ τὴν Θεσσαλίαν· ἐκωλύθη γὰρ εἰς αὐτοὺς κηρύξαι τὸν λόγον: cf. xvi. 6, 7, 8.

15. 29.   After πράξετε D adds φερόμενοι ἐν τῷ ἁγίῳ πνεύματι.

19. 1.   For this D has θέλοντος δὲ τοῦ Παύλου κατὰ τὴν ἰδίαν βουλὴν πορεύεσθαι εἰς Ἱεροσόλυμα, εἶπεν αὐτῷ τὸ πνεῦμα ὑποστρέφειν εἰς τὴν Ἀσίαν. διελθὼν δὲ τὰ ἀνωτερικὰ μέρη ἔρχεται εἰς Ἔφεσον καὶ εὑρών τινας μαθητὰς εἶπεν. The first and last are especially interesting.

nor Archdeacon Hare have at all forcibly or clearly expressed it.[1] Of the Johannine doctrine, and of the Pauline doctrine of the Holy Spirit, we have heard much. Our conception of the work of the Holy Spirit has been almost confined to the revelation of truth, of holiness, of church government and order. Missionary work as an expression of the Holy Spirit has received such slight and casual attention that it might almost escape the notice of a hasty reader. A few strong expressions here and there incidentally introduced do not satisfy the case. So treated, Acts remains an enigma unexplained.

For it is in the revelation of the Holy Spirit as a missionary Spirit that the Acts stands alone in the New Testament. The nature of the Spirit as missionary can indeed be observed in the teaching of the gospels and the epistles; but there it is hinted rather than asserted. In the Acts it is the one prominent feature. It is asserted, it is taken for granted, from the first page to the last. Directly and indirectly it is made all-important. To treat it as secondary destroys the whole character and purpose of the book. It is necessary to any true apprehension of the Holy Spirit and His work that we should understand it and realize it. This revelation embraces one whole hemisphere of the Spirit. If we ignore it, or treat it less seriously than the revelation of truth or of righteousness, we lose sight of the perfection of the Spirit. Our view is necessarily one-sided, our understanding of the past is robbed of its true foundation, our conception of our present duty is incomplete, and our hope for the future is rendered doubtful and indistinct.

[1] Nor the best writers of the other Christian bodies: Denney, Buchanan, Candlish, Adamson, Smeaton and Irving Wood.

III

The Revelation of the Spirit as Creating an Internal Necessity for Missionary Work

When the Holy Spirit descended upon the apostles, His first gift was a gift of tongues. Men, gathered from every nation under heaven, marvelled to hear the apostles speak in their tongues the wonderful works of God. Much learned ingenuity has been spent in attempts to explain what exactly happened. Into this controversy I do not propose to enter. To me, I confess, these discussions seem curiously uninteresting and unprofitable, and their conclusions equally dubious and barren. They tend rather to divert the mind, and to lead it away from the point of real significance and importance. From these learned disquisitions we gain little insight into the nature and work of the Holy Spirit given at Pentecost; but from the fact that a gift of tongues was given we ought to learn much, and what we learn must affect profoundly our life and conduct; because that fact must affect profoundly our conception of the Spirit which is given to us of God. The fact, clear and unmistakable, is that the apostles, when the Holy Spirit descended upon them, began at once to address themselves to men out of every nation and language, and that the Spirit enabled them so to speak that men understood. Thus, at His first coming, the Holy Spirit revealed His nature and His work as world-wide, all-embracing. He revealed His nature as a Spirit who desired the salvation of all men of every nation; He revealed His work as enabling those to whom He came to preach Christ to men of every nation.

The Holy Ghost was given: forthwith the apostles began to preach Christ. They began to preach Christ to those who did not believe. There is in the Acts only one speech after Pentecost addressed to believers: it is the farewell speech of St Paul to the Ephesian elders. As for the rest, all are missionary sermons.

The first of these is St Peter's speech to the people in Jerusalem on the day of Pentecost (2.14-36). In that speech he begins by explaining the strange conduct of his fellow apostles, saying that it is a fulfilment of the words of the prophet Joel (2.14-21). He then tries to bring home to his hearers their crime in crucifying Jesus by reminding them of His mighty works, which in the common thought of the day were unquestioned signs of the approval of the God in whose name they were wrought, adding to these the last and greatest sign that though slain by wicked hands He could not be holden by death, but rose from the dead (2.22-24). He appeals to Scripture to show that this had been foretold of the Christ, and urges that the fulfilment of the Scripture should prove to his hearers that Jesus was the Christ (2.25-36). When by these words he had touched their consciences, he urged them to repent and be baptized in the name of Jesus Christ, promising them remission of sins and the gift of the Holy Ghost (2.38-40).

In the sermon preached by St Peter in the temple after the healing of the lame man, the same note is struck (3.12-26). Again he proclaims that the miracle wrought in the name of Jesus reveals Jesus as the Prince of Life; again he tries to touch the consciences of his hearers, persuading them that they preferred a murderer to the Holy One and the Righteous One; again he proclaims the Resurrection as the sign of God's approval; again he declares that the Passion of Christ was the fulfilment of prophecy, and again he promises forgiveness and salvation in Him; ending with the assurance that God, having raised up His Son Jesus, has sent Him to bless them, not to condemn them (3.26).

Similarly, before the Council itself he proclaims the name of Jesus as the name of power in which the lame man was healed, and so is led to the great declaration that there is none other name under heaven, given among men, wherein we must be saved (4.12). Here again the denunciation of their crime is closely connected with the promise of salvation in Jesus.

Once more before the Council he repeats the same truth: 'The God of our fathers raised up Jesus, whom ye slew and hanged on a tree. Him hath God exalted at his right hand to be a Prince and a Saviour, to give repentance to Israel and remission of sins. And we are witnesses of these things' (5. 30-32).

It has often been observed that we have here examples of that practice which became universal amongst the Christians of searching the Old Testament to find in it words and sentences which could be interpreted as prophecies of events in the life of Christ or of their own experience as Christians. St Luke, at the end of his Gospel, says that Christ Himself opened their minds that they might understand the Scriptures (St Luke 24.45); and no doubt there is here a revelation of the Holy Spirit enlightening the minds of the apostles and leading them into truth.

But there is something much more remarkable. It is the understanding which St Peter shows that Jesus could be exalted and His claim vindicated, not so much by the condemnation of those who crucified Him, as by their salvation. St Peter does not attempt merely to prove the innocence of His Master. He does not attempt merely to glorify Him in the eyes of his hearers. He does not attempt merely to persuade them that they have committed a crime. He wishes rather so to convert their minds and their hearts that they may be brought into such a relation to Jesus Christ that they may be saved by Him, partaking of the Spirit which He has shed forth.

This conviction that Jesus could be exalted and His claims vindicated only by the conversion and salvation of man is indeed noteworthy. St Luke, at the end of his Gospel, tells us that Jesus Himself so taught His disciples, saying that repentance and remission of sins should be preached in His name unto all the nations (St Luke 24.47). When the Holy Ghost was given they immediately began to practise that teaching. To those who had rejected the teaching of Jesus Himself, to those who had been blind to the significance of His works, to those who had cast Him out and crucified Him, they proclaimed salvation in His name. It was not enough to refute calumny, it was not enough to assert His innocence, it was not enough to silence enemies, it was not enough to convict His murderers of crime. Only to guilty minds was it possible that the apostles should appear to be striving to 'bring this man's blood upon them' (5.28). The apostles themselves were concerned with far larger and deeper issues. To them Jesus was already 'the Saviour.' The Saviour could only be vindicated by the 'salvation' of men. It was salvation in the name of Jesus that they preached, even in the face of the very men who had been foremost in the persecution and condemnation of Jesus.

There is here a profound understanding of the nature and work of Jesus Christ; of His nature, both in respect of His attitude towards sinful men, and of His power to save them; and of His work in securing remission of sins to all who come to believe in Him.

Now these were precisely the points which during His life-time on earth the disciples most signally failed to grasp. Even after His Resurrection the redemption of Israel, the restoration of the kingdom of Israel to worldly power were still in their minds the chief work of the Messiah: the salvation of men was understood mainly as admission to a place in that kingdom. The apostles had preached repentance before, but mainly as the path by which men should be prepared to enter into that kingdom.

It is probable, indeed, that they still failed to grasp the full significance of Christ's redemption. It is clear that, as yet, neither the universality of His power to save, nor the universal application of His work to all men everywhere, under all circumstances, was yet apparent to them. But already they had attained to an understanding which had in it the promise of the larger understandings. It had in it the promise of that larger understanding in such measure that they actually used words capable of a far wider application than they themselves put upon them. When St Peter said, 'The promise is to you, and to your children, and to all that are afar off, even as many as the Lord our God shall call,' he no doubt had in his mind Jews only; but the expression which he used was capable of a far wider application, and before very long it received that wider application. Similarly, when he proclaimed that there is 'none other name under heaven whereby we can be saved,' he proclaimed a truth of universal application, and before very long he and the others learnt to realize the full meaning of the truth which he proclaimed.

How, then, did the apostles arrive at this knowledge? It seems to me a wholly inadequate explanation to say that, meditating upon the words and works of Jesus Christ, they began to perceive the real significance of them first for the Jews, and then for the world, as though this were purely a matter of intellectual apprehension. An intellectual apprehension which is partial is expressed in partial terms; a spiritual affection which is only partially understood is expressed in spiritual terms. But the spirit is not bound by the terms as the intellect is bound. Expression of a spirit only perceived in part by the intellect is often far from partial; because the spirit really embraces more than the intellect can grasp, and consequently the mind uses terms which exceed its own measure at the time.

So here, the apostles had received more than intellectual illumination: they received the Spirit of Christ. The wealth of that Spirit they knew intellectually only in part. But because they were moved by it they expressed more than they knew. The Spirit of Christ was a Spirit which embraced the whole world, desiring the salvation of all men. The apostles received that Spirit. They too desired the salvation of men; but intellectually they were bound by their early habits of thought. They thought only in Jewish terms; but the Spirit which moved them was a Spirit which desired the salvation of all men in Christ; and when they came to express that Spirit in words, it did not lend itself to limitations. The limiting terms with which the mind was familiar, the negative terms, were instinctively avoided, and positive terms were used to express the positive Spirit which now demanded expression. And those positive terms were capable of universal enlargement. The apostles were moved by a Spirit which desired the salvation of men. The only men before them, to whom, and for whom, they could express that Spirit, were Jews. They therefore appealed to Jews; but the Spirit, because it really embraced more than Jews, found expression in words which embraced more than Jews, whilst those who spoke the words and those who heard them were conscious only of their application to Jews.

There were limitations. 'Even as many as the Lord our God shall call' (2.39) is a limitation: 'Save yourselves from this untoward generation' (2.40) is a limitation. But the calling of God and the crookedness of men were limitations which the Spirit of God in the apostles, as in Christ Himself, recognized as necessary limitations which did not conflict with the love of the Spirit.

There was, then, more than understanding: there was community of Spirit. The apostles not only realized what Jesus would approve, what was in harmony with His nature and purpose; they themselves shared His Spirit. It is perfectly clear that St Peter, in these speeches, was not simply bowing to a command. Once, when men rejected Christ, he had begged leave to call down fire from heaven upon them, even as Elias did (Luke 9.54); now he had the mind of Christ. He was obviously speaking out of a full heart. He not only promised remission of sins in the name of Jesus; he desired it. He, like his lord, was full of the spirit of redeeming love, a Spirit which impelled him to speak to the people that they might be saved. 'We cannot but speak,' he said, 'the things which we have seen and heard' (Acts 4.20).

This Spirit is manifestly the motive power which actuated the apostles in all their dealings with men. We need not examine all the preaching of all the apostles as set forth in this book. It became more and more clear as time went on to what lengths the Spirit would carry them; but it was never more powerful than at the very beginning. Intellectual apprehension of it and of its universal application grew, but the Spirit itself did not grow. It was given an abode in the hearts of the apostles, and wrought there its necessary effects. That is why it seems inadequate to express the gift of the Spirit in terms of intellectual apprehension of truth. Intellectual apprehension of truth ebbs and flows; the Spirit is constant, and governs all. Intellectual apprehension of truth can and does sometimes remain sterile; the gift of the Spirit is living and active and potent, as we see it to be in the apostles.

The Spirit given to the apostles is thus seen to have created in them an internal necessity to preach the Gospel. 'We cannot but speak,' they say. Throughout this book the Spirit is revealed primarily as a Spirit impelling those to whom He comes to carry to others that which they have received. He is revealed as a Spirit of redeeming love active in those to whom He comes rather towards others for their salvation than in themselves for their own personal perfection. The revelation of Him as a Spirit of personal holiness is brought out more clearly in St Paul's epistles. The first sign of the Spirit's presence in the Acts is activity for the salvation of others; conviction of His personal work is the second and later sign. Many missionaries, I believe, would say that in their experience this is still sometimes the order.

This is in strict harmony with the revelation of the Spirit in the gospels. In the gospels the first mention of the Holy Spirit is of a Spirit of active redemption towards mankind, the agent of the Incarnation of the Redeemer, the Saviour. Only later is He revealed as the purifier, the truth-revealer, the comforter, the strengthener.

Obviously there is no actual priority of the one or of the other aspect of the Holy Spirit's work. The Spirit is Love expressed towards man as redeeming love, and the Spirit is truth, and the Spirit is the Holy Spirit. Redemption is inconceivable without truth and holiness. But the mere fact that the Holy Spirit's first recorded action in the gospels is an expression of redeeming love should cause us to suspect a teaching which represents His work as primarily, if not solely, the sanctification of our own souls to the practical exclusion of His activity in us towards others. It is important to teach of Him as the Spirit of holiness; it is also important to teach of Him as the Spirit which in us labours for the salvation of men everywhere.

IV

The Spirit Revealing the Need of Men

We have seen that the apostles, inspired by the Holy Ghost, began to preach Christ as the Saviour. Under the influence of the Holy Spirit, not only were their minds illuminated to see that the name of Jesus could be glorified and His claims vindicated in no other way than by the salvation of men in Him; they themselves were filled with a desire for the salvation of men akin to that desire which led Him to take upon Him human flesh.

But there was not only a great desire to glorify Christ by the salvation of men in Him; there was also a profound conviction that men needed Christ. The apostles were persuaded that the preaching of the gospel was of such vital importance to men that no pains or penalties could be allowed to postpone it. With the consciousness of power to give they attained consciousness also of the deep need of human souls.

This consciousness is shown not only by the fact of their preaching, but by the character of their preaching. It might indeed be possible to read the speech of St Stephen in the Council (7.) and to suppose that this preaching was simply the expression of a great loyalty to the Person of Jesus, such loyalty as we have often read of in history. His Master had been wickedly misjudged, wrongfully condemned, and ignominiously executed. He was full of righteous indignation. He was determined to defend His Master at all costs. He was determined to set the baseness of his opponents in the strongest light. He therefore searches the history of his nation for examples of the betrayal and rejection of God's servants to find a parallel for the iniquity of his opponents, and proclaims that He whom they cast out is now at the right hand of God. There is a certain fury in his speech which might justify such an interpretation. But the general course of the history recounted in Acts forbids us to think that St Luke intended to represent the apostles as moved by such motives. The preaching is begun in Jerusalem, but it is carried into wider and wider fields to men who had very little immediate connexion with the surrender of Jesus to Pilate. The preaching to them is not merely an appeal from the prejudiced to the unprejudiced in order to win a general recognition of the truth and goodness of a martyr. It is certainly inspired by a desire to win men to believe in Jesus as the Messiah, the Saviour; but it is equally certainly inspired by a conviction that the men to whom the preaching is delivered need Christ.

This becomes still more plain when we consider the conclusion to which the preaching always leads. St Peter, preaching to the people in Jerusalem (2), justifies Jesus; but his object is not merely the justification of Jesus. When the consciences of his hearers are touched and they ask, 'What shall we do?' he is not satisfied. His desire for the recognition of the grace and glory of Jesus takes a new form—desire for the salvation of his hearers. 'Repent,' he says, 'and be baptized every one of you in the name of Jesus Christ, unto the remission of sins, and ye shall receive the gift of the Holy Ghost' (2.38). Again in the Temple it is for the 'blotting out of their sins' that he urges them to repent (3.19). Even in the Council itself he is not content to argue from the healing of the lame man a justification of Jesus: it is 'salvation in his name,' which he proclaims (4.12). Again, in the Council he gives as his reason why he and his fellow apostles must continue to preach the truth that God exalted Jesus 'to be a prince and a saviour for to give repentance to Israel and forgiveness of sins' (5. 31). And so to Cornelius the end of his teaching is remission of sins (10.43).

In the account of St Paul's work, the need of men for Christ takes a most prominent place. Forgiveness of sins (13.38), 'eternal life' (13.46, 48), 'the way of salvation' (16.17, 31), take as important a place in his preaching as 'that Jesus is the Christ' (17.3; 18.5). Indeed, before Agrippa he sums up his work rather in terms of the need of men than in terms of the demonstration of the glory of Jesus. He says that his commission from the Lord was 'to open their eyes that they may turn from darkness to light and from the power of Satan unto God, that they may receive remission of sins and an inheritance among them that are sanctified by faith in me' (26.18).

The apostles preached as men who were convinced that men needed repentance and remission of sins. They preached repentance; they preached remission of sins in the name of Jesus; they preached a baptism in the name of Jesus Christ for the remission of sins.

The apostles had, in the early days of their discipleship, preached repentance and baptism; they had been familiar with the preaching of John the Baptist; but the repentance and baptism which they now preached were very different from the repentance and baptism which they had preached before Pentecost. Before Pentecost they had preached as the Baptist had preached. The Baptist had preached that men should turn from their sins, from those offences against the moral law of which they knew that they had been guilty; his baptism was a washing from these. Such repentance, such baptism, was essentially limited in its scope: it dealt only with sins known to the penitent; it referred primarily to the abandonment of evil courses; it left the penitent in the same spiritual state in which he began; it brought him no new power nor any new source of life. But now the apostles preached a repentance which was rather positive than negative. They preached not simply that men should turn from sin, but that they should turn to Christ. Repentance for sin which did not bring men to Christ was no longer adequate; for to turn to Christ is a far larger and more vital act than mere turning from known sin. To turn from known sin by turning to Christ is to do more than to turn from known sin; it is to turn from all sin known and unknown. What men turn to is more important than what they turn from, even if that to which they turn is only a higher moral truth; but to turn to Christ is far more than to turn to higher moral truth: it is to turn the face towards Him in whom is all moral truth; it is to turn to Him in whom is not only the virtue which corresponds to the known vice from which the penitent desires to flee, but all virtue; it is to turn the face to all holiness, all purity, all grace. It was this repentance which the apostles preached after Pentecost.

And the baptism corresponded to the repentance. Baptism was no longer the mere symbolical washing away of known sin; it was baptism into Jesus Christ. It was translation into a new spiritual state. It brought the promise of the gift of the Holy Spirit. It brought new life, new power. It brought men into touch with Jesus Christ, the source of all truth and grace. It opened to them the inexhaustible treasures of the life of Christ. It bound them to Him. However little they might understand at the moment of their baptism, by that baptism they did actually enter upon that new life of union with Christ, of obedience to Christ, of grace derived from Christ, which must inevitably draw them from all sin into the holiness and love of

Christ. Baptism into Christ implied a new conception of salvation, a new way of salvation, a way which was to be found only in Christ.

Because repentance, which is a turning to Christ, is a turning from and a forsaking of all sin, because baptism into Christ is not only a washing from known sin but the creation of a new relationship to Christ, because that union brings with it the promised gift of the Holy Spirit, the source of all holiness, the assurance of perfect holiness, because all salvation is in Christ and in the reception of His Spirit, the repentance and baptism which the apostles preached was 'unto remission of sins.' There was a real release.

That was why people who had repented, people who had been baptized with John's baptism, must repent again in a very different way, and be baptized with a baptism which could never be repeated. That was what men needed, not simply sorrow for past sin and a putting away of their wrong-doing and a resolve to amend, but a coming to Christ, an acceptance of Christ, the gift of the Holy Spirit. Men needed this repentance, this baptism unto remission of sins, this gift of the Holy Spirit. In the very beginning of the Acts the baptism of John is contrasted with baptism with the Holy Spirit. In the very first sermon of St Peter the Holy Spirit is promised to those who were baptized in the name of Jesus Christ unto the remission of sins (2.38). This note rings through the Acts. St Paul at Ephesus found certain disciples, and asked, 'Into what were ye baptized?' And they said, 'Into John's baptism.' Then said Paul: 'John verily baptized with the baptism of repentance, saying unto the people that they should believe on him which should come after him, that is, on Jesus. When they heard this they were baptized in the name of the Lord Jesus. And when Paul had laid his hands upon them the Holy Ghost came upon them' (19.2-6). Here clearly John's baptism is contrasted with baptism in the name of Jesus unto remission of sins and the gift of the Holy Ghost. Repentance was good, but it was not sufficient. Men needed remission of sins and the Holy Ghost.

The Apostles preached as men who were convinced that the need of men could only be satisfied by the gift of the Holy Spirit. It is here, in the close connexion between the preaching of the remission of sins and the gift of the Holy Spirit, that St Luke reveals most clearly his understanding of that hemisphere of the Holy Spirit which St Paul's epistles more clearly state. The hemisphere of redeeming love is in the Acts more definitely revealed; but the hemisphere of sanctification is not unrevealed. Remission of sins was preached in the name of Jesus; in the name of Jesus converts were baptized; in the name of Jesus the Holy Ghost was given. In Jesus was remission of sins, in Jesus forgiveness, in Jesus justification, in Jesus partaking of the Holy Ghost, whose presence in the soul makes remission and forgiveness and sanctification possible.

They preached as men who were convinced that the need of men could be satisfied only in Jesus Christ. 'There is none other name under heaven given among men,' said St Peter (4.12), and St Paul's preaching was that 'by him every one that believeth is justified from all things, from which ye could not be justified by the law of Moses.' (13.39). There is in the preaching in the Acts a grave and solemn note. To reject Jesus is to forfeit the remission of sins. 'Save yourselves,' says St Peter, 'from this untoward generation' (2.40). 'Beware,' cries St Paul, 'lest that come upon you which is spoken in the prophets; Behold, ye despisers, and wonder and perish' (13.39, 40). It is possible for them 'to judge themselves unworthy of eternal life' (13.46). When they persistently opposed themselves he uttered the solemn warning, 'Your blood be upon your own heads' (18.6). St Paul did not hesitate to speak of 'the wrath to come' (I Thess. 1.10). The very notion of salvation on which the apostles laid so much stress implied a danger and a serious danger, a need and an urgent need. They preached Christ as the Saviour and as the only Saviour, 'knowing the terror of the Lord' (II Cor. 5.11).

This is also the attitude of the gospels. In them too the love of the Father who sent the Son, and the love of the Son who came, is associated with the forgiveness of sins, with a deep need of men which nothing but the Passion of the Son of God could supply. The love of God was so great, the need of men was so great, that nothing short of the Incarnation and the Passion could satisfy it. The realization of the one and the realization of the other are closely united. And as in the gospels it was the love of God which first discerned the need, not the recognition of his need by man which first made him send up a great cry to God for help; so in the Acts it was the coming of the Spirit of Christ into the souls of men which led them to see the need of their fellow-men. It was the Holy Spirit who taught St Paul to know 'darkness' and 'the power of Satan.'

The apostles were profoundly conscious of the need of men for Christ, yet there are sayings in Acts, as in the gospels, which seem to

D

make that need appear less. In the gospels, for instance, there is a description of the judgment of the nations (St Matt. 25.31-46). There, men are represented as accepted by Christ on the ground that they have done well, that their actions partook of His nature of charity. So in the Acts, St Peter declares to Cornelius that 'in every nation he that feareth God and worketh righteousness is accepted with him' (10.35). And St Paul, who says that he preaches to those 'who are perishing' (I Cor. 1.18), says also that God 'will render to every man according to his works: to them who by patient continuance in well-doing seek for glory and honour and immortality, eternal life . . . glory and honour and peace to every man that worketh good, to the Jew first, and also to the Greek' (Rom. 2.6-10).

Now there is certainly a difficulty in reconciling the apostolic insistence upon the need of men, the apostolic assertion that men are in darkness, under the power of Satan and can be saved only in Christ, with this more comfortable doctrine that everybody, everywhere, whatever their religious beliefs, whatever their ignorance of Christ, will yet be accepted with God, if they obey the law written in their hearts.

We are familiar with these two apparently opposite doctrines in their modern form, each overstated and brought into the most extreme opposition, and in this modern form we reject them both. We have heard men talk of so many millions of souls passing into a Christless eternity within the space of time occupied by their speeches. That has struck us as horrible. We have heard men argue that it is most intolerant to imagine that the heathen so need Christ that they cannot be saved without Him, that it is a libel on the fatherhood of God to speak of men as 'perishing in their ignorance.' That strikes us as extraordinarily flabby. It is certainly not conformable to our strongest convictions about the Incarnation.

Still, the opposition is perplexing. We can understand how the conviction that all men need Christ with the deepest and most strong need can make men zealous missionaries. But this world-wide optimism, this conviction that heathen who serve God as they have been taught, and work righteousness as they can, are accepted with God, seems to weaken the missionary claim. We can hardly expect people to be as fervent in the propagation of the gospel if the heathen know enough to be saved, and if it will be well with them if only they do what they now know to be right. And we see that, in fact, many use this argument to justify lukewarmness in the support of, or even active opposition to, missions to the heathen. We feel almost compelled to accept one alternative or the other, either the apostolic doctrine of need so urgent, so instant, that nothing can be allowed to delay, or to prevent, the propagation of the gospel at all costs, or the equally apostolic doctrine of 'glory, honour, and peace to every man that worketh good,' and then the need for the propagation of the gospel seems to be less urgent.

In face of this difficulty it is well to return to the Acts and to read again the history recorded by St Luke. The apostolic missionaries, in his story, saw both sides of this question, they stated both sides, yet their zeal was not diminished at all. On the contrary, they lived and died in earnest, eager effort to bring the world to Christ. That is the fact set before us in the Acts. Obviously hope for the heathen does not necessarily weaken zeal for the propagation of the gospel.

The solution of the difficulty does not lie in the intellectual, but in the spiritual sphere. It is to be found in experience of the Holy Spirit, in an experience of His influence like theirs. It was the Holy Spirit who came to them with the fire of divine love. It was His presence which made them missionaries. Missionary zeal does not grow out of intellectual beliefs, nor out of theological arguments, but out of love. If I do not love a person I am not moved to help him by proofs that he is in need; if I do love him I wait for no proof of special need to urge me to help him. Knowledge of Christ is so rich a treasure that the spirit of love must necessarily desire to impart it. The mere assurance that others have it not is sufficient proof of their need. This spirit of love throws aside intellectual arguments that they can do very well without it. But if this spirit is not present, a man is easily persuaded that to impart a knowledge of Christianity (for it is noteworthy that such men always speak of Christianity rather than of Christ) is not necessary, nay, is superfluous expense of energy which might be better used in other ways.

The Holy Spirit is revealed in the Acts as the teacher of the need of men for Christ, because He illuminates men so that they see Christ, and know Christ for themselves. For themselves knowledge of Christ is an unspeakable necessity. When once the Holy Spirit reveals Christ to the soul, whatever the previous religion or morality of the man may have been, he is conscious that he could not do without Christ. Rob him of Christ, and he is robbed of all. It is wholly inconceivable that he should look back with satisfaction upon himself as he was without Christ. It is wholly inconceivable that he should think of himself as being saved without Christ then, and being saved in Christ now. 'Perishing in his ignorance' is not too strong a description for him. He knows that is exactly what he was. Then if he looks out into the world he sees men who do not know Christ. Their religion may be better or worse than his own early religion was; but he sees that in heathen lands men are living in sin, in sin which they know to be sin, in a social order where sin is an all-pervading force. He sees that they do not know Christ. He knows what his own state was before Jesus Christ was revealed to him. He knows that they have not that revelation of Jesus Christ. What can he say? 'Perishing in their ignorance' is not too strong an expression.

Yet, knowing the hopelessness of his own case without Christ, knowing the hopelessness of their case without Christ, there is, nevertheless, a hope. The Spirit of Christ is a Spirit quick to recognize and welcome signs of goodness, even as the spirit of love in human hearts is quick to welcome and recognize the least sign of goodness in those whom they deeply love. 'A cup of cold water' appears to the Spirit of love a sign of kinship with Christ; alms and prayers appear to that Spirit proofs of capacity to receive Christ; any striving after truth, any seeking after God if haply they may feel after Him and find Him will open at once the door of hope. Here is the sign. Here is a soul not remote from Christ. The Spirit of Christ goes out to him, with love, and approval, and thankfulness. It welcomes him. God accepts him. 'In every nation he that feareth God and worketh righteousness is accepted with him.' The Spirit of Christ knows it and rejoices in it.

This is no intellectual solution of the apparent opposition. If we treat the question as one to be viewed from the outside, impersonally; if we are content to weigh the one argument against the other; above all, if we welcome the sense of freedom from responsibility which a benevolent optimism might seem to induce, there is little doubt that we shall explain away the sterner teaching of the apostles, and welcome their expressions of universal hope as the larger truth. But then, since that attitude relieves us of all sense of need for active propagation of the gospel, it undermines all true understanding of the activity and zeal of the apostles. Their fervour must seem to us rather exaggerated and, we cannot possibly understand the Acts of the Apostles.

Nay, more, if we allow the consideration of heathen morality and
heathen religion to absolve us from the duty of preaching the gospel
we are really deposing Christ from His throne in our own souls. If we
admit that men can do very well without Christ, we accept the
Saviour only as a luxury for ourselves. If they can do very well without Christ, then so could we. This is to turn our backs upon the
Christ of the gospels and the Christ of Acts and to turn our faces
towards law, morality, philosophy, natural religion.

We look at the moral teaching of some of the heathen nations and
we find it higher than we had expected to find it. We ask, 'What more
do they need? They know what is right. They know enough. They
know more than they can practise. To teach them more would only
be to set them a standard still further above them.' Or we look at
morality in Christian lands, and we begin to wonder whether our
practice is really much higher than theirs, and we say, 'They are very
well as they are. Leave them alone.'

When we so speak and think we are treating the question of the
salvation of men exactly as we should have treated it had Christ
never appeared in the world at all. It is an essentially pre-Christian
attitude, and implies that the Son of God has not been delivered for
our salvation. It suggests that the one and only way of salvation
known to me is to keep the commandments. That was indeed true
before the coming of the Son of God, before the Passion, before the
Resurrection, before Pentecost; but after Pentecost that is no longer
true. After Pentecost the answer to any man who inquires the way of
salvation is no longer 'Keep the law,' but, 'Believe in the Lord Jesus
Christ.' The one question of vital importance is not, 'Do you keep
the law?' but, 'Did you receive the Holy Ghost when you believed?'

Similarly, we look at the religious systems of the East, and we find
in them much truth. We say, 'How beautiful! How good! What sub-
lime thoughts about the Deity are expressed here! Why should we
disturb the confidence of the people in such a belief as this?' The
answer is equally clear in the gospels and in Acts. No belief which
men had ever held was superior to Judaism, if there was any to equal
it; no philosophy was better than that of the best Greek teachers. Had
they sufficed, there had been no Passion of the Son of God. The
apostles, inspired by the Holy Ghost, were troubled with no doubts
whether the monotheism of the Jews or the philosophy of the Greeks
were sufficient for their salvation. Filled with the Spirit, they were

certain that both Jews and Greeks needed Christ, and that neither Jewish monotheism nor Greek philosophy would do instead.

When, then, we speak as though heathen moral teaching and heathen philosophical speculation absolved us from the duty of preaching Christ, if this is anything more than an excuse of idleness, if it really represents our religious belief, then it is a turning back from Christ to another gospel, which is not another, to a way of salvation well known before Christ came. When once men have done that in their own souls, it is not surprising that what they choose for themselves they find sufficient for others. We ought not to preach Christ, men say, because the morals and philosophy of the people are good! How does that absolve us? To those who so speak Christianity is a system of morals and philosophy, perhaps a little better than others, but essentially of the same order, better suited to us perhaps from any other system, but not essential, and therefore not of sufficient importance to justify us in disturbing ancestral beliefs.

Such conceptions of Christianity have nothing in common with the conceptions which lie at the back of the book of Acts or with the spirit of its author. They are the flat contradiction of the whole teaching of the Acts, and the denial of the Spirit there revealed as the 'Spirit of Christ and of God.' If they had been prevalent in the Church in the days which immediately followed Pentecost the history of the Church would have been a very different one. To read Acts with understanding, we must know, with the real knowledge born of experience, that the Spirit of Christ, the Spirit of the Incarnation and the Passion, the Spirit given at Pentecost, is the answer of God to a real need of the world, that is of every single soul in the world; for in the Acts these two meet, the redeeming Spirit and the utter need, and it is the redeeming Spirit that reveals the utter need.

V

The Administration of the Spirit

The apostles, moved by the Spirit, went forth as ministers of the Spirit. As ministers of the Spirit, they did not simply preach Jesus and the Resurrection, and so lead men to repentance and to faith in Christ; they communicated to others the Spirit which they themselves had received. They not only revealed the Spirit by their words and deeds, they not only convinced men that they had received the Spirit, but they administered the Spirit.

There are in the Acts a few accounts of the setting apart of Christians for special work in the Church by the laying on of hands. The seven were so ordained in Jerusalem by the apostles (6.6); Paul and Barnabas were so set apart in Antioch for their missionary work (13.3); and it is almost universally agreed, though it is not definitely stated by St Luke, that the elders were so ordained in the churches of Galatia (14.23).

In these accounts it is interesting to note:

First, that in none of these cases does St Luke assert that there was any gift of the Holy Spirit then given. Such a gift, a special gift for special work, there probably was. Such a gift is certainly suggested by St Paul's words to the Ephesian elders when he reminded them that the Holy Ghost had made them overseers (20.28); such a gift is certainly suggested by St Paul's charge to Timothy: 'Stir up the gift that is in thee through the laying on of my hands' (II Tim. 1.6), 'and of the presbytery' (I Tim. 4.14); but, if there was a gift, St Luke does not call attention to it.

Secondly, it is noticeable that St Luke constantly tells us that the persons upon whom hands were laid for some special office in the Church were men who had already received the Holy Spirit. This is definitely stated in the case of the seven (6.3) and of St Paul (9.17) and of Barnabas (11.24). Similarly, we are told of the disciples at Antioch in Pisidia that they were 'filled with joy and with the Holy Spirit' (13.52) before their elders were appointed (14.23). Indeed it is apparent that men were everywhere chosen for special office in the Church because they were full of the Holy Spirit.

These two considerations, that St Luke does not mention any gift of the Holy Spirit at the time of ordination, whilst he does notice the fact that the men so set apart were men already full of the Holy Spirit, must be enough to satisfy us that is was not in these cases that St Luke perceived the peculiar glory of that administration of the Spirit which began at Pentecost. Every reader of the Old Testament was familiar with passages which spoke of the imparting of a Spirit to men appointed to special work, by the laying on of the hands of inspired men, or by an anointing. The idea was quite familiar. What was not familiar, what was indeed peculiar to the new dispensation, was the communication of the Spirit to the whole body of Christians, and to every individual member of the body. That those who were possessed with the Spirit should lay hands on common men that they might be filled with the Spirit for their common daily life as Christians, was marvellously strange. It exalted the common life of common men to heights before held only by some special and important service of God. It exalted men occupied in humble tasks of daily toil to the position before peculiar to prophets and kings and priests. Christians all became kings and priests (Rev. 1.6; I Pet. 2.9); the Church became a kingdom of priests.

This laying of hands upon all who were baptized that they might receive the Holy Spirit seems to have been the universal practice. It is true that St Luke does not repeat again and again in every place that the apostles laid their hands on their converts that they might receive the Holy Spirit. But he begins with a promise made to the multitude by St Peter that if they would repent and believe in Jesus, they should receive the gift of the Holy Spirit (2.38); and he goes on to declare that St Peter asserted to the Council that this promise had actually been fulfilled (5.32). He then particularly explains what happened in Samaria: 'Now when the apostles which were at Jerusalem heard that Samaria had received the word of God, they sent unto them Peter and John, who when they were come down prayed for them, that they might receive the Holy Ghost; for as yet he was fallen upon none of them, only they were baptized in the name of the Lord Jesus. Then laid they their hands on them, and they received the Holy Ghost' (8.14-17). He further tells us what happened when St Paul met at Ephesus disciples who had been baptized into John's baptism, how he directed them to be baptized in the name of the Lord Jesus, and laid his hands upon them and the Holy

Ghost came on them (19.5, 6). Though he does not repeat again the like event in the case of each convert, he implies that they all everywhere did receive the gift, as when he says of the disciples at Antioch in Pisidia that they were filled with joy and with the Holy Ghost (13.52), though he has not mentioned any laying on of hands. This is borne out by the epistles of St Paul, who writes to his converts in Galatia, or in Thessalonica, or in Corinth as to men perfectly familiar with the gift of the Holy Spirit.

That St Luke considered the gift of the Holy Spirit necessary for every Christian is certain; consequently it seems strange that, in his account of the missionary preaching of St Paul, he never once mentions the promise of the Holy Spirit nor any teaching concerning that gift. I have before pointed out that the sermons and speeches of St Paul, as recorded in Acts, do not contain any complete statement of St Paul's gospel, and that a fuller statement can be gathered from the I Thessalonians alone than from any speech or sermon in Acts.[1] The fact that in these speeches and sermons there is no teaching about the Holy Spirit, a teaching which St Paul certainly gave to his converts, and which he certainly considered vital, makes this conclusion the more secure. St Luke, in reporting St Paul's speeches to particular people in particular places, was not setting forth his gospel in any fullness, but was accurately reporting what St Paul actually said under the special circumstances to the particular audience before him.

St Luke certainly teaches that the Holy Spirit was given to all the members of the Christian body; his language would certainly lead us to believe that the gift was administered by the laying on of hands of the apostles; nevertheless, it is remarkable that of the four cases in which he actually gives us any details there should be two in which the laying on of hands by one of the Twelve is definitely excluded. In the first of these St Luke tells us that St Paul, after his wonderful conversion, received the gift of the Holy Spirit by the laying on of hands (9.17); but he also expressly states the name of the minister, and the minister is not one of the inner circle of apostles. In the second case he expressly states that the gift was given without any human intermediary at all (10.44; 11.15; 15.8).

It is indeed strange that St Luke should have given us such very different accounts of the manner in which the gift was given; once by

---

[1] *Missionary Methods: St Paul's or Ours?*, chapter 7.

the laying on of the hands of St Peter and St John, once by the laying on of the hands of Ananias, once by the laying on of the hands of St Paul, and once in the presence of St Peter without any laying on of hands. When we consider how frequently reference is made in this book to the Holy Spirit, and how important St Luke manifestly considered the gift to be, it is indeed hard to escape from the conclusion that he was far more profoundly concerned with the reality and universality of the gift than he was with the mode of the administration of the gift. That which was of primary importance in his eyes was the presence of the Spirit, the gift of the Spirit, the certainty of the presence, the certainty of the gift; the means by which the gift was received seems to have been stated rather to assure us of the certainty of the fact than for its own importance.

In saying this I do not deny that there was a normal manner and means by which the gift was administered. That means doubtless was the laying on of apostolic hands. I do not wish to deny that St Luke teaches us a very important fact when he assures us that the gift was administered by the laying on of the apostles' hands. But I think it is useful to observe how the emphasis is laid by St Luke; for I perceive that we are often in danger of laying the greater emphasis on that upon which he laid the less. Some of our teachers speak of the allusions in the Acts as though the laying on of apostolic hands was the one point of vital importance, whereas St Luke writes as though the gift of the Holy Spirit were the one thing of vital importance, by whatever means that gift was conveyed, whether with, or without, the external act.

The apostles, then, did manifestly go forth as men moved by the Spirit to communicate the Spirit to others. The Holy Ghost was promised, the Holy Ghost was ministered. 'If the ministration of death written and engraven in stones was glorious, so that the children of Israel could not steadfastly behold the face of Moses for the glory of his countenance; which glory was to be done away: how shall not the ministration of the Spirit be rather glorious?' (II Cor. 3.7, 8). Glorious it was, glorious it remains.

This administration of the Spirit is the key of the apostolic work. It alone explains the promise of remission of sins in the preaching of the apostles. It alone explains the assurance of forgiveness which filled the hearts of their converts. It alone explains the new power which was manifested in the life of the Christian Church, the new striving after holiness, the new charity expressed in organized form for the amelioration of the sufferings of the poorer brethren. It alone explains the certainty of the hope of eternal life which filled the souls of the Christians and enabled them to face persecution and martyrdom. It alone explains the new sense of the value and dignity of the body which led to a new enthusiasm for purity of life and created hospitals for the care of the diseased. It alone explains the zeal for the salvation of men, which carried the gospel of Christ throughout the then known world.

VI

The Spirit the Source and Test of New Forms of Missionary Activity

In the Acts there is revealed a most curious change in the conduct of the apostles before and after Pentecost. Whether St Luke deliberately desired to call our attention to this change is not clear; but in his narrative the change is very apparent. Before Pentecost the apostles are represented as acting under the influence of an intellectual theory; after Pentecost they are represented as acting under the impulse of the Spirit.

The only event recorded after the Ascension before Pentecost is the appointment of Matthias. This appointment was made, we are told, at the instigation of St Peter, and the speech in which he urged it upon his fellow apostles is reported. St Peter found a passage in the Old Testament which seemed to him to foretell the defection of Judas. This passage ended with the words, 'His office let another take.' From this St Peter concluded that the apostles ought to choose a man to fill the position left vacant by the death of the traitor. Here there is implied an argument which is yet more clearly expressed in the prayer which follows: 'Thou Lord, which knowest the hearts of all men, show of these two the one whom thou hast chosen, to take the place in this ministry and apostleship, from which Judas fell away.' The argument is that Christ appointed twelve apostles: that one had fallen away and perished: the number of the apostles was therefore incomplete: consequently it was the duty of the apostles to restore it by appointing a new member.

Convinced by this argument, they resolved to appoint one of those who had been with them from the beginning and was a witness of the Resurrection. There were many who satisfied these conditions. In order to determine which of these should be appointed to the vacant office, they first selected two, and then adopted a method commonly practised in the Old Testament to discover the will of God: they cast lots. The lot fell upon Matthias, and he was numbered with the eleven apostles.

By casting lots the apostles revealed that they had not that clear and intuitive apprehension of the will of God which sometimes marked the actions of some of the Old Testament prophets. When Samuel, for instance, went to Bethlehem, and Jesse made his sons to pass before him, the prophet, as he viewed each one, was perfectly clear that he knew the mind of God. 'The Lord hath not chosen this,' he said again and gain, until it almost appeared that he had rejected the whole family. At last, when David was sent for and brought in, he recognized at once the man whom the Lord had chosen, and anointed him. The apostles had not this certain knowledge: they adopted a method used by those who were in doubt as to the mind of God.

Thus, in the account given by St Luke of the appointment of Matthias, these two points stand out with remarkable clearness: first, that the action of the apostles was based upon an intellectual theory, and secondly that they had no definite spiritual guidance which revealed to them unmistakably any individual disciple as called by Christ to the apostolate.

After Pentecost a very remarkable change is to be seen. The apostles no longer argue: they obey a spiritual impulse. They do not act in obedience to the dictates of an intellectual theory; the one and only guide, both in their own actions and in their judgment of the action of others, is their recognition of the Spirit in themselves and others.

I have already pointed out that St Peter expressed a great understanding of the nature and work of Jesus in his first sermon; but neither he nor his fellow apostles had intellectually grasped the truth which he expressed. They did not begin their work with a reasoned theory. They did not argue that, the nature and work of Christ being universal, they must embrace the whole world in their view. Christ taught this; but the apostles did not grasp it at once. Their view was limited, their understanding partial. But neither did they begin with a theory of the nature and work of Christ, or of the character of their mission which excluded the greater part of the human race, a theory which needed to be revised and corrected as time went on and larger and truer conceptions were admitted. Their view was partial, but it was not false; it was limited, but it was not misleading. So far as they could see, they spoke truly of Christ and of their work; nay, more, they spoke in terms which embraced more than they understood.

This was due to the fact that they did not begin their work under the direction of an intellectual theory, but under the impulse of the Spirit. This Spirit was in its nature world-wide, all-embracing. Consequently they did not gradually enlarge their sympathies, and extend their activities in obedience to the demands of an intellectual progress; the world-embracing spirit enlarged and expanded their sympathy, and intellectual illumination followed. They then perceived the wider and larger application of truths of which they had hitherto seen only the partial application, Study of the doctrine did not lead to the wider activity; enlarged activity led them to understand the doctrine.

Similarly, their sense of the need of men for Jesus Christ was essentially the apprehension of a universal truth. Wherever they might meet men, the men whom they met would share that need which they knew first for themselves and for their fellow countrymen. If they knew the need at all, they knew it for the world. Consequently, when they expressed it, though their thoughts at the moment were turned to a special limited class of men, yet the expression took universal form. They did not argue that the need of this class of men, or of that race of men, was great, and that therefore they must take steps to supply the need. They were moved, not so much by an intellectual apprehension, as by a spiritual illumination. They met men, and the need of those men whom they met cried aloud to them. Their own desire for the revelation of the glory of Jesus in the salvation of men went out towards those whom they met, and was immediately answered by the recognition of the need of those whom they met for Jesus Christ.

Again, Christ had given them a world-wide commission, embracing all the nations; but intellectually they did not understand what He meant. They found that out as they followed the impulse of the Spirit.

They did not base their action upon any intellectual interpretation of the nature and work and command of Christ. Neither did they base their action upon any anticipation of results which might be expected to follow from it. They did not argue that the conversion of any particular class or race of men might be expected greatly to strengthen the Church for her work in the world and therefore they ought to make special efforts to win the adhesion of this class or race. They did not argue that the relaxation or abandonment of familiar rules would inevitably result in serious injury to the Church. They did argue that any particular action of a missionary was to be condemned because, if it were approved, it would seem to undermine some generally accepted doctrine, or would greatly disturb the minds of a large body of Christians, or would lead to developments which might be undesirable. The apostles acted under the impulse of the Spirit; their action was not controlled by the exigencies of any intellectual theory.

This is most manifest in those steps towards the evangelization of the Gentiles upon which St Luke lays special stress. Philip the Evangelist went to meet the Ethiopian under the direct influence of the Spirit, and baptized him without apparently drawing, or expecting others to draw, any conclusions from his action which might involve the whole Church in a policy. In the crucial case of the visit of St Peter to Cornelius, St Peter himself was prepared by a special vision, and evidently realized that his action was liable to be called in question; but he acted under the impulse of the Spirit, though neither he nor the others really understood what consequences were involved in his action. St Peter certainly did not think the matter out, decide that the Gentiles were within the terms of Christ's commission, and then, and therefore, proceed to preach to them. Even St Paul himself did not begin with argument. It was repeatedly revealed to him that he was called to preach to the Gentiles; but only after his action had taken effect, when men disputed and opposed him, did he begin to formulate a theory that results which he saw to be blessed were in truth the fulfilment of Old Testament prophecies and teaching, and a true revelation of the nature and work of Jesus Christ.

Thus the path by which the apostles reached the truth was submissive obedience in act to the impulse of the Holy Spirit. When the moment came, when the Spirit in them moved them to desire men's salvation, and to feel their need, they acted, they spoke, they expressed that Spirit of love and desire, not knowing what the result of their action might be, nor how to justify it intellectually, certain only that they were directed by the Holy Spirit.

This seems to us very disturbing and dangerous. It looks like acting upon the impulse of the moment. 'First act, then think,' sounds strange doctrine in the ears of men like ourselves brought up to live very much within the bounds of the proverb, 'Look before you leap.' But there are two points at which men may look before they leap; one without and one within, or one above and one below; and the proverb suggests to us rather the outward and the below than the inward and the above. The apostles did not act thoughtlessly, because they did not base their action upon a nice calculation of the probable consequences. To calculate consequences and to act solely with a view to consequences, is worldly wisdom. The apostles were not guided in their action by worldly wisdom. They were guided by the Spirit. Care and wisdom are as clearly shown in consideration of the source as in consideration of the probable result of an action. It was this care and wisdom which the apostles showed. They did not consider consequences so much as sources. The important question was not what result would follow, but from what source did the action spring. Persuaded that they were guided by the Spirit, they acted, and the result proved their wisdom.

This also was their defence when they were attacked. This was the ground upon which the whole body approved of the action of one of their number. When the Jews in Jerusalem disputed with St Peter concerning his action in going to the house of Cornelius, St Peter's answer was not to allay the anxiety of his opponents with regard to the possible consequences of his action, but to reassert the source of the action. He recounted his vision, he maintained that the Holy Spirit sent him, he declared that God gave the Holy Spirit to Cornelius and his household. His action was necessary. 'What was I, that I could withstand God?' (11.17). Convinced of the source of his action, the Council at once upheld it.

Similarly, St Paul defended his action before the Jerusalem Council. He had nothing to say of consequences possible or probable. He strove to convince his hearers that he had acted under the guidance of the Holy Spirit. To the apostles and elders he declared 'all things that God had done with them' (15.4); to the multitudes he declared 'what signs and wonders God had wrought among the Gentiles by them' (15.12). Signs and wonders were enough to prove to the multitude that God was with them; for all believed that 'no man can do these signs except God be with him.' The source of his action was more important than the probable consequences which worldly wisdom could foresee. When his hearers were convinced of the source of his action, opposition broke down. The leaders of the church accepted it and approved it.

Today we are more anxious about consequences, less sure of sources. When new and strange action is proposed, or actually effected, and questions are asked, the first question is, Is it wise? What will be the result of permitting such things to be done? We hear men argue, If we allow such and such actions to pass uncondemned the Church will have denied her faith, or her orders, or her sacraments, and the faith will be overthrown, the orders cease, the sacraments be destroyed. This was the sort of judgment which the apostles refused to admit. Only one other judgment is possible, and that is the judgment of the Spirit which led to the action. From this judgment the Church today shrinks. The Christian body does not seem to feel sure of its ground. Men say, We can judge actions: these are open. In judging these they seem to feel that they are dealing with something concrete. They feel at home with what they call facts; but the spirit which impelled the action seems to be something intangible and rather nebulous. They do not feel sure of themselves in dealing with that. If Christians take some unusual line of conduct and say, We felt impelled by the Spirit of God to do this, voices are heard on all sides, crying of precedents, and consequences. None seems to dare to inquire by what Spirit these men were impelled to their action. But this was the one question with which the apostles were wholly concerned in such a case.

When we turn from considerations of Spirit to considerations of policy and expediency we base our judgment upon the unknown; we forsake the way of the Spirit; we are in danger of losing the path which leads to the revelation of truth.

Of the results of action we are not capable judges. The Council of Jerusalem could not have foretold the results which would follow upon its decisions. St Paul himself could not foresee the results which would follow his journey to Jerusalem. Results are seldom exactly what we expect; they are often very different from our expectations. We assert boldly that such and such consequences will follow; they very seldom do. The man who anticipates with any approach to accuracy the consequences of any critical action is justly admired as a wonderful prophet. To base our judgment upon anticipation of consequences is to base it upon the most unstable foundations.

And the sure foundation we reject. Nowhere is the Spirit revealed as the Spirit who guides men by enabling them to anticipate the results of their action. Once and again the Spirit inspired prophets to foretell coming events so that the servants of God might prepare to take the right action when the event actually came to pass; never did

E

He cause men to foresee what the providence of God would cause to result from their action. But constantly, again and again, He inspired them to judge the spirit behind actions done. St Peter so judged the spirit of the lame man at the Beautiful Gate, and of Ananias and of Simon Magus; so Stephen judged the spirit of his opponents; so the apostles chose men full of the Holy Spirit; so St Paul judged the spirit which moved Elymas to oppose the conversion of the proconsul; and so the Council of Jerusalem judged the spirit which moved St Peter and St Paul when their actions seemed questionable. St John indeed exhorts Christians to try the spirits. In truth, this is the one thing that Christian men can judge. Spirit answers to spirit. Christian men inspired by the Holy Ghost can know the spirit which inspires such and such a man to do such and such an action. The Spirit was given to the Church that the Church might so udge spiritually spiritual things. To decline to question the spirit and to give our whole attention to the material form is to depart from the Spirit.

But it will perhaps be objected that we cannot be bound to approve every action which good men perform from high motives. Certainly we cannot. It is one thing to recognize that good men, moved by good motives, often do foolish, or even wrong, things; it is another to decline to appeal to the Spirit, preferring to base our judgments rather upon imagined consequences than upon recognition of spiritual guidance. Some actions are at once apparent: they could not be the result of the Holy Spirit's inspiration. Some are in doubt. It is these that we are to judge and to support or to oppose. My point is, that in arriving at a decision in a question of doubt, the apostles in the Acts were guided solely by their sense of the Spirit behind the action, not by any speculations as to consequences which might ensue.

And so they found the truth. Gradually the results of the action manifested themselves, and, seeing them, they perceived what they had really done, and learnt the meaning of the truth revealed in the action. But if, from fear of the consequences, they had checked or forbidden the action, they would have lost this revelation. They would have missed the way to truth. And that is the danger which besets judgments based upon expediency, or upon anticipations of results. Such judgments close the way to the revelation of new truth. The unknown is too fearful, the untried too dangerous. It is safer to refuse than to admit. So the possibility of progress is lost, and the opportunity. From this the apostles were saved by their recognition of the supremacy of the Spirit.

VII

The Gift of the Spirit the Sole Test of Communion

Moved by the Holy Spirit given to them, the apostles went forth as missionaries. The Holy Spirit filled them with a desire for the salvation of men in Jesus Christ; He revealed to them the need of men. As they came into contact with different types and orders of men, so the Holy Spirit filled them with desire for the salvation of these and with the sense of their need. They could not but preach. Hence arose the great controversy over the admission of the Gentiles into the Church, a story which occupies so important a place in the Acts of the Apostles.

We have already seen how the apostles were led to preach to the Gentiles, how they justified their action on the ground that they were guided by the Holy Spirit. It now remains to point out how the church in Jerusalem was led to admit these Gentiles as members of the body.

The difficulty to be overcome was great. Before Christ came, a revelation of God had been made to men. One nation had been chosen by God to be the recipients of that revelation. The people of that nation had been brought near to Him. He had established His covenant with them. He had ordained the rites and ceremonies by which they should be admitted into His covenant and preserved in it. Christ, the Christ in whom the Apostles believed, whom they preached as the only Saviour, appeared in that nation, within that covenant. He came in fulfilment of promises made to the covenant people alone. He Himself accepted the authority of Moses, the great mediator of the covenant; He upheld the authority of the Mosaic system by word and by example. He obeyed the law, He observed the feasts. He learned the Scriptures, He quoted them with approval, He commanded obedience as a duty. Some traditional interpretations He rejected as calculated to overlay and hide the real force of the teaching contained in the Mosaic code; but no one, not even His enemies at His trial, contended that He broke the law, or undermined its authority, or that He attempted to lead men to despise, or to escape from, the covenant made by God with the fathers. He was condemned within the covenant on the ground that, within the covenant, He made a claim which His opponents declared to be blasphemous. Even St Paul, in his controversy with the Judaizing party within the Church, never attempted to argue that Christ in His life overtly, or by implication, had overthrown the law or had taught His disciples that they need not keep it.

Christ appeared within the covenant, and when He appointed His apostles He appointed only men who were within the covenant. He had found faith among Gentiles. Of one of these He had said that He had 'not found so great faith, no, not in Israel' (St Luke 7.9); but He called no Gentile to preach the gospel to Gentiles. He himself and His chosen Apostles were all within the covenant.

How, then, could disciples of this Christ do otherwise than He had done, or be other than He was? How could any one outside the covenant be the disciple of Christ who was within the covenant? The very notion was absurd. Could he be outside and inside at the same time? Could he follow a Christ who was within the covenant, whilst he remained outside the covenant? Could he accept Christ and not accept Moses whom Christ accepted? How could Christ's apostles overthrow the covenant, abandon the covenant themselves, and admit or recognize as servants of Christ men who were not within the covenant? Christ and His salvation were to be found only within the covenant. Who dare venture outside it? This argument alone should be sufficient to hinder any who called himself a Christian from preaching Christ without the law.

If such a dangerous experiment were tried, nothing but disaster could follow. The Mosaic teaching had been a preparation for the gospel invaluable and necessary. Outside the covenant what sort of ideas of God prevailed? The gods of the heathen were degraded and degrading abominations, devils, whose worship and everything connected with it was contamination for a righteous man. A few happily escaped out of the slough, but they escaped, not by listening to the teaching of philosophers, but by becoming proselytes. If, then, Gentiles were to become Christians, that was the path by which they must approach Christ.

If Gentile ideas of God needed to be corrected, their morals needed correction as fundamental. The immorality of the Phrygian scandalized the Greek; the immorality of the Greek scandalized the Roman of the old school; the immorality of them all scandalized the Jew still more deeply. Fornication was not even thought to be a vice. Men practised it openly, unashamed. It was not only condoned by religious men; it had a place in their religious rites. And vices more degrading still were commonly practised and condoned. Thus to the Jew the restrictions of the law were not merely valuable customs, designed to preserve the unity and purity of the people of God from contamination by intermixture with others, they were not merely safeguards of a ritual purity, they were the only possible and absolutely indispensable safeguards against positive and flagrant immorality. They were the foundation and pillar of sound moral life, both for the individual and for the people.

How, then, could the gospel be preached without the law? How could men accept Christ and not accept the law on which all purity of life depended? How could men be promised salvation in Christ without being directed to undergo the rite which symbolized adherence to the moral life, without being compelled to keep the law? Was immorality of life agreeable to Christian faith? Was Christ the minister of sin? Christ and holiness were inseparable. To teach men to believe in Christ, to teach them that they could be saved by Christ, without teaching tham the law was to separate these two. It was to ensure that the Christian faith would be divorced from purity of life.

To attempt to teach the heathen to keep the moral law without binding them to the Mosaic Law was to attempt the impossible. The Jews needed the law to direct them even at home; abroad they needed it still more. How, then, could new converts in an atmosphere of heathenism be expected to maintain any moral standard without the law? If they deliberately accepted the Jewish code, if they bore in their bodies the marks of their dedication to the moral life, if they associated themselves as closely as possible with those who, by tradition and inheritance and the long discipline of centuries of training, through much suffering had learnt the necessity of a high moral standard, then there was hope for them; but, without that, how could belief in Christ alone suffice? The temptations of their surroundings, the customs of their people, the inherited tendencies of ages would be too strong for them. They must fall. Christian morals would be no better than heathen morals. This was surely enough to secure that the Gentiles could never be admitted into the Church by Jews until they accepted circumcision and confessed themselves bound by the law.

But this was not all. If uncircumcised Gentiles were admitted into the Church what was to be their relation to faithful Jews? If Jews received them and shared with them in the Breaking of Bread, they themselves would lose their own position, they themselves would cease to be within the covenant, they would be unclean. For a keeper of the law to associate on equal terms with one who did not keep the law was impossible. Jewish Christians would, in accepting Gentiles, put themselves outside the pale. In order to admit men who, on every reasonable ground, ought not to be admitted, those who by birth and education were within must be exiled. What could be more absurd than to cast out the children in order to receive strangers who could never really be received, even at so great a price!

If the Jewish Christians received the uncircumcised they themselves and their children would lose the great safeguards which strict observance of the law provided. The weaker brethren would become worse than Grecian Jews. Already they had seen the dangers of laxity; they had seen a despised race of Jews who sought to compromise with heathen surroundings. Their history provided them with a fearful warning and a strong incentive to resist to the uttermost any approach to uncircumcised life. The story of the Maccabees might well deter them from weakness and persuade them to fight to the last for the strictest obedience to the law.

But even if they avoided the Gentile converts and refrained from communion with them, they could not escape. The mere fact that uncircumcised men were admitted into the Church, by whomsoever they might have been admitted and wherever, that mere fact that uncircumcised men were members of the Church of Christ would involve the acceptance of the principle that men could be saved without the law. The Church would be a body in which circumcised and uncircumcised members alike hoped for, and received, a like salvation. Then, if some men could be saved without the law, so could all. If the heathen who knew not the law could be saved by Christ in the Church, then the Jew too could be saved by Christ without the law, if he chose to abandon the law. The observance of the law was certainly a burden. Some, at least, would be glad to escape from the burden. Such an escape would be a great relief and a great convenience. Some would certainly escape. And so there would be Jewish Christians living like heathen, and a great temptation to follow their example would lie in the way of every young Christian who lived in a Roman or Greek city. There was really no alternative. To admit the uncircumcised meant that the Church of Christ forsook the covenant rather than that the Gentiles were received into a church within the covenant.

The example of Christ, the duty of disciples, the religious privileges of the Jews, the foundations of morality, were all to be abandoned. Any heathen who could show that he had been baptized might claim to be in as good a position as the Jewish Christians. Surely it was absurd and wicked to suggest such a thing; and for what end was the sacrifice to be made? Merely that heathen who were accustomed to live licentious lives might escape from a burden which every Jew and every proselyte knew that they ought to bear.

How was this argument answered? By one fact: God gave them the Holy Spirit. 'They of the circumcision which believed were astonished, as many as came with Peter, because that on the Gentiles also was poured out the gift of the Holy Ghost. For they heard them speak with tongues, and magnify God. Then answered Peter, Can any man forbid water, that these should not be baptized, which have received the Holy Ghost as well as we?' (10.45-47). The gift of the Holy Spirit to these men convinced and satisfied St Peter that they must be received into the Church. When his action was called in question at Jerusalem this was his answer: 'The Spirit bade me go with them' (11.12); 'the Holy Ghost fell on them as on us at the beginning' (11.15); 'Forasmuch, then, as God gave them the like gift as He did unto us who believed on the Lord Jesus Christ, what was I, that I could withstand God?' (11.17). That answer silenced his opponents.

Later, when the preaching of St Paul and the rapid extension of the Church in heathen provinces and the admission of large numbers of men who had not even been taught the Jewish code caused the question to be raised again, it was St Peter who, after hearing the account given by St Paul of his work, brought forward this first answer to all objections. He simply recalled his own earlier experience. 'God, which knoweth the hearts, bare them witness, giving them the Holy Ghost, even as he did unto us' (15.8). If God gave the Holy Spirit there was no more any possibility of refusal on the part of the apostles to receive those to whom the Holy Ghost was given. No argument could stand in the face of that one fact.

The gift of the Holy Ghost is thus seen to be the one necessity for communion. If the Holy Ghost is given, those to whom He is given are certainly accepted in Christ by God. All who receive the Spirit are in reality and truth one. They are united by the strongest and most intimate of all ties. They are all united to Christ by His Spirit, and therefore they are all united to one another. Men may separate them, systems may part them from the enjoyment and strength of their unity; but, if they share the one Spirit, they are one.

In this case the new converts desired communion with the apostles. The apostles acknowledged that they had the Spirit. Being led themselves by the Spirit, they put aside all the countless and crushing objections which could be raised, they put aside all the serious disabilities under which these new converts laboured, they recognized the fact and accepted the consequence. God gave the Holy Spirit; they admitted at once that nothing more was needed for salvation, nothing else was needful for communion.

NOTES TO CHAPTER VII

1. Perhaps some one will say that all who were received into the Church by the apostles accepted the apostolic doctrine and order, none were admitted who did not accept these, and that consequently there is here another test of communion.

'To this I would answer: (1) The whole point of the story of Cornelius and of the admission of the Gentiles lies in the fact that these people had not accepted what up to that moment had been considered a necessary part of the Christian teaching. The question was whether they could be admitted without accepting the teaching and undergoing the rite. It was that question which was settled by the acknowledgment that they had received the Holy Spirit. (2) When the apostles spoke of men with whom they were not in communion, they used language which showed that they were convinced that those with whom they were not in communion had not the Spirit.[1] The moment it was admitted that they had the Spirit they were accepted.

The difficulty today is that Christians acknowledge that others have the Spirit, and yet do not recognize that they ought to be, and must be, because spiritually they are, in communion with one another. Men who hold a theory of the Church which excludes from communion those whom they admit to have the Spirit of Christ simply proclaim that their theory is in flat contradiction to the spiritual fact. Their theory separates those whom the Spirit unites. In other words, they and the Spirit differ on the question whether certain persons ought, or ought not, to be admitted to communion with Christ. The Spirit accepts them and dwells in them; the theory excludes them.

[1] In Jude 19 this is expressly stated. Many passages in St Paul's and St John's epistles manifestly imply it.

We must then distinguish carefully tests which prove whether the Spirit is given like St Paul's 'No man can say that Jesus is the Lord, but by the Holy Ghost' (1 Cor. 12, 3), and tests which are applied after it is admitted that the Holy Ghost is given. The first is a true test: for there can be no communion between those who have and those who have not the Spirit of Christ. The second is the introduction of a test to subvert a spiritual fact already acknowledged. This is exactly what the Acts of the Apostles teaches us not to do.

2. It will perhaps be said that in our present state of schism this assertion of spiritual principle can give us no definite guidance for action, can provide us with no clear programme, and must remain unfruitful. Surely that is not wholly true. It certainly must help us if we recognize that it is the presence of the Holy Spirit which creates a unity which we can never create. If men believe in the existence of this unity, they may begin to desire it, and desiring it to seek for it, and seeking it to find it. If, when they find it, they refuse to deny it, in due time, by ways now unsearchable, they will surely return to external communion.

It is not true that the assertion of spiritual principle is vain, because we cannot see at the moment how to express that principle in action. It would assuredly make a difference if Christians, in their approach one to another, realized that, in spite of appearances, they were in fact one. If, in their seeking after external reunion, they realized that they were seeking not to create a unity which does not yet exist, but to find an expression for a unity which does exist, which is indeed the one elemental reality, they would approach one another in a better frame of mind. The common recognition of the principle would in itself be a unifying force of great value, and would dispose those who shared it to approach questions of difference in a spirit of unity which would immensely assist their deliberations.

VIII

Conclusion

In the preceding chapters I have tried to show that the coming of the Holy Spirit at Pentecost was the coming of a missionary Spirit; that the Spirit stirred in the hearts of the disciples of Christ a great desire to impart that which they had received; that He revealed to them the need of men for that which He alone could supply; that He enabled them to hand on to others that which they themselves had received; that He led them to reach out farther and farther into the Gentile world, breaking down every barrier of prejudice which might have hindered their witness, or prevented them from receiving into communion men the most remote from them in habits of thought and life.

Those who received the Holy Spirit became witnesses. The gospel was spread not only by men set apart for this work, but also by the general body of disciples. After the death of Stephen 'they that were scattered abroad went everywhere preaching the word' (8.4); and the apostles are expressly excluded from the number of those who were so scattered (8.1). In Galatia, after St Paul's second visit, it is said that the churches were established in the faith, and increased in number daily (16.5). From Thessalonica 'the word of the Lord sounded, and not only in Macedonia and Achaia,' but far beyond (I Thess. 1.8). The whole history of the Church in the early centuries witnesses to the fact that the disciples were missionaries to the heathen among whom they lived.

The Spirit, the missionary Spirit, was given to all. Whosoever received the Holy Ghost received that, and, in some degree, if only by approval and support of the missionary efforts of others, expressed it. Some in the Church received special direction to special work in a special way or in particular places. So St Paul and Barnabas were called to evangelize the West. So St Peter was sent to the circumcision, so Timothy was taken from Lystra to help St Paul. Simeon and Niger and Manaen, and others like them, received no such special call. Yet they did not fail to manifest the missionary spirit within them.

The Spirit was given to all. Whosoever received the Holy Spirit in some degree, if only by approval and support of the efforts of others, expressed that desire for the conversion of the world which the Spirit inspired. What was wholly unknown, what was unthinkable in the early Church, was that Christians should oppose, or deride, or even fail to support, men who were labouring to spread the knowledge of Christ in the regions beyond. Not even the Judaizing party in Jerusalem did that. The Judaizers protested strongly against the form in which the gospel was preached to the Greeks; they sent out their own emissaries to attack, to undermine, and to destroy, so far as they possibly could, the influence and teaching of St Paul; but their opposition was directed, not against the conversion of the heathen, not against missionary work as such, but only against a particular form of teaching which they deemed to be dangerous. It was universally agreed that the gospel must be preached to all the nations.

All who received the Spirit were more or less conscious of the missionary impulse of the Spirit. They all truly obeyed the command to go into all the world, for they all possessed a Spirit which impelled them to desire the world-wide manifestation of Christ. And it is the world-embracing Spirit which obeys the command rather than the wandering body. Christ came into all the world, though in the flesh He never went outside Palestine. It is obviously necessary to avoid the mistake of thinking that the reception and expression of the missionary Spirit necessarily involves going on missionary journeys, or that missionary journeys are necessarily truer and fuller expressions of the missionary Spirit than any other. The Spirit of redeeming love is manifestly expressed as truly in striving for the salvation of men at home as in preaching to the heathen beyond the seas. It is the reception and the expression of redeeming love which is of importance, rather than the manner or the form of the work in which that Spirit is expressed.

The Spirit of desire for the salvation of the world may be expressed in any form of Christian activity; but that Spirit is not revealed to others with equal clearness by every form of activity. In the Acts, as I have tried to point out, St Luke makes the revelation of the Spirit clear to us by setting before us the acts of those men in the early Church whose lives were devoted to what we, today, call 'missionary work. If he had dwelt upon the labours of those others who were not engaged in this special missionary work the revelation would have been less clear. The work of those who organized the Church may well have been as true an expression of the Spirit of redeeming love as the work of those of whom St Luke tells us most; but if he had written at length of church organization we should probably have missed the revelation of the Spirit as the Spirit which labours for the salvation of the world. When, by the insistence of St Luke upon the missionary aspect, we have learnt to know the Spirit as the Spirit who inspires active zeal for the salvation of others, we can then easily perceive the same Spirit in other forms of activity, and we can understand that the organization of the church and the amelioration of social conditions are equally forms in which that Spirit finds expression. We then find that every form of Christian activity may be used to express that Spirit. Every form of work can be undertaken in that Spirit, each individual finding in his own proper work the best way to manifest that desire for the salvation of men which the Holy Spirit inspires.

In this large sense, if we believe in the Holy Spirit as He is revealed in the Acts, we must be missionaries. We cannot accept the teaching of the Acts, we cannot believe that the one thing of importance to our souls is to receive and to know the Spirit, without feeling ourselves driven to missionary action. We cannot believe that the Holy Spirit reveals our own need and the need of men without beginning to feel that need of men for Christ laid upon us as a serious call to action. We cannot believe that the Holy Spirit is given to us that those who so need Christ may be by us brought to find the one way of salvation for their souls and bodies in this world and in the world to come, without feeling impelled to action. We cannot believe that men everywhere, whatever their previous education or ignorance, whatever their civilization or barbarism, are capable of receiving Christ and His salvation, without being moved to take a world-wide view of our responsibility. We must embrace the world because Christ embraces the world, and Christ has come to us, and Christ in us embraces the world. Activity world-wide in its direction and intention and hope and object is inevitable for us unless we are ready to deny the Holy Spirit of Christ revealed in the Acts.

2

Non-Professional Missionaries

Editorial Note
The whole text of Non-Professional Missionaries *is printed, apart from the Preface.*

Non-Professional Missionaries

It is an interesting fact that missionaries intensely dislike being called professionals. Doctors do not feel any such abhorrence: teachers do not feel it: lawyers do not, neither do military or naval officers. It is by evangelistic missionaries that it seems to be felt most strongly. Missionary doctors and teachers apparently have no objection to the term as doctors or teachers; if they feel this dislike at all, they feel it only when the term is applied to them as missionaries; and by 'as missionaries' is meant as missionaries of the gospel.

By a 'missionary of the gospel' I understand a man who having found the secret of life in Christ is eager to impart it to others. The gospel is for him the only way of life; there can be no other: men who do not share his secret are living in darkness and perishing in their ignorance: that is the difference between a missionary of the gospel and a lecturer on comparative religion. A missionary is therefore an evangelist.

It is true that the modern division of missionaries into three classes or faculties, medical, educational and evangelistic, implies on the face of it that evangelization is not the work of the medical, or of the educational, missionary; and it is true that some of the medical and educational missionaries definitely decline to be called evangelists. I shall have occasion to examine the inner meaning of this attitude later; for it is an important matter and throws no small light on the subject which we are discussing; but here all that I need say is that all missionaries sent out by Christian missionary societies are sent out as men who desire the conversion of those to whom they are sent, and to that extent must be evangelists. If a missionary sent out by a Christian missionary society is not an evangelist in this sense, it is hard to know what he is a missionary of, or what his mission really is. I know that today confusing voices are heard at great missionary conferences; but I think that my readers will agree with me that a Christian missionary ought to be a man who has found the great secret of life in Christ and is eager to share it with others; and that it is as such that medical and educational missionaries feel a shrinking

F

from being called professional missionaries. The dislike, so far as they feel it, is a dislike which they as evangelists share with the evangelistic missionaries technically so called, and its meaning must be sought here, rather than in their medical or educational profession. We must enquire then why a man devoted to the propagation of the gospel should resent the suggestion that he is a professional.

A professional is a man who is recognized and accepted as duly qualified to practise some vocation or calling which requires learning or technical skill: that is the first and essential meaning of the term. To this is commonly added the conclusion that he makes his living, or may make his living, by the practice of his profession. Is there anything here which should properly cause a missionary to shrink from the term professional? If there is, what is it?

On the face of it, at the first glance, it would appear that nearly all missionaries today are professionals and are properly so called. They are nearly all attached to some society and, missionary societies accept only men whom they consider properly qualified. Most of them are trained specially for the work: nearly all of them make their living by the practice of their profession. So far is this the case that the term 'missionary' is now employed almost exclusively of those who have been so trained, or recognized by a society as duly qualified, and are supported by a society, or work in connection with a society.

What then is there in the application of the term to missionaries which causes them to shrink from it?

(1) They do not dislike the emphasis on efficiency which the term suggests. They themselves at their conferences are constantly insisting on the importance of technical efficiency, deploring the inefficiency of untrained, or unsufficiently trained, workers; and demanding that some subject which they think would add to the efficiency of missionaries, such as psychology or anthropology, for instance, must be either added to, or given a more important place in, the preparation of missionary students. Indeed in this we might well say that the professional instinct is very apparent, seeking its own true line, creating a strictly professional class as opposed to the untrained laity, and raising the standard of that class by raising the standard of technical qualification.

Modern missionary societies exist to create and maintain such a professional class. They are highly organized bodies, and they require year by year large numbers of recruits to fill vacant posts in their missions. Missionaries on furlough are sent up and down the country appealing to young people to offer themselves. Moved by their appeals young men and women are filled with a desire to go out as missionaries, and they offer themselves. Such immature, inexperienced, young people must be tested and trained before they are sent out as missionaries; that is certain. If that is the way in which God directs that His truth revealed in Christ is to be propagated throughout the world, then there is no escape: a professional technical training is inevitable. The directors of the institutions no doubt lay stress on spiritual qualifications, and they provide opportunities for establishing habits of devotion; but that does not alter the professional character of the training. The training institution is essentially professional: the distinction between the professional and the layman is the very reason for its existence. So much is this the case that Christian people today can scarcely think in any other terms. When they speak of missionaries they think of training and connection with a society and qualifications; they think in professional terms. This is so true in my experience that I have generally found it quite impossible to make myself understood when I speak in any other terms.

The very study of religion in such an institution must be professional. Students can no doubt experience their own religion, in an institution as well as outside it; but the meaning and purpose of the institution is to produce men and women who have learnt the technical side of their religion and *how* to propagate it. The students receive lectures on: How to present the Gospel to Buddhists, or to Hindus, or to Moslems, or to people who profess some other religion, and textbooks are prepared for them on those religions. Missionary conferences insist that missionary work is an art which must be practised by qualified practitioners.

The stress which is laid upon technical training as a qualification is manifest in the division of missionaries into the three or four specialized classes to which I referred above. Missionary doctors and teachers and social workers, as I said, often insist that they are not evangelists. Each class has specialized in its own subject. The doctor has not received the training of the teacher, or of the evangelist; the teacher has not received the training of the doctor, or of the evangelist; though they may have attended a few courses of instruction in common. The doctor, or the teacher, consequently does not call himself an evangelist, because he has not had the technical training of an evangelistic missionary, any more than an evangelistic missionary would call himself a doctor, though he might have attended some lectures on the commoner diseases prevalent in the country to which he goes; nor call himself an educational missionary because he has attended a few lectures on teaching methods or on child psychology. Missionaries express no dislike to this division, which is plainly a technical, professional division; and it is far more reasonable and charitable to think that missionary doctors and teachers and social workers refuse to be called evangelists because they recognize this technical, professional, distinction, than to suppose that they have not the same secret of life as the evangelists, nor the same desire to impart it to others. Their unreadiness to be called evangelists is simply an unreadiness to assume a technical knowledge and practice in which they have not as a matter of fact qualified, and perhaps have no desire to qualify.

(2) Neither do missionaries object to making a living by practising their profession. Candidates trained and accepted by a board as duly qualified are appointed to posts and given regular stipends and agreed allowances[1]; and, so far from objecting to this, missionaries argue that it is the right and proper order, and they teach all their converts in the missions to which they go that it is their duty in like manner so to support their own native missionaries. I suppose that if we asked a large number of laymen why they look upon missionaries as professionals, many more would fix upon this point that they are paid, than upon the element of professional training of which I have just spoken, though that is, I believe, the more important. But missionaries do not object to payment, any more than they object to training; and they can hardly object to the use of the term professional on that ground; for they are unquestionably in the position which the term suggests, and they themselves constantly emphasize the fact when they meet together.

To what then do they object? Many of them, I think, object be-

---

[1] It is true that there are some missionaries who do not receive any guarantee of a fixed stipend or allowance from their society, but they are supported by their societies, and only an intimate knowledge of the actual terms of their agreement with the societies under which they serve would reveal the distinction. It is true also that there are a certain number of missionaries who, having private means, do not draw any stipend or allowances; but they form a very small minority of the whole number of missionaries, and the fact that they exist does not affect the rule. They work within the stipendiary system, and if they lost their private means would willingly be stipendiaries themselves.

cause they imagine that the term professional necessarily implies that a man does his work to earn his living, or for what he can get out of it. That is far from being the case. When we talk of a professional doctor, or of a professional cricketer, we are not asserting that either does his work simply because he is paid to do it. It is true that, if we want to assert that a man does his work for private gain, we call him a 'mere professional.' In that form 'professional' sometimes means narrow, incapable of seeing outside his own particular work, but it also sometimes means that the man so described is doing his work not for the love of it, but for what he can get out of it. In that form it is used as a personal judgment; and it may be so used sometimes of individual missionaries; but we are not discussing whether there may or may not be 'mere professionals' in the missionary body; and 'professional' unqualified seldom carries any such implication.

Nevertheless, many missionaries feel that the term is distasteful. They oppose it to divine vocation. They say that a missionary is a man called by God to communicate to others the great secret of life in Christ Jesus, and that such a man cannot be called a professional preacher, or teacher, without a disparagement. To obey such a divine call is not to adopt a profession, in the sense in which men habitually use the phrase. That call is independent of any training which the man may, or may not, receive, and independent of any stipend which he may, or may not, receive. It is a direct personal revelation, and men who obey it are qualified by that: it is a direct personal impulse of the Holy Ghost, and is obeyed as such, and can never be made subject to the earning of a stipend. There is no place for that talk about qualified missionaries, as if a knowledge of psychology, or of anthropology, or of comparative religion, was a qualification. There is no qualification but one, the divine call. Qualifications make professionals, the divine call makes missionaries. That is what they say.

That is a great position to take up. We cannot fail to see that when men speak like that they are in a different world from that of the missionary conference in which the qualifications and training of missionary candidates are discussed: we are breathing a different air from that of the Board room in which the stipends necessary to attract suitable men to fill vacant posts are measured out.

But if that is, as I think that it is, a position commonly taken up by missionaries, it is desirable to reconcile it with the facts which certainly suggest not that ideal, but the ideal of the qualified professional missionary. How can this be done?

The answer generally given is that the training is not training of men to be missionaries, but training given to men and women who have already heard the divine call and are missionaries by call before they are trained. As good missionaries they seek to equip themselves as well as they possibly can for the work to which God has called them. Men who are called by God do not despise education, as if God needed their ignorance, and societies which send out men, knowing that, give them the best assistance possible, because there is no advantage in sending out a man to a foreign land totally ignorant of all the conditions which he will meet when he gets there. So far from being opposed to the other ideal, it is the complement of it. The mistake made by those who oppose the two ideals lies in their use of the word qualification. The training given is rather equipment than qualification. To speak of a man as qualified to be a missionary by his training, as we speak of a qualified doctor, or teacher, is false: the first qualification, the essential qualification, is conviction of the divine call; all the rest is only secondary, though of such importance that it cannot be despised, or neglected, without disaster.

Similarly with pay, they argue that missionaries do not receive their stipends, or allowances, as pay for doing their work, but as mere support allowed them, or given to them, to enable them to devote their lives to it. They appeal to the example of St Paul. They say that he accepted gifts to set him free from the bondage and restraint of having to spend much of his time in labouring to earn his livelihood. They say that they can see no difference in principle between such gifts and a regular salary, and that in fact it is both simpler and better that each missionary should receive a regular allowance than that one man who achieves notoriety should be loaded with gifts whilst his less observed neighbour receives none.

Here, I think, we can begin to see light. The distinction between gifts and a stipend opens our eyes; for there is a distinction, and a real distinction. Gifts are given to a man who is doing a work to which he feels called, a work which he would do, gifts or no gifts; the stipend is a regular payment agreed upon before the man begins to do the work. It is a distinction which the Income Tax collector recognizes. And St Paul, whose example is cited, knew it. The charge was brought against him that he did not preach the gospel for nothing, that he was not wholly disinterested. How did he answer it? Not by saying that an apostle was a man called by God to preach the gospel, and that it was wicked to suggest that such a man could possibly be preaching for his living; not by saying that the gifts which he received were mere assistance to enable him to carry on his work without distraction; but by saying that he had refused to receive them. It was not his acceptance of gifts which proved his disinterestedness but his refusal of them.

The example of St Paul does not help missionaries who receive regular stipends, because they cannot use his argument; and it does not answer the difficulty raised by the engagement of candidates by missionary societies, because St Paul was a missionary first before he received any gifts at all, and candidates are not missionaries, but young people who think that they might well become missionaries. Individual missionaries today certainly can refute any suggestion that they are doing their work to earn their livelihood, but they can refute it, not by saying that missionaries are men who are obeying a call, but only by conduct which manifestly cannot be paid. Being disinterested, their words and acts reveal it; but that is in spite of the salary, which in the case of lesser men creates a suspicion beyond their capacity to overcome.

Now the same line of thought helps us when we consider the training. There is a distinction between training given to candidates and training sought by men who are already missionaries and know what they seek. In the missionary institutions most of the students are candidates, and if at the end of their training they were not accepted by a society, most of them would not become missionaries. If rejected, they would themselves probably say that they had hoped to be missionaries, but unfortunately that had proved impossible, because the board to which they applied had not been able to offer them support, or had refused them on some other ground.

But if, as has been suggested, all who enter those institutions are obeying a divine call and are simply equipping themselves for their service, how can any of them say that? The answer given is that young people who enter those institutions are seeking to find out whether they are, or are not, truly called of God, and acceptance or rejection by a board is the means by which the will of God is made plain to them. If they are accepted, they are called of God; if they are rejected, they are not called to be missionaries.

It follows inevitably that the training given is not training given to missionaries who are seeking to equip themselves for their work, but a training given to men and women who may, or may not, be missionaries, young people whose vocation is still in doubt. And what are we to make of those cases, happily rare, in which men, after being accepted and sent out as missionaries, come to the conclusion that they have mistaken their vocation, and that the board made a mistake; and what are we to make of those cases, also happily rare, in which the board comes to the conclusion that it made a mistake? And are there no doubtful cases? Such cases break down at once the position that all missionaries are called of God because acceptance by a board proves the call. All that acceptance by a board can prove is that at the moment when the board accepted the candidate, the board thought that the candidate was a suitable candidate.

The fact is that when we say that all missionaries are men who are wholly disinterested followers of a divine call, we are begging the question. Simply to assert that a missionary is unquestionably not a professional, in spite of the appearances created by the training and the stipends, and in spite of the resolutions of conferences on qualifications, is not sufficient. It may satisfy the man who says it, but it will not, and cannot, satisfy the man who asks the question. Training, like stipends, may be assistance given to missionaries, but the only possible proof that it is so is when the training or the stipend is given to a man who has proved himself a missionary by becoming one *before* he received either the training or the stipend. Even then the man or woman who has received them is thereafter in the position of the professional, and can only prove that he or she is not a 'mere professional' by doing his or her work in such a way that no one could possibly in reason pass that judgment upon him, or her. That he, or she, is a professional in the proper sense of that word is certain.

I cannot help thinking that most of those who object to the application of this term to missionaries are really more afraid of the appearance and of the name than of the thing itself. As I said, they do not object to the qualifications, or the efficiency, which the term implies, nor do they object to the stipends. They do object strongly to the appearance of being paid to propagate the gospel. They know that the term professional embraces not only men who do their work for the love of it, but also men who work for what they can get out of it, and they cannot bear the least suspicion that any missionary could belong to the latter class. Therefore they dislike a term, which embraces both, to be employed of them as a body, or of any one of them as an individual. They feel that missionary work is essentially work which demands not only disinterestedness in those who undertake it, but unquestioned disinterestedness.

Such unquestioned disinterestedness cannot be theirs. They may, and often do, rise above it, but they cannot escape the question so long as training and salaries hold the place which they now occupy not only in the minds of men who are not missionaries, but in the missionary body itself. St Paul himself did not escape, and they, who certainly cannot give his answer that he was neither trained nor paid by men for his work, cannot hope to escape.

I am inclined to believe that the unwillingness which medical and educational missionaries sometimes express to be called evangelists is due not merely to that technical distinction of which I have spoken above, but to the hope that they may escape. They do not mind receiving their salaries for teaching in a school, or for working in a hospital, or for organizing and directing social welfare institutions, but they will not admit that they receive their salaries for preaching the gospel. Some of them, perhaps, do not want to preach the gospel, some of them possibly do not feel that strong impulse to impart to others the secret of life in Christ which makes the missionary of the gospel: but many of them do feel it and do obey it; only, because it is a secret of life, a Divine secret, they will not allow it to be supposed that they are paid to impart it. They receive their salaries for doing work which is done by others as secular work: then, if they do that other work, they feel that they are doing it freely.

As missionary societies give themselves up more and more to sociological, medical, educational, scientific work, which can be done by good men who are not necessarily missionaries of the gospel in the sense in which I have been using the word throughout this chapter, a time may come when that position is recognized, but, at present, whilst the societies are largely, if not almost wholly, supported by people whose supreme purpose is that others may share their faith in Christ and their hope in Him, they cannot openly send out men except as missionaries of the gospel, and they can hardly help making the work of imparting to others a knowledge of Christ, if not a specified duty, yet an understood obligation. They expect their missionary educationalists and doctors and social workers to be evangelists at heart. However much, then, these men may protest that they are not sent out as evangelists, yet, if they do anything directly to impart to others the knowledge of Christ, all that they do is, so to speak, within the terms of their contract. They cannot escape outside it when they do evangelistic work. They are not in the position of men employed by a purely secular organization. Consequently their position must be ambiguous. But their existence is very suggestive, and the increase in their numbers shows in what direction the thoughts of Christian young men and women are moving.

The only missionary who is manifestly and unquestionably a non-professional missionary is the man who has no connection with a society which sends out professional missionaries; and Christian young men in increasing numbers are inclining to take up that position. They see the ambiguity in the position of the men supported by the societies, and they shun it. They see that the connection between preaching the Gospel and earning a living is a dangerous one; they see that the communication of a secret of life is not a proper subject for payment. They see that the calling of God is above all questions of professional equipment, and that the communication of the Spirit is not wrought by methods of presentation. They feel that missionary work is essentially a work dealing with souls, and that in dealing with souls not only disinterestedness but manifest disinterestedness is essential. They cannot let it appear that they are even seeking to increase the numbers of their own flock, or working for the aggrandizement of their own church, much less that they themselves are making a living. They feel that there is something nauseous in offering to others a way of life in Christ except on terms which wholly preclude any possibility that they are seeking anything whatsoever except the other man's salvation.

All men know that there are professional missionaries today working in that spirit; and they do not judge them, nor wish to question their way of life, any more than St Paul condemned those who lived of the gospel; but for themselves they will give the only answer which really satisfies the question, What are you paid for doing this work? that is, Nothing. And that answer can only be given in unmistakable form when they earn their living openly by some other means.

There have always been, and there always will be, such men. They live their lives outside the body of professional missionaries, unknown to selection boards and society committees, quietly earning their own living by trades and professions, and imparting to others their secret of life, as they have opportunity, freely. They are not called missionaries. It is quite possible that the term missionary has already become so technical that they will themselves more and more decline it. They are often spoken of by the professional missionaries as 'men who do a little Christian work in their spare time,' or as 'men who would be all the better if they joined up'; but they are doing real missionary work, and it is they who prove that Christians do not only try to give their gospel to others when they have made that work their profession. Technically they are not missionaries, but spiritually they are missionaries of great importance, both to the church and to the professional missionaries, and to the non-Christian world. Therefore I have called them non-professional missionaries.

Missionaries are a class apart. At home and abroad when a man is spoken of as a missionary, it is understood that he has joined that class. The work of a missionary is a profession which a man takes up; but it is a profession unlike any other because it includes within itself many professions. A missionary may be a doctor, or a cleric, or an engineer, or a schoolmaster, or practise any other art, but he is not considered to be a missionary unless he has joined that peculiar class. Generally speaking, a missionary works for a society, and is supported by a society, and in this sense missionary work is a profession. It is this body of men, professional missionaries, which forms the class of which I speak.

It is a class apart. Ordinary Christians think of it so, the missionaries themselves think of it so, and the people of the lands to which missionaries are sent think of it so.

In the countries to which they go, missionaries, except a few individuals, mix little with men of any other class; they live a life apart. Men of any other class, except a few individuals, mix little with them. Some of them try to enter into the life of the ordinary lay folk around them, but they are not 'of' them; there is always a certain restraint, and constraint, in the intercourse.

The native Christians distinguish them sharply from all other Christian white men whom they may meet; and sometimes think that they are the only Christians and all others men of the world. The native population distinguishes them equally sharply from all other

Christian men, and thinks of them as peculiarly their friends or peculiarly dangerous enemies, as the case may be; happily, most often as peculiarly their friends; but always peculiarly, as a special class of white Christians. They belong to a class apart.

They act as a class apart. They often meet in conference and pass resolutions which they forward to governments. They do this, not as ordinary citizens, but as a special class with special interests; and sometimes government officials attend their conference and address them on those social and political questions in which they are peculiarly interested, and occasionally listen to their debates. The class is a large and influential class, and its decisions carry some weight. Even in the state this class is a class apart.

No doubt this position of being a class apart from all others has some advantages. Missionary groups are not unlike medieval monastic groups. As the monastics lived a life apart from the general body of Christians, and devoted themselves to the care of the sick, the ignorant, and the down-trodden, so do these; as the monastics devoted themselves to study and the production of Christian literature, so do these; as the monastics devoted themselves to a peculiarly religious life, so these missionaries represent the life of religion in a special sense, and certain peculiar outward piety is expected of them by those who are outside, even when they deride it. As monastics might be doctors, or teachers, or farmers, or traders, or students, or statesmen, but never belonged to any of these professions as they existed outside the monastic orders, so the missionary body embraces all these while yet it separates them by a subtle and invisible gulf from their fellow labourers in the same work outside. And as membership of a monastic group had certain advantages, so has membership of the missionary group; and as the monastic groups did great service to the church and to the state, so do these missionary groups.

But the position has also its dangers. In the days of their early struggles and poverty the monastic groups kept close to their simplicity of purpose, but in the day of their wealth and power they lost it. The days of the early missionary struggles are passing; missionaries are becoming a very large and influential body, and their voice is heard, as I said just now, in high places. Just as the monastics were individually poor, whilst many of their monasteries represented great wealth, so missionaries are still for the most part individually poor, but many of the societies to which they belong are wealthy. The power of money is behind them, and the power of numbers, and these have their dangers.

There is always a danger in the formation of a special class apart. The special class absorbs elements which ought to be at work in the wider fellowship of the whole Church. The monastic bodies arose, at least to some extent, because good men despaired of the Church and sought an escape from the dangers and tumults and toils of an un-Christian Christian society which could not be brought to do the will of God. Just so, missionary societies arose, at least in part, because good men despaired of an un-missionary church, and so organized themselves apart. But as the formation of the monastic bodies took the leaven out of the unChristian Christian society of the Middle Ages, so the formation of the missionary societies has taken the leaven out of the un-missionary church of modern days. I am not denying that the monastic groups exercised a great influence over the world and the church outside, I am not denying that the missionary groups exercise a great influence over the world and the church; all that I am saying is that their constitution was essentially a taking away of the leaven from the lump, and it had to be preserved there by others who did not go apart into the monastic groups or, into the missionary groups.

Today the missionary group as such absorbs far too much of the missionary spirit in the church, to our serious loss, and to the grave hindrance of the progress of the gospel. Today it is hard to find anyone who has any missionary zeal who does not take it for granted that he can express it only by supporting one of these societies financially, or by taking service under one of them. That a divinely inspired desire for the salvation in Christ of men who know Him not should be so restrained is very serious. Canon Gairdner, of Cairo, expressed the danger as the danger of 'Foreign Missions by proxy,' and he warned us that if we do not amend 'we shall beget native communities in our own likeness who will also insist before long in doing this work by proxy.'[1] He might have gone further and said that that is what is actually happening, that we are, and have long been, training all who become Christians through our missions to imitate us in this and to think that the spread of the gospel and the conversion of the world is the work of a special body of professional missionaries.

[1] *Brotherhood—Islam's and Christ's*, by W. H. T. Gairdner. Edinburgh House Press, 1923.

Canon Gairdner declared that 'we shall never win Islam (at any rate), nor even attract it preliminarily, until we can get this primitive ideal (that is every Christian a missionary) right back into the consciousness of the Church, pervading and permeating all its members individually and collectively.' 'More missionaries, certainly'; he cried, 'but above all more unofficial missionaries.' But he contented himself with the cry 'Every Christian a missionary,' and did not say how a firmly established convention that no Christian is a missionary unless he is an official missionary was to be broken down. To break down a convention so firmly established, and supported by all the influence of a long tradition, by the practice which almost drives anywho is strongly imbued with the missionary spirit into the life of the professional missionary, is no mean or easy task. It cannot be done by saying that all Christian men ought to be missionaries.

I suggest that the first step is to find men and women who have a strong and deep missionary spirit and to persuade them that the highest and best missionary work that they can do is to go out into the mission field as 'unofficial missionaries,' refusing to join themselves officially to the professional missionary body. They should go into government service, into the offices of the great trading houses, into the farming community, into the society of the great cities and towns of non-Christian lands with this deliberate purpose—to show that it is possible for a man, or a woman, to be in the fullest sense 'in' that life and yet to be a missionary, to prove to the foreign community and to the native people amongst whom they dwell, that it is possible, and so to leaven the whole lump.

There are already men quietly doing this work, but what is needed is that their number should be increased, and increased by men and women who are acting consciously and deliberately and know at what they are aiming. The increase in number of such men, farmers who know that they are missionaries, officials who know that they are missionaries, traders who know that they are missionaries, would work wonders. Men would cease to be astonished when a member of one of these professions acts as a missionary. They are not unfamiliar with the man who 'takes an interest' in missions and supports them financially, but they expect him to be taking an interest in a work which the mission is doing and he is not doing. What is needed is an increase not so much of laymen in the field who 'take an interest' in missions, as an increase of men who are really missionaries themselves, whether they take an interest in the official missions or not, whether they support official missions financially or not. That is what is needed, so that non-Christian and Christian communities alike may become accustomed to the fact and think it not strange that an official, or a trader, or a farmer, cares for the souls of his people.

I can see no way to that other than the deliberate refusal of missionary-hearted men to become official professional missionaries. Young men and women who are just starting in life should be encouraged to seek their vocation and to exercise it in this way. The difficulty is that now, when any young man or woman is moved by the Holy Ghost to take thought for the souls of the heathen, everyone conspires to drive him into the position of a professional missionary, and they do it in the most powerful way, by simply taking it for granted. Here is a man who cares for the souls of non-Christian folk; of course he is going to be a missionary, and by 'a missionary' is meant a professional missionary. The power of that tacit assumption is incalculably weighty. It ought to become natural for a man who cares for the souls of non-Christians to be asked what sort of a job he is looking for, and where, and the assumption behind the question should be the assumption that he is probably looking for a post under government or on a farm or in a trading corporation, an assumption only to be avoided by the assertion that he is proposing to apply to a missionary society for a post as a professional missionary. If only we could get to that stage the evil which Canon Gairdner deplored would be largely removed. The way to attain it, is to begin.

The difficulty is that religious people in England are very timid. They think that if missionary-hearted men went abroad as missionaries on those terms, and lived among men who were not missionary-hearted, they would cease to be missionaries. Some of them might. What then? There are, no doubt, some professional missionaries abroad today who would have ceased to be missionaries long ago if they had not been professionals; but is that fact a source of strength or of weakness? A missionary who can only be kept a missionary by being kept in a professional ring is spiritually a failure. So outside the professional body some might fail; but that is no reason for timidity. What is the good of saying, as we nearly all say with Canon Gairdner, Every Christian ought to be a missionary, if the moment that anyone proposes to act as that saying demands, we cry, He will be lost. The saying demands just what he is proposing to do.

The difficulty is that the great societies think that they cannot afford to support any such movement. They need all the men they can get, and they hunt for every man who is missionary-hearted, and try to catch him. The societies cannot present the case to the young men and women of today—the great need for non-professional missionaries. The Student Christian Movement might do it. Canon Gairdner is quite right when he says that what is needed today is Christians who will *welcome* a convert, Christians who will care for the souls of men, Christians who will present Christ to the non-Christian world, Christians who will not be content to do the work by proxy, unofficial missionaries. Then let us present this missionary life to young men and women, and urge them to adopt it.

It is not an easy path. It is far more easy for the missionary-hearted man to join the professional body and to live all his days with those who are in sympathy with him. It is far more easy to be a missionary in a missionary society's school or college than in a government office, in a mission hospital than in a government medical service, in a mission station than in a trading station. But we are not seeking an easy path; and it is necessary that the non-Christians should learn that a Christian trader can be a missionary as well as a Muslim trader, a government official as well as a Muslim official, and that it is not only a comparatively small body of paid professionals who know how to care for the souls of others.

Hitherto I have attempted to show the need for non-professional missionaries, and the danger which has arisen from the fact that missionaries have become a professional order: I now wish to consider the work of the non-professional missionary and a misconception of it which is common.

I received the other day a letter in which I was told of a certain bank clerk who had been converted, and of the influence which his life had upon his fellows. My informant added: 'Of course now he wants "to do some work for the Lord." I tell him that he *is* with a vengeance; but the . . . people have got tight hold of him and have persuaded him to "join up"—alas!' There is an example of the practice which I described earlier in the chapter. Professional missionaries are naturally inclined to draw any man who shows any care for the souls of his fellows into the professional body. In so acting they are violating the doctrine of St Paul when he urged men to abide in the calling wherein they were called. 'Let each man,' he said, 'wherein he was called, therein abide with God' (I Cor. 7.24). It is true that the apostle was speaking of slavery, but the teaching has a wider application. The leaven should be left in the lump; and my correspondent felt that in this case something was lost when the leaven was taken out of that particular office.

But in the saying of the man who wanted 'to do some work for the Lord,' and his ignorance of the work which the Lord had given him to do, lies an illustration of the misconception of the work of a non-professional missionary of which I wish to write now. It is expressed even more clearly in another letter which has come into my hands in which the writer, speaking of non-professional missionaries, talks of such men as 'attempting to do missionary work in their spare time.'

The idea here expressed is that there is a certain peculiar class of work which is called 'missionary work,' all the rest of the work which a Christian man does in a heathen land being non-missionary work. The missionary work is distinguished sharply from all other work and is described as 'work for the Lord,' and is sometimes almost defined as 'preaching.' Just as 'missionary' has been made the title of a peculiar class of men, so 'missionary work' has been assumed as the title of a peculiar class of work. We hear the expressions that a man is 'engaged in missionary work,' that he is 'going to undertake missionary work,' that he is 'retiring from missionary work,' as if 'missionary work' were a special occupation, as specialized as banking or mining or farming. These expressions take it for granted that a missionary is in a class apart, engaged in a special work peculiar to him, exactly in the sense which I argued before to be pernicious.

Now this assumption needs some consideration. In the letter which I quoted above, the words 'I tell him that he *is*' (doing work for the Lord, when the man was abiding in the calling wherein he was called), show plainly that my correspondent did not agree with the assumption; the words 'do some work for the Lord' and the reference to missionary work done in spare time show that those men did agree with it. The assumption then is not universally accepted; nevertheless it is sufficiently common to need some examination.

If we are prepared to believe that every Christian ought to be a missionary, we must also be prepared to admit that every Christian ought to be a missionary *in* his ordinary daily work, all the time, not merely outside it, and part of the time; that 'work for the Lord' in-

G

cludes his ordinary daily work, and is not to be treated as something which he can do only when he escapes from the work by which he earns his living.

The missionary work of the unofficial missionary is not the same work which a paid professional missionary does. The paid professional missionary leaves the ordinary work of the world and devotes himself to what he calls 'religious work'; the non-professional missionary realizes that the ordinary work of the world ought to be done religiously, and does it religiously, and calls it 'religious work.' The professional missionary secularizes all the work which he does not recognize as religious work; the non-professional missionary consecrates all work. The professional missionary exhorts others to consecrate their lives in the common work which he forsakes in order to consecrate his own; the non-professional missionary sets an example of the consecrated life by refusing to forsake his work. The professional missionary preaches by exhortation; the non-professional missionary preaches by example.

I shall be told that professional missionaries preach by example; that their lives speak louder than their words. That is true; but what we are here considering is the restriction of the term 'missionary work' to the work of the professional missionary. The professional missionary preaches by his example that the way to convert the world is to forsake the common life of men and to live in a special class doing a special work. It is neither possible nor desirable that all Christian men should follow his example. Consequently, if a 'missionary' is a man who does that, the exhortation that every Christian should be a missionary becomes absurd: only a few can live the 'proper' missionary life. But if a Christian who lives among non-Christians and consciously seeks by his life and conversation to reveal to others the secret of Christ's grace is a missionary, then indeed every Christian ought to be a missionary and do missionary work. Thus the example of the professional missionary, as such, is not an example for all; whilst the example of the non-professional missionary is an example for all—an example of universal application. It is in this sense that the non-professional missionary preaches by example a lesson which the professional missionary does not. The one preaches by example a lesson which all men can follow; the other a lesson which few men can, or ought, to follow.

But it may be said, on that showing, all evangelists, all prophets and teachers who forsake all other employment to busy themselves about the preaching of the word set a limited example, and therefore their work is less admirable than that of the Christian who consecrates the common life and occupations of men. It does not follow. I said nothing about the one form or the other form of expression of Christian life being 'more admirable'; all that I said was that the idea that only the one was to be called, or ought to call himself, a 'missionary' was a dangerous and misleading idea. St Paul said: 'Let each man wherein he was called, therein abide with God'; but he also said: 'God hath set in his church some apostles and some prophets and some evangelists.' He did not make any distinction such as we make when we speak of 'missionary work' as peculiarly the work of a special class. In his day the church, as a society, was a missionary society, and each man in the church was a member of a missionary society, and his work, whatever its character, was to be consecrated so that the missionary influence of the church might extend into all departments of life. When we draw our modern distinction between 'missionary work' and 'secular work,' we divide life precisely as the apostle taught us not to divide it. That all the members in the body have not the same office is not in conflict with the statement that whatever any Christian man does should be done to the glory of God.

The missionary influence of the Church is strengthened, not hindered, by this teaching. There is no work which a Christian man does which is not missionary in this sense; and it is this sense of the missionary duty of Christian men which needs to be restored and strengthened today; and it is as a matter of fact destroyed, or weakened, by the common teaching and belief that 'missionaries' are men in a class apart, and that 'missionary work' is their work and not the work of others. It is as a matter of fact destroyed, or weakened, by the struggle of missionary societies to draw into their own professional body every man who shows any sign of religious care for the souls of others. It is as a matter of fact weakened, or destroyed, by the idea that if a man cares for the souls of others and lives such a life as to exercise a strong religious influence upon others, he ought to forsake his calling, to do 'missionary work,' blind to the truth that he is doing missionary work where he is, and as he is.

We shall never make any great progress in the mission field until this one-sided idea of missionary work is broken down. As I said that it is not enough to preach 'Every Christian a missionary,' but it is necessary that men with strong missionary convictions should go out deliberately into distant lands as officials and farmers and traders; so now I say that it is necessary that they should go out with the clear conviction that *all* the work they do is missionary work, and is to be done with a missionary motive, rather than with the idea that missionary work consists in preaching or teaching, and that they may find opportunity to do such 'missionary work' in their spare time. It is no answer to say that government officials or agents of business houses are not encouraged to preach the Christian faith, or that there is an understanding, or even a definite order, that they shall not do so, and that consequently it is impossible for a 'missionary' to be in such employment. No government can prevent a man doing his work in Christ and for Christ, nor hinder him from answering the question which inevitably arises, Why is your life so different from that of other men? I know a man in a foreign land who answered the question, Why do you not do what other young men out here do? by saying, I believe in Christ and Christ does not approve of that conduct. Was not that missionary work, and could any government prevent him from giving that answer, or reprimand him for giving it? But what was the 'missionary work'? Was it the explanation which the man gave of his conduct (which was a form of preaching), or was it the conduct which led to the question being asked? Obviously it was both. The whole life of the man was 'missionary work' among the people with whom he had to do. And if he had thought that he was a missionary only when he was doing some special and peculiar work, public preaching, or something of that sort, he would have been far from the truth, and he might possibly have earned a reprimand. He was a missionary in his daily life; that was the secret, and that is the secret which the non-professional missionary must learn. If a man were to go out as a non-professional missionary thinking that to be a missionary he must engage in the work which professional missionaries call 'missionary work' and consider their special province, he would only be a missionary for part of his time, and often not a very successful missionary at that. The missionary work of the non-professional missionary is essentially to live his daily life in Christ, and therefore with a difference, and to be able to explain, or at least to state, the reason and cause of the difference to men who see it. His preaching is essentially private conversation, and has at the back of it facts, facts of a life which explain and illustrate and enforce his words.

That is the essential work of the non-professional missionary, and any further preaching or teaching which he may do is not immediately in question. He may do such work, or he may not do it, but the addition is not necessary to his missionary purpose, or usefulness.

It is such missionary work, done consciously and deliberately as missionary, that the world needs today. Everybody, Christian and pagan alike, respects such work; and, when it is so done, men wonder, and enquire into the secret of a life which they instinctively admire and covet for themselves. Much that is done as 'missionary work' by professional missionaries they do not admire; still less do they covet the spirit which they see inspiring the preaching of some professional missionaries; but the spirit which inspires love of others and efforts after their well-being, both in body and soul, they cannot but admire and covet, unless, indeed, seeing that it would reform their own lives, they dread and hate it, because they do not desire to be reformed. In either case it works.

A great host of such missionaries doing such missionary work would transform the whole missionary situation. There are, as I said, already many Christian men so working today; but what I urged then I would urge again, that men who are full of the missionary spirit should deliberately and consciously go out into the world to do that work, instead of allowing others to persuade them that if they want to be missionaries they must join a missionary society and engage in what is called 'missionary work' by men who have narrowed that term till it means nothing more than work done by professional missionaries.

3

Mission Activities Considered in Relation to the Manifestation of the Spirit

Editorial Note
The whole text of Mission Activities *is printed.*

Mission Activities Considered in Relation to the Manifestation of the Spirit

The Question Propounded

In a series of questions prepared for the consideration of a Missionary Conference in Shanghai in 1926, I found one which struck me as peculiarly arresting and suggestive: 'Why is it that the Christian Movement in China has impressed people chiefly as a movement of activities rather than as a spiritual force?'

This Question is of More Than Local Importance

This question seems to me to have more than a merely local significance. Not only in China, but all over the world, our missionary societies are engaged in the activities to which the question referred. We ought, then, to ask whether we must not expect the same question sooner or later to arise everywhere. Our work is world-wide and we cannot afford to pass lightly over consequences which are very serious when they become so apparent in one country as to be made the subject of inquiry at a missionary conference. If the defects are inherent in the methods which we employ, we must expect similar consequences everywhere, and we ought betimes to take heed lest we multiply an evil which we deplore. If we found a leprous spot on one part of the body, we should not be content to treat it as a purely local trouble, and to regard the rest of the body as healthy because no sores had as yet broken out on the other members.

The Terms 'Activities' and 'Spiritual Force'

By the 'activities' spoken of I understand, as I said, nothing peculiar to missions in China, but activities which we universally employ in all our missions everywhere. It would be tedious to make out a complete list of them, but they include such things as the organization and direction of schools for the education of the people, of clubs for the welfare of young men and women, of institutions for the improvement of social conditions in towns and villages, of agitations for the removal or amelioration of evils such as opium smoking, or child marriage, or foot-binding, or forced labour, or overcrowding, of hospitals for the cure of the sick, of lectures on public health, of schemes for the improvement of agriculture and such like, an endless list.

By the 'spiritual force' of which the question speaks, I think that we cannot understand any or every spiritual force, because in that case the statement that the Chinese do not see a spiritual force behind the activities carried on by missions in their midst would be untrue. All men inevitably expect and seek for some spiritual force behind all human activities, and the Chinese have in fact lately been proclaiming that the spiritual force which they see in these activities is a capitalistic or an imperialistic spirit, or the spirit of a western civilization striving to bring them into bondage to itself. The conference in its discussion of the question certainly took it for granted that the spiritual force which ought to be revealed to the Chinese is not any spiritual force, but a particular spiritual force, the power of the Spirit of Jesus, of the Holy Spirit. I take it then that the 'spiritual force' meant by the writer of the question is that spiritual force, and no other.

The Danger of Vague Non-Christian Terms

Nevertheless, we ought to observe that there is a growing tendency among missionaries to use vague and comprehensive religious terms which are not essentially Christian in place of terms which are essentially, definitely and clearly Christian terms. This tendency is dangerous. As we shall see later, it makes no small difference whether we speak of a 'spiritual force' or of 'the Holy Ghost'. In the one case we think and speak, and in the event act, as if we had to do with an impersonal force; in the other we think and speak, and in the event act, as if we had to do with a personal force. The difference is not small.

The Statements Contained in the Question

The question implies four definite statements: (1) that the activities are so prominent that they absorb attention; (2) that the missions appear to exist for them; (3) that there is a spiritual force which might appear, and be made manifest; (4) that this force is obscured. We may also, I think, say that the question suggests that the revelation of the spiritual force is, in the mind of the author of the question, a matter of importance, and its obscurance a source of regret.

The Conference Accepted the Statement of Fact

The conference which considered this question did not deny any of the statements suggested by it. The question proposed was: Why is this so? And to that question three answers might have been given: (1) It is not so; (2) It is so, but we do not know why it is so; (3) It is so, because . . . The conference did not attempt to give the first of these answers. It did not deny the suggestion that the activities obscured the spiritual force; it suggested a solution of the problem, Why it is so. In doing this it accepted the assertion that the spiritual force was in fact obscured. I shall not attempt to prove the truth of the assertion. I shall accept it as the conference accepted it, for I believe it to be largely true not only in China but elsewhere; and I shall try to show the underlying causes of it.

The Solution Suggested by the Conference

The conference itself suggested a solution which seems to me inadequate. In its findings it warned missionaries that there was a danger of their becoming so immersed in the activities as to neglect the habits of prayer and meditation. In so doing, under an exhortation to piety of life, it suggested that the missionaries were themselves falling into the error which they deplored in the Chinese people, paying more heed to the activities than to the Spirit. It did not indeed directly say that this was so; it only pointed out that this might be so.

The Solution is not Sufficient

But is this so? Are we to believe that our activities fail to impress people as a spiritual force, because there is in fact little spiritual force behind them? Is it true that missionaries generally are so immersed in activities that they neglect their prayers and forget the Spirit which should inform all their activities? The missionary body is a large one composed of many different individuals of many different types, and in so large a body some may be, and probably are, so afflicted; but the great majority are sincerely desirous of being guided by the Spirit and of expressing the Spirit in all their activities; and behind them is a great host of Christian people who pray for them and subscribe money to help them, earnestly desiring the manifestation of the Spirit. I do not think, then, that we can possibly accept this answer as complete, or sufficient.

Putting this answer, then, on one side, not as unimportant, but as insufficient, we must consider that the activities may obscure the Spirit in three ways: (1) They may obscure it because they are made too prominent; (2) They may obscure it because they are used in such a way as to obscure it; (3) They may obscure it because they are in themselves of such a character as to obscure it. I propose in this paper to examine each of these in order.

The Place Given to Them in Missionary Conferences and Literature

The place given to these activities in our missions might at first glance appear a sufficient answer by itself to the question why the activities obscure the Spirit. That place is overwhelmingly great. In every missionary conference, in every missionary magazine and report, in every mission station all over the world, these activities occupy a large, and an increasingly large, place. They are constantly brought before us as though they were essential to the evangelization of the world, and we are sometimes even told that our definition of evangelization must be such as to include them.[1] Look where we will, we see missionary leaders constantly busy about these activities, and their appeals and their speeches keep them ever in the foreground. What we appear to put into the place of first importance, it is not surprising that others should think the most important.

The impression which we receive in reading missionary literature is very marked and clear. We do not indeed know, we are never told, what proportion of the funds, or of the agents, of missionary societies are engaged in these activities, but we do know that it is large, and we do know that those engaged in them are insistent in their demands for larger support, and we do know that each form of activity is presented in turn as the most important work to be done at the given time in the given place under the given conditions. We know also that when there is any hope of obtaining subscriptions from com-

[1] A great Conference at Le Zoute in 1926 stated this explicitly.

mercial firms or from the general public who are not likely to support evangelistic work, the beneficent activities are put in the foreground.

We, as Christians, Lay Special Emphasis on Certain Familiar Expressions
The impression which we receive is very clear, and it is only checked by a certain conviction and expectation on our part, based upon our knowledge and experience as Christians living in a Christian church and familiar with the Christian motive, that these social benefits are not the sole and complete object of missionary work. If we had no means of arriving at the truth other than a balance of statements, if we did not lay a peculiar emphasis on certain expressions familiar to us as Christians, which missionaries use in speaking of their work, we should be hard put to it to avoid the conclusion that large numbers of missionaries, and a larger proportion of missionary leaders, were really social reformers, seeking to overcome social evils simply because social evils are a social danger to the human race in this world.

The Place Given to Them Locally
We cannot then be surprised if people who have not our private and peculiar knowledge should reach that conclusion. Their sole means of judgment are the existence of the organizations and institutions in their country and the public utterances of the leaders of these activities who, in commending them, lay great stress upon the public evils which they are founded to combat and the public benefits which they confer upon the community as a whole. They see government officials attending the opening of these institutions and supporting these activities quite apart from any personal acceptance of the religion with which they are connected, and they hear them commending them as useful and important social activities. It is not surprising, therefore, if they receive the impression that these activities are of primary importance in the eyes of those who conduct them.

The Activities of the Local Churches are Overshadowed by Them
But it is still necessary to inquire why activities carried on almost entirely by foreigners and by a few nationals who have learned foreign ideas and have been trained by foreigners, so entirely absorb atten-

tion. Compared with the number of Christians in China, for instance, as in most other places, the number of foreign missionaries and Chinese Christians engaged in these activities is comparatively small. That so far as this minority represents anything that can be called the Christian movement, the Christian movement is a movement of activities, is so obvious that anyone might wonder how the question came to be asked. As I have said, these activities occupy such a place in the thought and the speech and the action of our missionary leaders that it would be almost impossible for anyone who began to study our work by reading missionary books or going about the world to escape from that conclusion. It is, therefore, not in the least surprising that non-Christian onlookers should receive it. But it is surprising that, when there are such large numbers of native Christians, the activities of this comparatively small body should bulk so large in the country that the Christian movement can be identified with these activities. We must, therefore, ask ourselves how it comes to pass that the activity of the native Christians is so completely overshadowed by these activities.

The Native Christians Take Little Interest in Them
It is well known that these activities are maintained almost entirely by us, and a small body of educated nationals who have learned our western habits of thought and action, and that the great bulk of the native Christians feel no responsibility whatever for their maintenance, looking upon them as essentially our work. This is so much the case that if we were forced to withdraw it is very doubtful if the native Christian community either would, or could, continue any of these activities in their present form, and it is certain that nearly all the larger institutions would collapse immediately. The Christian Church in the country certainly could not maintain them. They are essentially 'of' us. They represent our ideas of Christian work. When a Chinese Christian leader was asked the other day what the Chinese Christians thought of a problem which had arisen with regard to educational institutions, he answered that they never thought about them at all, that they did not consider these things as in any sense their business, but looked upon them as something which we carried on for our own purposes, with which they had nothing whatever to do. The activities, therefore, cannot possibly be thought to express the spirit of the native Church.

The Church is Identified With Committees

The activities are carried on by missionary societies from Europe and America, and by committees composed of Europeans and a certain number of western-educated nationals, almost wholly apart from the great body of the native Christians. Nevertheless the committees which carry on these activities speak as though they represented and really were the Christian Church in the country, and as though their activities really were and represented the activities of the Christian Church in the country. At this conference in China, for instance, of which I have been speaking, a question was propounded for consideration: 'Upon what few things should the church in China concentrate its strength today so as to be of the greatest service to the people of China?' It is quite impossible to understand that question at all unless we identify the Christian Church in China with the committees. A committee which commands the use of money and a number of agents can concentrate its use of these upon a few forms of activity by employing agents only of a certain type for certain specific work. But can the church concentrate its energies upon a few activities unless it is identified with the committee? Its members are engaged in every form of activity in their daily life, and none can be ruled out. And the Christian Church expresses the power of Christ in the lives of her members in everything that they do or say. It is only by identifying the church with the committee that we can understand this question at all.

The New Prelacy of Committees

Here we are face to face with a very remarkable phenomenon. In the middle ages the clergy came to occupy such a position in the church that they sometimes spoke of themselves as 'the Church.' The laity were in such a subordinate position that they hardly counted. The church, as represented by the clergy, spoke. It was the business of the laity to support the clergy. Today we see committees of 'leaders' in the mission field arrogating to themselves that same position. They call themselves the church, and they call their activities the activities of the church, regardless of the fact that they do not represent the great body of the church, and that the great mass of the Christians take very little interest in their activities, and certainly feel no responsibility for them. It is true that I have taken an example from China because it happened to be a convenient one, and the conference in question stated the horrid truth with singular precision. But we can see the same thing going on everywhere. There is arising a new prelacy, a prelacy of committees.

This Explains the Native Objection to the Church as Foreign
(If we want to understand, rather than to protest against, the widespread conviction in all lands that the Christian Church is a foreign institution, I am sure that we must take this position of the committees into account. In them foreign influence is concentrated. This is true even where a majority of the committees are natives of the country. The nationals who sit on these committees are all men who have been trained in western habits of thought; and the money upon which the committees depend to carry on their work is almost wholly derived from a foreign source. The committee is an institution of foreign creation and carries on its work in almost identically the same way whether its members are native or foreign. It is for that reason that foreign societies entrust money to it with confidence, assured that whether the majority of its members are foreign or native will make little difference in the conduct of the activities; the moment that there is any serious doubt whether this will be so, the foreigners demand safeguards. Thus, from the point of view from which we are now considering them, it makes no difference whether the committee is wholly foreign or composed almost entirely of nationals. The work is foreign and must be conducted to the satisfaction of foreigners.)

Since the committees assume this position and use this language and are in control of large resources, and carry on activities which naturally attract attention, and are in a position to advertise their activities in every possible way, the activities carried on by these committees completely overshadow the activities of the real church of the country, the daily activities of quiet simple Christian men. And the non-Christian world is misled into forgetting that it is the Christian life of the common quiet members of the church which is the real activity of the church, and think of the Christian Church and her activities, as these committees teach them, simply in terms of those showy and expensive activities which committees put in the foreground. And when they think of the Christian Church, they naturally think of her in terms of committees, and in terms of activities of a foreign type directed on foreign methods. Hence it is that the native peoples get the impression that 'the Christian movement' is a 'movement of activities.'

The manner in which we use the activities emphasizes the prominence which we give to them.

The Means Are Put in the Place of the Spirit

We use them as if we relied upon them to produce the results which we desire. That the Spirit may be revealed it is essential that men should plainly and unquestionably depend upon the Spirit; but in all our activities there is an apparent reliance upon the activity to produce the result. Do we not habitually talk of uplifting and enlightening men *by* education or *by* social work of some kind?

I have seen a letter in which a missionary wrote: 'How can we expel witchcraft from Africa? By preaching the gospel? Did that do it in England? A belief in witchcraft is carried over by Africans from paganism into Christianity. I personally believe that we can only free them by the God-given knowledge which we have of the germ causation of disease.' And I know that that sort of idea, though less clearly expressed, recurs in missionary literature and in speeches delivered at missionary conferences.

Do we not talk of creating leaders *by* training? What are we saying? We are saying that the means employed produce the effect. We say that our training makes leaders, our education enlightens the intellect, our social work ameliorates conditions of life. Well, suppose they do: these are not the ends which we set before ourselves: the end which we set before ourselves was a revelation of the power of the Holy Ghost. We have either lost sight of the end or we have put the means, our 'activities,' into His place. When the activities usurp the place of the Holy Spirit, the Spirit is obscured and hidden, because He is in fact deposed from His rightful place. It is He who creates leaders, it is He who enlightens, it is He who uplifts, it is He who teaches men to 'live', whatever the conditions in which they live. We cannot have it both ways.

Native Christians Are Taught to Rely Upon Our Activities

Do we not rely upon our activities? In relation to our converts, upon what do we rely for their spiritual, moral, physical progress? In the last resort on what do we rely? By 'in the last resort,' I mean to

H

express the point at which we say 'It is all up; failure must follow.' At what point do we commonly say that, and in respect to what aids' Do we not say 'newborn Christians,' or 'infant churches,' as we call them, cannot possibly stand secure without our 'activities' to support and train them? Do we speak, or act, as if we did in fact rely, and teach them by our own action to rely, upon the Holy Spirit for their guidance and keeping? We often talk to them and to one another of reliance upon the Holy Spirit, but do our acts support our speech? In the main? In our daily practice in relation to them? I think not. From our preaching they might learn to rely upon the Holy Spirit for the establishment and expansion of the church; but from our other speech, from our obvious fear of the consequences of the removal of our education and organizations, they do not learn it; for we do rely upon *our* guidance. Missionary conferences and appeals for men and money constantly proclaim it in explicit terms.

They Are Not Essential

We speak and act as though the maintenance of these activities were essential; but none of them is really essential to the propagation of the gospel. If we ask ourselves in regard to any one of these activities, Could there be a propagation of the gospel without this special form of activity? the answer must be in every case that there could; as a matter of fact there has been in the past a highly effective propagation of the gospel without it, and there might be such again.

With respect to many of our activities we often hear men speak of a 'worthwhile line.' A short time ago missionaries were discussing education in India and questioning whether under certain conditions it would be worthwhile to carry on their educational work. The same question might easily arise with regard to all our activities. Now when we speak of a 'worthwhile line' in relation to any activity we assert that it is not essential, because we say that under certain circumstances we shall give it up. In every undertaking there are certain things which are indispensable; the work cannot be carried on without them. So long as the work is worthwhile, these things are worthwhile. The moment that we admit a worthwhile line, the moment that we say: under such and such conditions we will dispense with this or that, we acknowledge that this or that is something that we can do without. Of course that does not necessarily mean that we can easily do without it, or can lightly dispense with it, but it does mean that its existence is not indispensable, essential, or necessary, to the conduct of the work. Now I venture to say that every one of our activities is in this position. The propagation of the gospel is the indispensable; nothing could induce us to say that it has a worthwhile line, but all these activities are expedients and have a worthwhile line.

We Speak of Them as Essential

This may seem a truth too obvious to need stating, but we are constantly in danger of forgetting it. It is quite pardonable in the leaders of these activities that they should sometimes forget it, and speak of their activities as worthwhile in themselves; but that is simply to make the activity an end in itself. It is to do precisely what the question which we are discussing, and the conference to which it was propounded, deplored. There is a larger purpose in which these activities are subordinate parts, and to fail to recognize that is to treat the part as the whole, the subordinate as the dominant. I should hesitate to write this, but it is needful to do so. Lately missionary leaders have been speaking often of education or of medicine, as if these were not subordinate to any higher dominant, as if they were ends in themselves, as if the practice of them were essential, as if they were in themselves the gospel. We need to be reminded that the gospel has been spread abroad without them, and we need to be reminded that they are not indispensable. If we forget it we make social progress our gospel and become more concerned about social progress than spiritual regeneration, and then it can scarcely surprise us if non-Christians see in our missions activities rather than the power of the Holy Ghost.

The Manifestation of the Spirit in the Native Churches is Obscured

I pointed out above that the position of the committees obscured the church; I pointed out also that our apparent reliance upon our activities does not teach the church to rely upon the Spirit. What I must here insist is that not only the people generally, but the Christians in the country learn the lesson so taught.

The Manifestation of the Spirit in the Native Church

The 'people' look upon the Christians and they see the influence of foreigners rather than the Spirit. For the revelation of the Spirit the activities of the Christians as individuals and as a body, the Church in the place, should be the most clear revelation of the Spirit. Christians living naturally in their old familiar homes must live their lives exactly as their neighbours and friends live, or they must show some change. If they live exactly as their neighbours, then no question will be asked, because all their neighbours will be familiar with the spirit which animates them. But if there is a change in the spirit in which they do familiar things, then a question at once arises. When men see a change in the lives of their neighbours who have previously lived a life in all respects identical with their own, and whose life is still in nearly all its outward aspects identical with their own; when they see such neighbours changed, doing the same things that they do themselves but doing them with a difference, in a different spirit; when they see them united in a Church which is a living body in the place and in which the Spirit resides which appears to affect the conduct of its individual members; then they inevitably begin to wonder and to question the cause. If these Christians are unlike their neighbours, the cause must be an object of curiosity. It must be some internal spiritual power which makes them unlike. If their neighbours judge the change to be a bad one, they will certainly ascribe it to some evil spiritual force which has seized upon them; if they judge it to be good, they must ascribe it to a spiritual force which is in its nature good. They are then face to face with a spiritual force previously unknown to them, but unquestionably a spiritual force. If the change is seen to be good, and the spiritual force which causes the change is judged to be good, then the people are face to face with the Holy Ghost.

This is a witness by activity which we find it extremely hard to appreciate. A change which is very visible to a man's heathen neighbours and friends in China, or in Africa, is often wholly invisible to us. We do not live, and cannot live, sufficiently close to the life of the people to see it. We should often say that a man was no better than his neighbours when his neighbours see a subtle change in him. Similarly a native church might well appear to us eaten through and through with pagan superstition when the people in the village or town would see that it was the home of a new spirit that was in fact changing the whole outlook of its members. We are very bad judges of such matters.

The Manifestation is Obscured

But suppose that the Christians are not free in this sense; suppose that they are led and guided by a foreigner, or by an agent trained by a foreigner; suppose that their church is a body ruled by such men and discipline is enforced by them, education carried on by them, lessons taught by them, then if there is any change in the lives of the Christians it can easily be ascribed to the influence of the foreigner and his teaching and his financial assistance. The witness to the Spirit is obscured. It is not, of course, annihilated, but it is obscured. The non-Christian onlooker has an easy explanation ready to his hand.

The Christians Accept the Position

And the Christians as individuals and as a body, the church in the place, are weakened. The activities of the foreigners and of their trained agents oppress them spiritually whilst they assist them. They learn to rely upon the activities of the foreigners or of the committees, at the best to follow and support them when they lead, at the worst to wait for them to act. They cannot act naturally, freely, in the Spirit. All their little simple activities are overshadowed by the comparatively great organized activities of the committees. They get the idea that the only proper way to do Christian work is to join a preaching band, or to support a great organization by contributions which are often wrung from them by exhortations or, still worse, by assessments. The force of the simple daily activities is lost to them. They do not do their own work, the work which all must do, as the proper Christian work of their lives. The church largely ceases to function as a Christian church in a heathen place, the Christians miss their way. The first and proper Christian activity of a Christian church is to carry on its own life Christianly; the first and proper activities of the church are the activities of its members, the common simple activities which all fulfil well or ill. That is what is lost by our manner of using our 'activities.'

It remains to consider the character of the activities in which we engage.

The Place in Them of Money

They all openly and unmistakably give great prominence to money and the collection of money. They all depend upon money for their existence. It is inconceivable that they could continue without large funds of money. This is true not only of those activities which are concerned with the material and physical welfare of the people at large, such as public education, or public hospitals, and the like; but it is true also of those activities which are more immediately concerned with the expansion and establishment of the church, such as training schools for evangelists, or pastors or teachers. It has invaded the very organization and life of the church itself. Today a propagation of the gospel, an expansion and establishment of the church, without large funds of money seems to us almost incredible. We cannot imagine any progress without paid agents: we cannot imagine any church without paid ministers: we cannot speak of self-support except in terms of finance. It may sound almost absurd, but it is true. Money so dominates all our ideas of missionary work that we have carried over this dependence upon money from spheres, such as our organized activities, where it is plainly true that without funds of money the work must cease, into spheres where it is obviously untrue that without funds of money the work must cease. For anyone can see that there might be churches without paid ministers, and evangelization without paid evangelists. What is even more strange is that we have so succeeded in impressing these ideas upon our converts that, in many parts of the world, they have learned this lesson against all their inherited religious instincts and traditions. It is truly amazing. Christian activity and the collection of money, the church and stipends, are now so inextricably bound together that is seems almost impossible for anyone anywhere to learn to be a Christian without learning this as one of his earliest lessons in the Christian faith. In producing this impression our missionary activities have had no small influence. They are costly tools; they keep money ever in the foreground.

They Are Not the Most Spiritually Costly

They are costly tools in the financial sense, but they are not costly in the spiritual sense. The management of institutions, social work, does not make the heaviest spiritual demand upon us. The suggestion made by the conference that missionaries might become so immersed in the activities as to neglect prayer and meditation reveals it. Many men and women feel that social work makes less demand upon their spiritual resources than prayer or meditation or reliance upon the

Spirit in the native churches. Social work is indeed often an escape from spiritual toil. I think that it would be true to say that immersion in social work, education or medical practice, or the management of clubs, has been a path by which many men at first enthusiastically evangelistic have contrived to escape from a task which they found difficult beyond their expectation into an easier task. They have more or less consciously tried to satisfy their souls by persuading themselves that this work, which was naturally to them more easy, was yet the proper expression of the Divine desire which the Holy Spirit inspired for the conversion of men to Christ and their establishment in the church. Social work is today for us popular and applauded, and comparatively easy; it does not make the deepest demand upon the spiritual force. It is not the most costly work in that sense. It can be undertaken without great spiritual effort.

They Present Subordinate Objects and Ends
These activities have each of them some immediate object peculiar to it, and that object is some form of social advantage which seems to us today desirable. Sometimes it is the propagation of a social, or political, theory, which is the theory of the moment and will almost certainly give place sooner or later to another which in its turn will be proclaimed as the only Christian theory. In our practice of these activities we apparently go to a country definitely and deliberately to improve social conditions according to our ideas of good social conditions. We constantly speak as if the improvement of intellectual and moral and physical conditions were directly the object of our work. The conference in Shanghai so spoke; the conference at Le Zoute so spoke. The impression which we receive in reading missionary literature is very marked and clear. Who has not heard that the YMCA, for instance, exists as an organization for supplying young men with healthy clubs, or that educational missions exist to produce healthy and moral and intellectually enlightened citizens, or that medical missions exist to lead the way in matters of hygiene and the cure of disease. The impression produced is that each of these forms of activity is a separate 'activity' with its own peculiar end in view, and that end some social advantage to the country. It is not surprising, therefore, if onlookers receive the impression that the object which missionary societies have in view in establishing and maintaining these organizations is what it appears to be, or that if they

have any inkling that the apparent object is not the sole object, the inkling takes the form of suspicious doubt as to its real character. For social reform is easily interpreted as interference with the habits and customs of the people, and, when advocated and led by foreigners, is easily interpreted as an interference with the sovereign rights of the nation, or the ancestral rights of the tribe, to manage its own life in its own way.

Contrast With the Apostolic Activity

That missionaries should set out to inaugurate and conduct social reforms is so familiar to us that we scarcely question it; but if we look at the New Testament account of the work of the apostles, we see at once how strange it appears. If we try to imagine St Paul, for instance, setting out to serve the people of Macedonia in the sense in which we set out to serve the peoples of China or of Africa; if we try to imagine him discussing the question, 'Upon what few things should we concentrate our strength so as to be of the greatest service to the peoples of Galatia or of Macedonia,' we find that we cannot imagine any such thing. It becomes inconceivable. And the reason? Because times have changed? Certainly not; it is because there is a great gulf between our idea of direct social service as the work of a missionary of the gospel and his conception of his work as a missionary of the gospel. He could not have contemplated the possibility of undertaking 'a few things.' He had one end, one purpose, one work. He could not have looked upon the service of the people of Macedonia, in our sense of the words, as his work; he could not have attempted to reform social evils directly; he could not have dreamed of attempting to impress the people of Macedonia with the excellence of his social activities, so that they might hail him as a benefactor and welcome him because he provided schools for their children, orphanages for their waifs, or hospitals for their sick; he could not have imagined the possibility of revealing the power of the gospel in any such manner, or by any such activities. The churches which he established did those things, or things like them; they soon began to bury outcast dead, to purchase the freedom of slaves, and to do other pious works which appealed to them as proper expressions of Christian charity; but St Paul himself never directly engaged in any such work nor endeavoured to direct the Christian churches of his foundation in the doing of them. He could not have done so. Social activity of this kind was a fruit of the Spirit and it could not be expected to appear until the apostles had done their work and had ministered the Spirit. Then the charity of the Spirit expressed itself in these forms. It was the business of the missionary to minister the Spirit, it was the business of the Church to express the Spirit in social service. It is hard to think, then, of St Paul and of these social workers whom we send abroad as missionaries in the same sense, though both are Christians and both go out. When we do this kind of work as missionaries we simply confound the work of a missionary with the work of a leader of a settled Christian church. But that is what we are always doing; and the result is hopeless confusion.

They Glorify Human Wit and Skill

In all these activities human wit and human skill are ever in the foreground. They are essentially activities to be carried on by men with specialized training. The deepest spiritual knowledge of the needs of the soul, of the power of the Cross, of the grace of God, of the love of our Lord Jesus Christ have no place in the equipment *necessary* for their conduct. They can be, and sometimes are, carried on by men who know none of these. They are not necessary any more than they are necessary in the equipment of a successful banker or lawyer. The equipment for the conduct of these activities is essentially a special training for that particular form of work—for medical practice medical training, for educational practice educational training, for the conduct of a club experience in club administration, and so on. It is true that to do any of these things Christianly it is necessary to be a Christian, but that is true of every action in life; what the special activity, as a special activity, demands, is the special skill, the special training. The increasing appeal for leaders, and for better trained leaders, keeps this ever before our eyes. The specialized activities demand it, they emphasize it. We are always being told that in education, which is the activity popular in missionary circles today, it is trained skill that counts. Tomorrow some other activity may be the one on which missionary conferences expand, but the demand will be the same. It will be a demand for special training and technical skill. Thus the human element is exalted in all our activities. Science, in its widest sense, is in the foreground. Without it the activities cannot be efficiently carried on; efficiency in the conduct of the activities is inevitably ascribed to it.

They Appeal to the Wisdom of the World

They are essentially the kind of activities which appeal to the wisdom of this world. They aim at and attain immediate social and economic advantages which attract the applause of statesmen and the support of the more far-seeing and wise-hearted merchants, traders and employers of labour. Men who have little faith in the Holy Ghost, who scarcely understand the meaning of the ministration of the Spirit, who certainly cannot see that the ministration of the Spirit is the secret of all true progress, or that, given the Spirit, the progress is inevitable; men who believe that true progress can be attained by the improvement of conditions, the teaching and practice of sound economic doctrines or by technical instruction; men who fancy that right relationships between man and man can be attained without the Spirit of right relationship; men who would certainly not support the propagation of the gospel as the power of God unto salvation; readily support these activities because they value the immediate social and economic advantages which are attained by their influence upon non-Christians who have not received the Spirit equally with Christians who have. The wisdom of the world can understand them.

The Teaching and Example of St Paul

Let us turn to the New Testament. It is always refreshing to do that, because we at once escape out of our modern confusions into a clearer atmosphere where first principles are kept first and expedients are put into their proper place.

I have already pointed out that it is impossible for us to imagine St Paul and those who followed him going about to propagate the gospel and to establish churches by embarking on all sorts of activities for the benefit of the peoples of the Roman Empire. He and his followers had one object, one purpose, and that purpose was, not to raise directly the social conditions of the people to whom they went, but to bring them to Christ, to minister the Spirit, to establish them in churches in which the Spirit lived and was manifested in and through the activities of the body and of all its members, transforming them from within, so that their activities became and appeared different from the activities of the heathen society and they themselves different from the heathen people amongst whom they resided. With that one object, with that one purpose, they were delivered from the confusions which arise in our missions through multitudinous activities, each aiming at some subordinate object. In the apostolic life and teaching and example first things were not simply first; they stood alone; there was no other object in the field, and consequently there was no possibility of confusion.

St Paul Met the Difficulty That the Spirit Might Be Obscured

But there is one passage to which I now wish to call attention particularly, because in it St Paul recognizes the possibility of a certain course of action producing precisely that result which the Shanghai conference deplored. He presents the case; he argues the point. St Paul then knew the danger of obscuring the spiritual force. Here, as in nearly all our modern missionary difficulties, he has faced the danger before us: he met it; he knew how to avoid it; and we might learn from him, if we would. But, unfortunately, we consider him out-of-date, and we do not foresee the danger as he foresaw it, and we discover it only when we have fallen into it. Then we begin to ask: Why has this evil come upon us? We begin to consider what we are doing, when it is already too late, when we have gone so far that to retrace our steps is difficult, and there are many to proclaim that we cannot afford to go back to apostolic principles, because we have already invested so much time and labour and money.

The Passage I Cor. 1.17-2.16

In the Epistle to the Corinthians St Paul says that there was a method of propagating the gospel, attractive to many, open to him, which he deliberately declined to use. He is not, of course, speaking of any of our social activities by which he might have presented himself as a social reformer, and his gospel as a gospel of social reform. As I have said, such a conception of his work would have been so alien to him that it is positively inconceivable even to us that he should have set before himself the service of the people of Achaia, in our sense of the word service, as the direct object of his work. He is speaking of a method of commending his gospel to his hearers which was very attractive in his day, as, indeed, it is to many minds in ours, and was in fact the common and natural method used by intelligent and thoughtful men in commending any new religious theory or way of life. This method he describes as 'wisdom of words,' 'the wisdom of the wise,' 'the wisdom of this world,' 'excellency of speech,' 'the wisdom of men.' He says that the use of this method would have 'made the cross of Christ of none effect.' Men would have accepted the preaching as a wisdom akin to the wisdom of other philosophical theories with which they were familiar; they would have made progress, so far as they made any progress in morality of life, or in theological truth, by it, and by their intelligent apprehension of it, rather than by the power of the Cross, the power of God, the wisdom of God. He says that it would have obscured the power of God, the wisdom of God, which was in the eyes of the Jews and Greeks weakness, foolishness and an offence.

The Relation of This Passage to Our Activities

Now I ask my reader to consider carefully whether our activities, our use of scientific methods, is not closely akin to what St Paul calls the 'wisdom of the wise,' the 'wisdom of the world.' Is it not in fact 'the wisdom of the wise,' the 'wisdom of the world' today? Do not 'the wise' who have little faith in the power of the Cross, little knowledge of the power of the Holy Ghost, expect from it progress and enlightenment, intellectual, moral and physical; and do not missionaries who use it enjoy their applause just so far as they appear to rely upon it, and do they not lose that applause just in proportion as they decline to rely upon it and exalt the power which is of God, the power of the Cross, the power of the Holy Ghost above it? When they do that, are they not smiled at as people who have much sound sense and an excellent knowledge of true science but a strange kink in their brains; or derided as men ignorant of all true scientific principles, and carried away by a foolish superstition? Read the passage with our modern scientific activities in mind and see where they stand.

The Fruit Seen in the Church

Then St Paul says that rooted in this foolishness of God there appeared in the church a true spiritual philosophy which far out-topped the philosophy of the world. We have used the philosophy of our day, the scientific methods of the wise, and we deplore the absence of true spiritual social progress in the church. We have exalted the philosophy and we miss the power; not of course wholly; that could never be; but in measure large enough to perturb us. If we could follow the apostle, we should see social activity in the church producing social progress of the deepest and strongest character, because rooted in the Spirit, in the innermost depths; and because deep, slowly manifesting itself by quiet growth; so deep that few of us would at first have eyes to see it, any more than the philosophers of St Paul's day could see the wisdom of which he spoke. But if we would see the the like, we must follow his rule, and know, as he knew, the power which is of God, and learn to rely upon that and to decline to use the method which obscures it.

Zeal Does Not Ensure the Propriety of the Means Which it Employs

We need to recognize that zeal for God is not a guarantee that the means used to express the zeal is divinely inspired. There was an age when Christians thought the sword a proper weapon for expressing their zeal and faith; but it did not follow that the sword was a proper weapon. Their zeal and faith had its reward; but growth in the knowledge of Christ taught us that the sword was not a fit weapon for the Spirit. So men today are earnestly desirous of following the guidance of the Spirit, and of revealing His power to men; and they employ these activities. Their faith and zeal is not lost: Christ's kingdom is advancing, men are being converted to Christ, Christ's Spirit is being shed abroad; but it does not follow that the activities are the proper weapon of the Spirit. Another age may learn to look upon our use of activities much as we look upon the use of the sword by an earlier age. Because in them money takes so prominent a place, ours may one day be known as the age of financial Christianity, just as we look upon that earlier age as the age of military Christianity. As we regard the sword so a later age may regard money. It may learn the wisdom of the Apostle and decline to use such an abiguous weapon. If the sword was an ambiguous weapon which might easily confuse the issue, money and activities which depend upon money, are not less ambiguous and may as easily confuse the issue. The time is not yet full. We have yet to learn the consequences of our use of money.

The Importance of the Character of the Spiritual Force

It makes a difference whether we speak of 'a spiritual force' or of the Holy Ghost in this way: If we think of 'a spiritual force' we naturally think of it as residing in a person and manifested to others in his activities. We can so think and we can stop there. The manifestation is complete. So when we speak of our activities as the service of the people, and think of the force which moves us to the activities as 'a spiritual force,' we can stop at the manifestation of that spiritual force in our activities. When we speak of the end of missionary activities as some service done to the people of China, or of India, or of Africa, we are thinking of what we do for them. In this sense our activities are curiously self-centred in spite of their apparent altruism. We stay at 'for them.' We cannot reach to 'in them,' But the ministration of the Spirit speaks not of what *we* can do, but of what *they* can do in the power of the Spirit. It is, therefore, something far more profound than our activities generally admit. Our activities are, indeed, in this sense superficial: the Spirit goes down to the roots in them. In proportion as we allow 'for them' to absorb attention, in proportion as we miss 'in them,' we are really losing sight of the Spirit; but are not 'for them' and 'to them' shouted aloud by our activities; and is not this the sound which we hear in all our missionary conferences, even when the subject under discussion is the manifestation of the Spirit? Are not *our* activities emphasized till we almost forget *their* activities?

Even when we are not satisfied with our activities for others and we educate them to sit on the committees, to run the institutions, to manage the clubs, or even to conduct the evangelistic activities which we have promoted, we fall short. For a master to teach a pupil the trick of the tools' true play is not the same thing as ministering the Spirit.

Nay, more, when we speak of encouraging or inculcating a spirit, as missionaries often speak of 'the team spirit,' or 'the public school spirit,' or the 'spirit of service,' because we think in terms of 'a spiritual force,' we miss the ministration of the Spirit. Not every spiritual force is the Holy Ghost. Men may catch a spirit of altruistic self-sacrifice and yet not know the Holy Spirit. The spirit of self-sacrifice is not necessarily holy, nor is it necessarily the Spirit of divine love. I may give my body to be burned, said St Paul, and yet not have that Spirit.

All these conceptions of our work as missionaries fall far short of the work in which missionaries of the gospel ought to be engaged. We cannot stop at 'for them' nor even 'with them,' or at a philanthropic spirit.

The Spiritual Force the Holy Ghost

The Spiritual force with which Christians have to do is a personal,

active, Spirit who works not only in us, as missionaries, but upon all
with whom we deal and in all who will receive Him. Any success to
which we may attain is His work. It is He who moves the soul, it is
He who enlightens, it is He who establishes and upbuilds. We attain
our end only when He is received by and revealed in another. The
manifestation of the Spirit is only fulfilled in the ministration of the
Spirit. That is, I suppose, the reason why St Paul speaks of his work
as a ministration of the Spirit. It is not enough merely to show forth
the Spirit of Christ by pious and beneficent activity on our part as
missionaries; it is the ministration of the Spirit which is our goal. It is
not enough that those with whom we have to do should see our
activities and recognize that they are inspired by a good spirit; it is
not enough that they should imitate our activities; it is not enough
that they should help us in them; there is no satisfaction until they
are actuated by the Holy Spirit and express the Holy Spirit in their
own activities.

Manifestation of the Spirit in Free Activity
Just as we ourselves only manifest the Spirit in our activities where
those activities are free and spontaneous, not forced or governed or
controlled (even in slavery, though then the actual work to be done is
controlled and forced, yet the Spirit is revealed only in the free spontaneous activity of the soul in the performance of the work; the Spirit
makes the work a free spontaneous expression of its own life), so
those to whom we minister the Spirit can only show forth His power
in their own free spontaneous activity. Action done under compulsion
or direction is no revelation of the Spirit. If we want to see what is
the character of any living thing, we must see what it does in free
conditions. To say that it is enough to see how it acts under ordered
conditions is only to confuse our minds; because the manifestation of
its character is made only so far as it is free under the ordered conditions. If then we want to see a manifestation of the Spirit in a form
which can be understood, it must be in the unfettered activity of
Christians under their own natural conditions.

The Key to Our Problem—Indigenous Churches
I believe that this is the key to the problem which we have set before
ourselves. The spiritual force, the Holy Ghost, will be manifested to
the people of any country to which we go when they see that Spirit

ministered by us manifested in the spontaneous activity of their own countrymen. They cannot see that so long as every sign of progress in Christians in their country can be ascribed to the influence of foreign governors and directors, exercised, either directly or indirectly, through ministers and officers trained and appointed and controlled by them; nor can they see it in the activities of fellow-countrymen who have received a foreign education and are engaged in directing organizations of a foreign type and largely financed with foreign money, exactly as the foreigners directed the organizations until they gave place to these trained natives.

It is here that we see the importance of the establishment of little native churches which are obviously and unmistakably not under our control, but fully equipped with their own ministers and possessing full spiritual authority to direct their own life. We should spend our strength in establishing as many of these as possible. The establishment of such churches would at once strike at the root of the difficulty which is presented to us. The people would see in those churches Christians possessed by the Spirit and showing forth the Spirit by being in some way different from other people who had not received the Spirit and acting in some subtle way differently from other people.

The Place of Mission Activities

Then mission activities would take a lower place and their influence be at once lightened, illuminated and counterbalanced by the activities of the local churches. In a short time the activities of the churches, though apparently small in any one place, would together bulk so large as to outweigh our activities; mission activities would be mission activities and would not overwhelm the activities of the Christians in their local churches, nor so overshadow them that men could any longer speak of foreign activities as if they were the sole examples of the Christian movement in the country. The Christian movement in the country would be outside them, more widely spread, and more effective. If any one looked for the Christian movement in the country, he would find it most powerfully expressed in the life of the local churches. And that is what it ought to be. But that it may be so, the local churches must be absolutely native and obviously and unmistakably free from our control—not in our speech, but in the eyes of every native.

The Work of the Missionary of the Gospel

And then I believe that we should gain enormously if we could see that missionaries of the gospel ought to have not many activities, but one activity.

I venture to insist that missionaries of the gospel have only one proper activity, the ministration of the Spirit of Christ. The material social, political, physical advancement of the nation is not their proper, direct work. Their sole direct work is to bring to Christ those whom He has called and to establish His church; and the social, political, physical, material progress of the people must spring out of that, and be the direct fruit of the Spirit in them.

We must not admit for one moment the truth of a statement often made that the man who devotes himself to the establishment of the church, declining to be involved in all sorts of activities for the improvement of social conditions, is indifferent to, or heedless of, the sufferings and injustices under which men suffer. He is nothing of the kind; he is simply a man who is sure of his foundation, and is convinced that the only way to any true advancement is spiritual, and is Christ, and therefore he persists, in spite of all appearances, in clinging to Christ as the only foundation, and in building all his hopes for the future on the acceptance of Christ. He is not content with attacks upon symptoms of evil: they seem to him superficial: he goes to the roots. He cannot be content with teaching men 'Christian principles of conduct,' 'Christian ideals of social life,' still less with the establishment of colleges and clubs. Nothing but Christ Himself, faith in Christ, the obedience of Christ, seems to him equal to the need, and nothing else is his work but the establishment of that foundation. In doing this he is not showing indifference to social evils, he is not standing aloof from beneficent movements, he is actively engaged in laying the axe to the roots of the trees which bear the evil. That is not indifference.

That is what I mean by saying that the sole work of the missionary of the gospel is the ministration of the Spirit.

I

4
St Paul and the Judaizers:
A Dialogue

Editorial Note

This is Part II of The Establishment of the Church in the Mission Field: A Critical Dialogue. *It illustrates pungently Allen's use of New Testament principle and practice for modern controversial purposes; and is further important because this particular New Testament issue is sometimes treated as if its significance were only historical.*

St Paul and the Judaizers

A. I wonder whether the Bible throws any light on the problem. It might help us to decide what it is wise for us to do. The apostle St Paul, for instance, had to meet this question, and his example and practice might afford some guidance. Have you ever looked at his work from this point of view?

V. Of course I have. I know perfectly well that St Paul established churches just as you seem to want us to do; but it cannot be done today. Some years ago the same man, whose article we were discussing at the beginning, wrote a book on St Paul's missionary method, and plenty of people pointed out at once that the conditions today are utterly different from those which obtained in St Paul's day, and that consequently you cannot argue from his action. I never heard that he made any answer to that.

A. Shall we consider the matter now?

V. If you like.

A. Where shall we begin? Were there any people in the Christian Church in St Paul's day who argued that missions to the heathen ought to be conducted on the same principles which you are maintaining, and for the same reasons?

V. Not that I know of.

A. Were there not people who followed St Paul wherever he went, arguing that Gentile converts must be compelled to keep the law?

V. Oh, you mean the Judaizing party! Of course they did that.

A. Why did they do that?

V. Because they wanted the Jew to be top dog in the church, and the Christian Church to be Jewish throughout, and the converts from the heathen to be admitted only on sufferance, and, in so far as they followed Jewish rules of life, as a species of proselyte.

A. Is that what they said?

V. No, of course they did not put it like that. They said the converts from heathenism could not be saved unless they were circumcised and kept the law. But it amounted to what I said. That would have been the result; and any fool could see it.

A.   Do you think those 'certain which came from James' were men who were consciously seeking nothing but to maintain the predominance of the Jews in the church? Do you think that all those who followed them were doing that?

V.   I should think they probably were. Anyhow, they were bitter opponents of the policy of St Paul which set the Gentiles free.

A.   Was not St Peter at one time inclined to think that they were right?

V.   Yes, that is true.

A.   And Barnabas also?

V.   Yes.

A.   And do you think those two men were ready to adopt a policy of which the obvious meaning was nothing but Jewish predominance in the church?

V.   No. I should not like to say that. St Peter had gone to the house of Cornelius, and Barnabas had been on a missionary journey with St Paul. I think that they must have had some reason for believing that it was better for the whole body of Christians, Gentiles as well as Jews, that all should be circumcised and keep the law.

A.   Do you think that the Galatian and Macedonian converts of St Paul were in danger of being led astray by an appeal which obviously meant nothing but Jewish domination in the church?

V.   That seems hardly likely. They must have had some more plausible reason to give.

A.   What reason could they have given? What sort of argument could they have used?

V.   I do not quite know. All that we are told is that they laid down the law and said that the Gentiles could not be saved unless they kept it.

A.   That sounds as if they were, at least professedly, anxious about the salvation of the Gentiles. Perhaps they really were anxious. They might well have been anxious; they might well have believed sincerely that St Paul was leading his converts along a very dangerous path and forsaking the way of Christ in telling them that they need not keep the law. Before the Jerusalem Council they might have sincerely believed that all the apostles would agree with them, and after the Council they might have sincerely believed that they were right. But they must have used some argument to maintain that position. You yourself said that they must have had some reason to give for their belief.

V. I am certain that they had some reason.

A. Well, what was it? There are some obvious arguments which they might have used. They might have said, for instance, that Jesus was a Jew and kept the law, and that men who wished to be saved must follow him in this.

V. They might certainly have said that.

A. And did not Jesus say, 'One jot or one tittle shall in no wise pass from the law, till all be fulfilled'? And did not He tell His disciples, 'The Scribes and the Pharisees sit in Moses' seat: all therefore, whatsoever they bid you observe, that observe and do'? Might not these people have argued that Christ the Saviour told His disciples to keep the law?

V. They might. It sounds a strong argument.

A. Might they not then have said that the Jewish law was the Christian law, and must be maintained by Christians?

V. I suppose they might.

A. And might they not have said that if heathen Gentiles were bound by that law the moral standard of the church would be no better than heathen?

V. Well, it is clear from his epistles that even St Paul himself was anxious about the moral standard of the Gentile churches; and that they gave him good cause to be anxious.

A. And might they not have argued that if Gentiles lived in heathen cities and were not bound by the law, the church would certainly be contaminated with heathen ideas of God, and be compromised by compliance with idolatrous customs?

V. I do not know whether they said anything about these things; but I imagine all men would see that strict adherence to the law involved a strict adherence to the idea of God as One and Holy, and would be a great safe-guard against the inroads of heathen conceptions of God, polytheism and idolatry.

A. They might have said so?

V. They certainly might have said so. It would have been a powerful argument.

A. Anyhow, they acted as if they believed it; I suppose I must say that?

V. Yes, you may say that.

A. And is it not more reasonable to suppose that men who plainly had great influence in the church were honest men and used good arguments, even if their hatred and fear of St Paul's doctrine and practice drove them to seek his life, than that they were men who openly and confessedly were fighting for nothing but domination over the Gentile churches? Which do you believe?

V.   I believe that they really were afraid that if St Paul's doctrine of freedom from the law won the day all those evils which you suggested must follow. It seems so perfectly obvious.

A.   Then they shared the fears which you expressed. They in their day and you in yours have felt the same fear, and the same need for a stout maintenance of a standard of morals and doctrine. There is, then, some likeness between the conditions in St Paul's day and in ours.

V.   Well, as far as that goes, there is a resemblance; but I think it ends there. The danger was not so great, because St Paul could always establish his churches with a nucleus of men, Jews and God-fearing Greeks, who really knew the discipline of the law. Now we have nothing of the kind; and that makes so great a difference that it breaks down all argument from St Paul's action.

A.   Let us consider that. What you are saying is that St Paul made converts from the synagogue, Jews and God-fearing Greeks, men who had been trained under the discipline of the law, and therefore he could rely upon them to maintain the Christian standard of doctrine and morals. Is that right?

V.   Yes, that is what I said.

A.   And if we had men like that in the churches today we could follow his example. Is that right?

V.   Yes; no doubt that would be true.

A.   Well, then, let us inquire first whether the converts from the synagogue had such influence in the church that there really was no danger in those days. Did not St Paul write to the Thessalonians as though they had heard of one God living and true from him first?

V.   Yes, that is true.

A.   And does he not write to the Corinthians of the right attitude of Christians to polytheism and to idolatry and idolatrous feasts?

V.   He does.

A.   Why should he do that? If the Pauline churches were really guided by men who had forsaken that sort of error long before he preached to them, if they were not in danger of falling into compromise with heathen ideas of God and heathen immorality, why should he write like that? Was the whole thing a delusion, and was there really no danger at all of the church going astray?

V. No doubt many of the converts were from the heathen outside the synagogue, and they needed this exhortation.

A. But still the nucleus was there, the well-taught, established Jewish converts and proselytes, and there was no fear of the church as a whole going astray. Did not you say that? Didn't you say that St Paul's churches were guided by these men and therefore he could rely upon them to keep the church straight? Was not that the difference between his work and ours which made the imitation of his missionary practice impossible today?

V. Yes, that is true.

A. Then why did they not do their work? Why did they not settle the question? You said that they were the men who saved the church from any danger of compromise with heathen customs and ideas, didn't you? Were these churches really being led by the men upon whom you stake so much? Or were those men comparatively few in number and not always the most influential men in the church?

V. I do not know.

A. But you know, don't you, that very early the breach between the synagogue and the Christian Church became accentuated, so that the Christian could no longer preach in the synagogues. What happened then? Did churches continue to multiply just as before?

V. They certainly multiplied among the Gentiles.

A. In spite of the fact that they could no longer be called 'offshoots of the local synagogue,' as a missionary bishop once called St Paul's churches?

V. Yes, in spite of that.

A. Then may I not conclude that St Paul relied upon neither the Jewish Christians nor Gentile proselytes, but upon something else to maintain and advance the true standard of doctrine and morals in the church? Or must I add further argument?

V. I do not know what further arguments you could adduce.

A. Let us see. I suggested to you a moment ago that the Judaizers must have used some rational argument to bring the Gentiles under the law.

V. Yes. You suggested that they must have taught that the law was the law kept by Christ and confirmed by Him, and that His followers must keep it because He kept it, and apparently told them to keep it.

A.   And did you not agree?

V.   I agreed that they certainly might have used that argument.

A.   And to whom would that argument most strongly appeal: to the Jewish Christians and the God-fearing Greeks who had already accepted the law, or to the Gentile converts who had never been attracted by the law sufficiently strongly to become proselytes?

V.   I suppose to the Jewish and God-fearing.

A.   Then you think that these classes would be most likely to accept the teaching of the Judaizers?

V.   I do.

A.   And St Paul was opposed to the Judaizers?

V.   Plainly.

A.   And he writes as if there were grave danger of his converts submitting to the teaching of the Judaizers?

V.   Yes.

A.   Then were not those converts from the synagogue rather a source of danger than a source of strength in this controversy? How, then, could St Paul naturally rely upon them? The converted Jews were of the same race as the Judaizers, and had been born under the law; the God-fearing had already submitted. They were the people who would feel least difficulty in acknowledging the truth of the Judaizers' argument.

V.   There may be something in that, but still I do not think it very convincing.

A.   You mean that you think the Gentile converts would be more ready to accept Jewish claims than the Jewish converts.

V.   No; I do not. I do not think either would easily have submitted.

A.   Yet you agreed with me that St Paul wrote as if there were grave danger.

V.   So I did; but I really do not know what to say about it.

A.   Well, let us consider the matter in this way. St Paul relied upon the presence of these converts from the synagogue to maintain the standard of doctrine and morality. You said that, didn't you? Your position was that St Paul's practice was impossible today because we had no such converts upon whom to rely. Is not that what you said?

V.   Yes, that is the great difference between his day and ours.

A.   May I say, then, that if there had been no converts from the syn-

agogue St Paul would have agreed that the Christian Gentiles must
be protected by the hedge of the law?

V.   No, certainly not. St Paul's argument was that men were not to
be saved by obedience to law, but by faith in Christ. It does not make
the smallest difference to his argument whether there were or were
not Jews and God-fearing Greeks in his churches.

A.   Do you mean that he would have spoken and acted exactly as he
did, had there been no Jews or God-fearing Greeks in his churches? I
thought you said that it was the presence of those men which made
all the difference, and that we cannot follow his practice now because
there are no Jews or God-fearing Greeks in the churches which we
found.

V.   You do not understand. We must have trained men on whom
we can rely to maintain some standard. St Paul found those men in
the synagogue. That is all that I mean.

A.   And did not find them outside the synagogue?

V.   I should hardly like to say that.

A.   But, surely, you must say that, if you are to maintain your position; because otherwise it is possible that we might find them outside the synagogue today, and that you say we cannot do.

V.   Well, anyhow, we do not. That is the only thing that matters.

A.   Perhaps we do not know, because we have never tried. But did
St Paul rely upon the training of the synagogue at all?

V.   Surely he did that. The Jews and God-fearing Greeks brought
into the church a well established standard of faith and morals which
the Gentile converts sorely lacked. You can hardly deny that.

A.   You mean that these men first learned the discipline of the law,
and then, being themselves established in character by that discipline, could accept the liberty of the gospel without danger, and
could maintain a standard in the church.

V.   Yes, that is what I mean.

A.   How does that differ from saying that for morality of life Moses
with his law is a better and more effective teacher than Christ? Is it
not the same as saying that when men have learned the fundamental
ideas of morality and of the unity and holiness of God from Moses,
then they can accept the faith of Christ without danger; but that the
faith of Christ and the teaching of Christ and the grace of Christ and
the gift of the Holy Spirit, are not sufficiently powerful by themselves
to do what the stern discipline of law alone can do?

V.   I cannot say that. I do not believe it. Faith in Christ's grace and His gift of the Holy Spirit are far more strong foundations for purity of life than any law. How can I say that Moses is a better teacher than Christ?

A.   But if that is so, it is possible to begin with faith in Christ and to rely solely upon Christ, even if there has been no previous discipline under the law. Does not that follow? And is not that precisely the position which St Paul took up? Did he not teach that for salvation of soul and body in this life and in the life to come, Christ is the only Saviour, and that faith in Him is the only way, and that any trust in the law is vain?

V.   That is, I think, what he taught.

A.   Then he did not rely upon the discipline of the law, nor did he rely upon the teaching of the synagogue to save the standard of morality in his churches. Whether his converts came from the synagogue or from the heathen world outside, he taught them that they must regard their past ideas as vain, and learn of Christ and of Christ alone, and follow and obey Him, and Him alone? Do you agree?

V.   Yes, I agree.

A.   May I conclude, then, that this assertion that St Paul's method depended on the presence of proselytes and Jews in his Churches is of no force at all; but is the flat contradiction of his teaching, and would have horrified him?

V.   I do not see how it can be avoided. But you must not forget that he preached for the most part to civilized people. Who can tell whether he would have run such risks if he had been face to face with people like those with whom we have to deal in many parts of the world, in Africa, for instance, men with no civilized history behind them, or outcaste tribes in India? There he simply could not have established churches as he did in Galatia or in Macedonia.

A.   Why not?

V.   Because the people are too degraded.

A.   When we hear modern missionaries speaking of their work I do not remember that they ever distinguish in that way. Do they generally say that in dealing with civilized races like the Japanese or the Chinese, they can follow the principles and practice of St Paul because these nations are civilized, but in dealing with outcaste Indians or Africans they cannot follow his example because the people are degraded and uncivilized? Have you ever heard them say anything of that kind?

V. No, I cannot say that I have.

A. Would it be possible for them to say it?

V. No, they could not say it, because we make no such distinction in our action. We follow the same practice everywhere.

A. But you said that we could not follow the apostolic practice because today the people to whom we go are not as civilized and enlightened as the people to whom St Paul went. Don't you think that the peoples of the Far East would feel insulted if they heard this answer, that they are more degraded that the provincials of Macedonia and of Achaia and of Asia Minor under the Roman Empire? Do you think they would like it?

V. I never thought of that. I was thinking of uncivilized people in Africa, and I said so.

A. You did, and I understood you. All that I wanted to do was to suggest that that answer is not a true one. If it were true we should be compelled to make distinctions which we do not make in our mission practice. May I say that whatever the true reason may be, that is not the reason why we do not follow the apostle?

V. As far as the civilized people are concerned, you may say so; but as for the uncivilized and degraded, it may still be true, that if St Paul had to deal with them he could not have founded churches as he did in the Roman Empire.

A. Upon what foundation did he build? Did he build on the foundation of the intellectual and social enlightment of the people to whom he went? Did he rely upon that any more than he relied upon the training which the law had given to Jews and proselytes?

V. No, I do not think that he did that. But still, just think of the conditions in outcaste Indian villages and in African kraals!

A. I am thinking of them. I am prepared to admit anything, however bad, that may be said of them. But I am thinking of St Paul's principles: circumstances do not alter principles. And was not his principle that Christ sufficed to meet all conditions?

V. No doubt; but there is a limit beyond which no man can go. Surely you recognize a *praeparatio evangelica*: the people to whom St Paul went were prepared by a long discipline under law, so that their moral and religious sense was cultivated. What Africa needs is a like preparation. I have heard missionaries say that what Africans need is a long discipline under the terrors of the moral law, then they might be prepared to receive the Gospel; but as it is they have had no moral training to keep them straight. To talk about Pauline principles in such a case is mere folly.

A.   I, too, have heard them say that; but is it true? I have heard others speak very differently; but I do not want to weigh authority against authority on this subject. That would be an endless and futile task. What you and I want to consider is, what is the truth of the gospel. And we agreed, did we not, that Christ is a better foundation on which to build than Moses?

V.   Yes, we did.

A.   And shall we not agree that when missionaries of the gospel go to any people, it is because in the providence of God the time has come for them to go?

V.   That is certain.

A.   And can missionaries of the gospel be missionaries of anything but the gospel?

V.   Certainly not.

A.   Then in the providence of God the time has come for these people to hear the gospel.

V.   Plainly.

A.   Then it is of Christ that they must hear, not of the law; for the law is not the gospel.

V.   Well.

A.   And moral advance must spring from faith in Christ and obedience to Him, not from fear of the law.

V.   Well.

A.   You say, 'Well,' but what do you really mean; do you mean that in the case of these degraded people the indwelling Christ is to be put first as the foundation of all, and not some external control?

V.   I really do not know what to say. It seems a fearful risk.

A.   Do you agree with me that St Paul's principle that the indwelling Christ is the one and only hope for men would have forced him to act in Africa today as he did in Macedonia and in Galatia twenty centuries ago, or do you think that he would have said that he could apply that doctrine in Galatia and Macedonia, but that in Africa external control was unavoidable? Is his doctrine one which could so change?

V.   Well, he might have done it; but we cannot venture so far.

A. Why not, if indeed we believe in Christ?

V. It is all very well to believe in Christ; we all do that; but to say that Africans can do without control from us, that is going too far. Didn't I tell you long ago that we are sent to control, and must control?

A. Now you are explaining why our practice is identical in principle in the Far East and in Africa; for if we believe that we must rely upon our control to save our converts, and if we teach our converts to rely upon our control, that can be applied universally. They are all new-born Christians, and we can easily be afraid for them all, and see at once that they all alike need our control.

V. That is right. You see that at last.

A. Do you remember that, when I asked you why the Judaizers acted as they did, you answered that they obviously wanted the Jew to be top dog in the church, and converts from the heathen to be admitted only so far as they followed Jewish rules of life. You are not afraid that our converts may one day say that of us?

V. Some of them say it now; they accuse us of importing western forms and civilization, and of keeping them down, but it is absurdly false. We do nothing of the kind. Our one care is for their progress and stability.

A. Did not the Judaizers say that, or might they not have said that, and yet you, looking at their work from this distance, said at once that it was plain that they were working to maintain the supremacy of the Jews in the church, and to keep all Gentile converts in the position of proselytes? Have those natives who accuse us of keeping them down no reason or excuse?

V. No excuse whatever. It is perfectly manifest to any impartial observer that we use our control solely for their uplift, and have no idea whatever of maintaining our supremacy, or of keeping them down. It is absurd and wicked to suggest such a notion.

A. Yet our converts say it. It is strange.

5

An Illustration from V. S. Azariah

Editorial Note

Educational Principles and Missionary Methods: The Application of Educational Principles to Missionary Evangelism, *published in* 1919 *with a somewhat cautious introduction by Bishop Charles Gore, is evidence of the serious study that Allen made at this time of what was then 'modern' educational theory (in particular, the work of Froebel, Pestalozzi, and Montessori) in order to put it to use in the cause of effective missionary work. The following extract, which is the final chapter of the book, sufficiently indicates Allen's point of view and affords evidence of a link with Bishop Azariah of Dornakal.*

An Illustration from V. S. Azariah

A few months before his consecration as Bishop of Dornakal, Mr Azariah, in a letter to a friend in England, said: 'At this place there is only one family of Christians . . . I was trying to tell the evangelists the new method of training the congregations; and I gave model lessons in this congregation. The man for the first time opened his mouth to pray. He said "Oh Father who art in Heaven, You are our Father, we are Your children. Keep us all well. Heal my rheumatism and my child's boil. Keep us from all wild animals, the bear and the tiger. Forgive us our sins, our quarrels, angry words, all that we have done since morning. Make us good. Bring all the castes to kneel down to You and call You Father." He did not know that he ought to finish it in a set fashion and I thought I would not trouble him with the Greek "Amen". For two months the catechist had tried to teach the Telugu Lord's Prayer, but "it will not come" to him. The young boy was the only one who could proceed unaided up to "Lead us not". We felt greatly encouraged at this result. On the second day his relation, an equally brainless man, joined and offered another beautiful prayer.'

We have here an interesting example of the educational method which I have tried to set forth in the preceding pages.

I. The pupil is put into his proper place in the thought of the educator. The first and sole consideration is his progress. He is not subordinated to his subject, or to any policy. Mr Azariah is not concerned to set forth his subject in any predetermined order. He is not concerned with any desire to create a Christian of any certain type. His sole object is to assist his hearers to learn the meaning of prayer. Consequently in his statement the thought of the learner occupies the first place.

II. The lesson is based on real knowledge of the people with whom the teacher had to do. It is extremely simple. It is based of course upon true and deep Christian ideas. But in form it is designed rather to lead up to Christian ideas, and to strictly Christian practice, than to enforce the precise observation of these at the moment. Christian prayer is prayer in the Spirit, through Jesus Christ our Lord. In a sense there can be no Christian prayer till this is known. But the practice of prayer is not postponed until the converts have a large knowledge of Christ. The teacher knows what is in the mind of his hearers. He knows how much he can teach them in this lesson. He is content in this short lesson to base his teaching on that knowledge, and to leave it there for the moment to become familiar to his hearers' minds. Its incompleteness does not trouble him. His knowledge of his hearers is deep enough to enable him to judge how much they can grasp at this lesson, and to enable him to present that lesson in such a way that they do grasp it.

III. There is a true conception of the end, a real end is attained in that one lesson. This lesson is not simply a preparation for another lesson. It is not merely a part of an education which is to be carried on hereafter. The end is to be attained here and now, and the hearers arrive at it. If the teacher never came near them again, his end, so far as he had gone, would have been attained. So far their education was complete. They could have gone on praying by themselves in the light of this lesson.

IV. Here is development. This lesson prayer is based upon the known nature and history of the learners. We can see an enormous advance made by them. They themselves have developed under this teaching. They have grown. Their minds, their hearts, have opened. They are conscious of powers of which they had before the most dim conception. If they had any conception at all. But this growth arises naturally and harmoniously. There is no sudden break, no beginning as though there had been no past. The men who pray this prayer are the same men who a little while before seemed incapable of any prayer.

V. There is real instruction resulting in knowledge. Knowledge of God, knowledge of the relationship in which the learners stood to Him, knowledge of His nature, of His power, of His willingness to hear prayer, of the proper attitude in which to approach Him, of the need of forgiveness, of the relation of men to their fellow men, all this and much more is strongly apprehended. It is real knowledge, it is significant, it is intimately connected with life and experience.

VI. There is activity. The educands are active throughout. The only test that they have learned the lesson is their capacity to put it into practice. If these people had been put through a verbal examination on the subject of prayer they would probably have been speech-less.[1] Yet there is no question that they had learned the lesson.

VII. There was liberty; external liberty to express themselves as they pleased without interference; internal liberty, the attainment of power to direct their own actions. And with liberty came discipline, self-control, consideration for the needs of others.

VIII. There was experiment. There is here an excellent example of the experimental method of education, experiment both on the part of the teacher and of the taught, experiment which enlightened both teacher and taught. There is a note of gratified expectation, if not of joyful surprise, in Mr Azariah's remark that he felt 'greatly en-couraged at this result.' And I suspect that if these Telugu outcastes were capable of giving us their version of the story we should find in it a similar note of delight if not of surprise—a certain joyfulness in the sense that the experiment involved in the lesson had succeeded. The result of the lesson was a true experience.

It is noticeable that Mr Azariah contrasts this teaching with the teaching of his catechists—that is, with the common practice of those whom we send out to educate converts. This suggests at once that profound gulf which lies between our accepted missionary method, and true educational principle. There is all the difference in the world between teaching people to say a prayer, or to attend meetings where prayers are said, and this teaching. *This* is religious education.

---

[1] Amongst illiterate people the best examination for confirmation would probably be to hear the candidates pray extempore and to note their prayers, not to find out whether they were well expressed so much as to discover whether they prayed at all. It should also be inquired carefully whether the candidates were of good reputation.

6

The Case for Voluntary Clergy

Editorial Note

The Case for Voluntary Clergy *was published in 1930: it incorporated in revised form the substance of two earlier books,* Voluntary Clergy *and* Voluntary Clergy Overseas. *It is a substantial work of over 300 pages, now very rare. The selections that follow, which are entirely in Allen's words apart from the occasional addition or omission of a phrase to smooth a transition, are quotations from chapters 1-3, 5-7, 10, 11, 13, 15, 18, 22 of the original work. In making the selection we have eliminated much that appears elsewhere in Allen's writings (chapter 19 for example is a version of the pamphlet* Mission Activities, *which appears on pp. 87-113 of this volume) or is now dated illustrative material, and have borne in mind that in the Church of South India, the Church of England, and elsewhere, the question of voluntary clergy is now at last practical politics.* Part-Time Priests? *edited by Robin Denniston (London, 1960) surveys the current practices, proposals and objections.*

Principles, not Expediency, the Apostolic Rule of Judgment

My contention in this book is that the tradition which we hold, forbidding the ordination of men engaged in earning their own livelihood by what we call secular occupations, makes void the word of Christ and is opposed to His mind when He instituted the sacraments for His people. It is also opposed to the conception of the Church which the apostles received from Him, and to the practice by which St Paul, of whose work God has given us the fullest account, established the churches. The stipendiary system grew up in settled churches and is only suitable for some settled churches at some periods: for expansion, for the establishment of new churches, it is the greatest possible hindrance. It binds the church in chains and has compelled us to adopt practices which contradict the very idea of the Church.

In this book I have examined the practice which follows the maintenance of a tradition which has no biblical authority, and I have tried to show that the doctrine involved in our practice is not the doctrine of the gospel; I have tried to show how great a burden the maintenance of our tradition lays upon us; I have contrasted it with the freedom and power of the apostolic practice and teaching, and have answered objections which have been raised to the reformation which a return to biblical principles demands. That reformation is the ordination after ancient and biblical order of men who maintain themselves by their own trade and profession, whatever it may be; voluntary clergy as they are now commonly called.

I do not want bishops to practise the ordination of voluntary clergy as a plausible policy, for which something can be said. If by persuasive speech I could induce all the bishops in the world to adopt that practice, I think that I should refuse. I do not believe that Christian men should base their action upon such a foundation: I believe that the first blast of difficulty would overthrow them if they did. I try to set forth a truth of Christ which demands obedience. I call upon the church not to adopt a plausible policy, but to repent of a sin; for to make void the word of Christ is sin.

It is important to notice how the apostles approached grave questions touching the organization and order of the Church. See how they dealt with the subject of the admission of the Gentiles when they met in council in Jerusalem as recorded in the Acts (C.15). The question then was whether it was necessary for Gentile converts to be circumcised and to keep the law of Moses. That question could have been discussed as a question of church policy. The dangers and difficulties inherent in the admission of uncircumcised Gentiles could have been endlessly debated—indeed, the arguments on the side of those who opposed such an innovation must have appeared almost irresistible.

The example of Christ, the duty of disciples, the religious privileges of the Jews, the foundations of morality, were all to be abandoned. Any heathen who could show that he had been baptized might claim to be in as good a position as the Jewish Christians. Surely it was absurd and wicked to suggest such a thing; and for what end was the sacrifice to be made? Merely that heathen who were accustomed to live licentious lives might escape from a burden which every Jew and every proselyte knew that they ought to bear.

How did the apostles meet such an argument? They declined to discuss the subject as a matter of policy: they found a principle, a rock, upon which all such debates were broken. That rock was: 'God bare them witness, giving them the Holy Ghost, even as he did unto us.' There was an unshakable rock of truth. Where God gave the Holy Spirit, there no debate was possible. The fact once admitted, the conclusion was inevitable.

That is the way in which the Christian Church ought always to meet questions touching its life. It is for men of the world to debate policies on the basis of expediencies: the Church ought to build upon the truth of Christ.

II

The Apostolic Qualifications for the Ministry

In any discussion of voluntary clergy it is of the utmost importance that we should realize clearly the difference between the qualifications demanded by the apostles for the ministry and those which we now demand; because, as we shall see, the apostolic conception of the clergy, their work and their relation to the Church, is utterly different from ours.

The most definite and important passages in the apostolic writings are those in the Pastoral Epistles, I Tim. 3.2-7, and Titus 1.6-9.

It is obvious that in these passages 'bishop' is synonymous with 'elder.' It is obvious that, when St Paul and his followers ordained elders in every city, those whom they ordained had not been ordained to any sacred ministry before (e.g. Acts 14.23).

Now if we analyse these passages which I have quoted we are struck at once by the great emphasis on moral qualities. Of the fifteen items in the first passage five are personal virtues, six are social virtues, one is moral-intellectual, one is experience, and two are concerned with reputation. Five are personal virtues: temperate, sober-minded, orderly, gentle, not a lover of money. Six are social virtues: first, at home; constant to one wife, ruling the children well, given to hospitality; secondly, abroad as well as at home; no brawler, no striker, not contentious. Two refer to reputation: first, generally, without reproach; and secondly, particularly, in the eyes of non-Christians. One is a moral-intellectual power: apt to teach. One is experience: not a novice.

In the second passage there are fifteen items of which eight are personal virtues: not self-willed, not soon angry, not greedy of filthy lucre, lover of good, sober-minded, just, holy, temperate. Four are social virtues: constant to one wife, given to hospitality, no brawler, no striker. One refers to home conditions: having faithful children who are not accused of riot or unruly. One refers to reputation: blameless. One is a moral-intellectual qualification: holding to the faithful word;

to which is attached a power to exhort in the sound doctrine and to convict gainsayers.

We see, then, in both passages the same emphasis upon moral qualifications first of all, and upon social virtues next, both at home and abroad.

Anyone who has been in the mission field will instantly recognize the portrait. The man lives before our eyes. He is a man of mature age, the head of a family. He has been married long enough to have children who are old enough to believe, and to be capable of riotous and unruly conduct. His wife and children and household are well governed and orderly. He is a man of some position in the community. Strangers and visitors, especially Christians on their journeys, are naturally directed to his house, and he knows how to entertain them and can do so. He is a man of a certain gravity and dignity whose words carry weight. He can teach and rebuke those who would slight the exhortations of a lesser man. He is a man of moral character: he can attend a feast without getting drunk; he can control his temper; he can rule without violence. He has no temptation to be always dealing blows, because his moral authority is sufficient to secure obedience. He is sober-minded and just: he can settle disputes with a judgment which men respect; and he is not ready to take a bribe. He is a Christian of some standing. He has learned the teaching of the apostles and he holds it fast. He can teach what he has learned, and when some one propounds a strange doctrine, or a morally doubtful course of action, he can say: 'That is not in accordance with what I was taught'; and men listen to him, and pay heed to what he says.

There, in the mission field, it suits the surroundings to say that a man who is to be admitted to the sacred ministry should be the husband of one wife: there the danger of covetousness and grasping after gifts has a peculiar significance, when nearly all men in any official position of any kind are seriously tempted to use their authority and influence to acquire money by means which, if not exactly dishonest, certainly do not tend to improve a man's character, or to strengthen his spiritual influence. There, in the mission field, where Christians are scattered in little groups, a man like this stands out with a prominence which is not so easily marked at home. When we read the apostle's description of the man whom he directed his followers to ordain, we instinctively say: We know that man.

Take first the one plain contradiction. The apostle demands that the candidate must be of mature age and proved experience: we commonly ordain the young and inexperienced. I put this first because it seriously affects those points on which we seem to follow the apostle's rule. Age and experience make a great difference even where there is seeming agreement.

Let us consider the points on which we apparently follow the apostle. We demand, as he did, that the candidate must be of good moral character; at least so far as that he can produce testimonials to his good conduct. We demand, as the apostle demanded, that he must hold fast the faithful word; at least so far as that he shall not write deliberate heresy in his examination papers, and shall profess belief in the Creed. We demand, as he demanded, that the candidate must be apt to teach; at least so far as an examination of his verbal memory can prove that he knows what he ought to teach. But there is some difference between the 'without reproach' of the apostle and our testimonials; and there is a difference between the holding fast of the faith by a man tried in the furnace of life, and the soundness in the faith of a youth fresh from a theological school; and the aptness to teach of a man of experience and social authority is not quite the same thing as the aptness to teach of a young man who has just passed an examination in the subject-matter.

Then we must consider the qualifications which the apostle demands, but we omit. We omit hospitality, children well brought up, and the good testimony of those without. It would be adding insult to injury to demand that young men beginning life on very small stipends, or that middle-aged men struggling to meet the expenses of a family on wholly inadequate stipends, should be given to hospitality.

Similarly it would be absurd to inquire how a man has brought up children and governed a household when he is being constantly warned against the disastrous consequences of marriage without the means to support a family; but it is quite otherwise when men are proposing to ordain persons of mature age. Then the way in which they govern their households is a most important sign of their capacity to guide the church.

We are now learning daily that even at home those without the church are more numerous than we imagined, and abroad we are face to face with churches composed of mere handfuls of Christians in the midst of great heathen populations. We are back again in the conditions which led the apostle to lay down the rule; it is possible that with the conditions the rule also should return. We may refuse the rule, but we cannot refuse the conditions. It is of no small importance in what estimation candidates for ordination are held among those outside the church.

These, then, are the qualifications which the apostle demanded and we ignore. What are the qualifications on which we insist, and the apostle ignored? Obviously they are readiness to pass an intellectual test in which the power of a verbal memory is prominent, and readiness to resign all other means of living. The apostle said nothing whatever about any such qualifications. There is not in his list one single item which is purely intellectual. Aptness to teach is far from being a purely intellectual quality, even if we understand the word 'teach,' as we usually employ it, in the sense of purely intellectual instruction.

The second qualification which we demand and the apostle omits is a readiness to resign all means of living other than that of the sacred ministry. Of this there is not a trace in the apostle's list of qualifications: there are, on the other hand, many points which suggest the opposite. The men whom he desired to see ordained were all men who were capable of maintaining themselves and their families without any assistance from the church. They had in fact been doing so, and there is nothing to suggest that they would cease to do so. They were men of a well-established position in life. They might, of course, cease to earn their living in their accustomed way when they were ordained, but it is hard to imagine that they would necessarily do so; for there is no hint that it was considered necessary or desirable by the apostle. It would have been quite simple, and to us quite natural, to have put in a clause to the effect that the bishop must abandon all worldly pursuits and give himself wholly to the care of the church, but there is not a word about it. Such silence rather suggests that the man will continue to live his life as he has been living it and providing for his family as he has been providing for it.

III

Vocation

Nowhere in the Bible do we find that men were invited to offer themselves for the priesthood. In the Old Testament the example of Korah was presented as a warning: the priesthood was given to a family chosen by God through Moses. In the New Testament we hear nowhere of men being invited to offer themselves for any office in the church. The apostles did not offer to be apostles, the seventy did not offer themselves, St Matthias did not offer himself, the seven deacons in the Acts did not offer themselves: in no church of apostolic foundation was there any suggestion that anyone was appointed because he offered himself. In the Pastoral Epistles, Timothy and Titus were not told to invite men to offer themselves.[1]

In the Old Testament it is true that prophets obeyed an inward and direct call to speak in God's name, but that was not a vocation to offer themselves for the position of officers in the church. In the New Testament and in the early Church, apparently some of the evangelists and some of the prophets obeyed a purely inward vocation to preach Christ, but that was not a vocation to accept the office of a deacon or of a priest—still less an office to which a stipend was attached. To apply these examples to the case of men who are asked to seek offices of dignity and emolument in the church is to misuse them. The call of Isaiah is often taken as a test to urge young men to offer themselves for Holy Orders; but Isaiah did not offer himself for a priesthood and a stipend.

Vocation to the ministry of the church has two sides. If it is important that a man should be convinced that he is called by God to serve, it is also of importance that the church which he is to serve should be convinced that he is the best man to serve it. Now if we set out to establish the church in every little group of communicants all over the world we should recover the reality of the local church, and with that we should recover once more that side of vocation which we have lost. The local church would be compelled to consider who were the best men to serve from among its own members. It

---

[1] 'If a man desire' does imply that there were men eager to be appointed; but that is quite a different matter from appealing to men to offer.

would be incredible folly to invite anyone who liked to offer himself, as if the office could be filled by anybody. The local church must be led by men whom it respected and whose services it would accept. Many of the best men would decline to put themselves forward. They know that to fulfil the office they must have the moral support of their congregation, and that it would be fatal to open the door to the jibe that they were putting themselves on a pedestal. The church would be driven to propose the men: the bishop would certainly take counsel with the body of the communicants, and when he was sure that the best men in the group were before him he would solemnly call upon those men to serve. The call so presented would be a vocation which no one could doubt or deny.

Under our present system we still retain some hints and relics of that external vocation, but the appeal to young men to offer themselves for ordination has so obscured the reality of it that it is practically lost. The young man is invited to offer himself before the church has called him; and he is expected to know and be sure of his vocation before one half of it exists. Were the call of the church put first, the internal vocation could respond to that. If the man was internally convinced that the call of the church through the mouth of the bishop did not express to him the call of God, if he were internally aware that a mistake was being made, if his secret knowledge of his own life and character assured him that he was not a proper person to serve, he could refuse to do so; if, on the other hand, he recognized that he ought to fulfil the duty he would accept it. He might, indeed, believe that he was the best man to serve before the call came to him, and he might wish to be chosen; but that would not justify him in offering. The two sides of vocation ought to correspond to make a true vocation. Then all doubt is removed.

Some men say that this is pure congregationalism, but it is nothing of the sort. The congregation does not simply elect its ministers. The presence and action of the bishop make all the difference. The call of God is established through His church. If bishops appealed to men of goodwill; if they went to the place and told the congregation the plain truth: 'You know quite well that you cannot have a stipendiary minister; I have not the men and you have not the money'—if they asked them, 'Have you not here two or three men fit to serve who between them could lead the church and minister the sacraments: men whose ministration you will accept?' often they would be answered: 'Yes, we have.' And if the bishops then solemnly and openly put it to those men: 'It is your duty to do this service: in the name of Christ and in the name of the church I demand that you shall serve,' not many men would refuse.

But it is objected that such men would be untrained, and that under our present system we can persuade young men that they have a vocation and then train them. To that I must answer that this conception of training is, like our conception of vocation, one-sided. If we read the instructions given to Timothy and Titus in the Pastoral Epistles, and consider the qualifications there laid down for the ministry of the Church, we see at once that the apostolic writer lays great stress on the training upon which we lay very little, and scarcely hints at the training on which we lay so much. The training on which the apostolic writer lays the greatest stress is the training which God alone can give, the training of life and experience; the training on which we lay the greatest stress is the training that *we* can give, the training of the school or the college. The training on which we lay stress is the training which is suited to the young; but God does not call only the young to be his ministers. Men are not only converted to Christ in youth: they are converted often late in life and, in the apostolic conception, they are generally called to the ministry of the church after years of experience. The training on which we lay stress is almost wholly intellectual; the training on which the apostle laid stress is almost wholly spiritual and practical. The training upon which we lay stress is comparatively superficial; the training on which the apostle laid stress is vital and fundamental.

Our conception of the relationship between the clergy and those to whom they minister is one sided. We always look at the matter from this point of view: Here are so many parishes, here are so many clergy; if there are not enough clergy for the parishes then there are still only so many clergy, and they must be sent to the parishes which, for one reason or another, seem to be the most important. But surely that is not the true way of looking at the matter; surely we ought to say: Here is a group of Christian people: this group of Christians must be properly organized with its own clergy; the only question before us is, Who ought to serve this group? If a suitable man is willing to go there and they are willing to receive his ministrations, well and good; but, if not, they must still have clergy, and the only question is, Who are the men who ought to serve them?

L

The responsibility for their religious life must rest upon them. If they decline to take any interest in the matter, then we cannot make them take a proper interest by sending someone to minister to them; when they do not want church life, we cannot make church life simply by sending a man to hold a service. Something far more fundamental than that is needed. A man may go to them as a visitor and urge upon them the importance of church life, but he cannot create it by going to minister to them when he knows, and they know, that at any moment he may go away, and the church life will thereupon cease. If the people really desire to live in the church, then it ought to be made possible for them to do so. In other words, we must think first and foremost of the group as the church in the place, and of the ministers as naturally and normally members of that group, attached to it by every tie, spiritual and social. When we put the church first and see that the clergy come out of the church (and I am speaking of the church in that local sense), then at once we recover the family aspect of the church. The church is at once a local entity as certain and clear and distinct as the village or the group, and we escape at once from that imperfect loose relationship of cleric and people which finds expression in such terms as 'We will starve him out' and 'He does not belong to us', for those expressions are a sore weakness.

IV

The Meaning and Place of Voluntary Clergy

Voluntary clergy are men who earn their living by the work of their hands or of their heads in the common market, and serve as clergy without stipend or fee of any kind.

(1) Since stipendiary clergy are voluntary in one sense and voluntary clergy are only opposed to stipendiary in another, we ought not to oppose them as if one excluded the other. It must be plain to anyone who has read my chapter on the apostolic qualifications that I did not there attempt to prove that the clergy should never be paid. The apostolic qualifications are quite compatible with dependence for livelihood upon the offerings of the faithful, either in the form of endowments, or of subscriptions. The means by which the minister gains his living is not in the picture. He may earn it by a trade, or inherit wealth from his ancestors, or enjoy a salary, or receive dues as an official, or be supported by the church. How he is supported is a mere external detail, which is not even mentioned. His call of God and his service do not depend upon such things as that.

The church unquestionably needs some men who give themselves wholly to prayer and the ministration of the Word and Sacraments, and such men must be supported by the faithful. She needs also some men whose time is wholly occupied with the care of parishes, and these she must maintain. She needs also scholars who give their whole time to study, and these she must maintain. But there are countless small groups of Christians needing pastors, which cannot afford to maintain clergy nor to provide them with sufficient occupation to save them from the temptations of idleness. There are also many large town parishes where the church needs assistant priests of varied capacity, drawn from many classes of the people, who can speak, each to his own class, in the language familiar to it, understanding by experience the difficulties and temptations of that class. It is also important that many services and sermons should not be heaped upon one man: the stipendiary ought to be able to leave his parish at proper intervals for rest and refreshment without feeling that his people are neglected and his work left undone; he ought also to be relieved from a pressure which drives him to minister when he is sick and unfit. It is in such cases that the assistance of voluntary clergy would be invaluable.

(2) The ordination of such men would give no additional excuse to anyone to question the disinterestedness of the stipendiary clergy. Men sometimes think that voluntary clergy would appear to be disinterested labourers for love, whilst the stipendiary clergy would be thought to be hirelings, and that invidious comparisons would be made. But all men know that those who give up their whole time to a particular work must have the wherewithal to live. Every one would know that the work of a stipendiary cleric precluded his labouring in the market. Every one would know that the work of the stipendiary was not the work of the voluntary cleric. All sensible men would know that the church needs both. The argument that the ordination of voluntary clerics would lead men to question the disinterestedness of the stipendiary is very weak. If men questioned it then, it would be because they question it now. Disinterestedness is not proved by the exclusion of voluntary workers. Wherever it is, there it makes itself felt; and it does not manifest itself by building a hedge round itself. Men do not question the disinterested zeal of paid prison visitors because there are many unpaid visitors: they do not question the disinterested zeal of paid secretaries of philanthropic societies, because there are many unpaid secretaries. They question disinterestedness only when the conduct of the stipendiary suggests that he is more concerned about securing his own position than he is about the cause for which he works.

The ordination of voluntary clergy would not cause men to question the disinterestedness of the stipendiary clergy: it would indeed enlighten them, because they would escape from that confusion between vocation to serve and a means of livelihood of which I spoke in the previous chapter. If once men saw that vocation to serve was not necessarily vocation to a certain means of earning a livelihood, they would distinguish between vocation and livelihood, and they would understand vocation, and they would respect it in all in whom they saw its fruits. Thus the ordination of voluntary clergy, so far from bringing the service of stipendiary clergy into disrepute, would exalt it; because the stipend would drop into its proper place as a mere accident, and vocation to serve would stand out clearly in its purity. The difficulty which we have been considering arises not from the presence of voluntary clergy, but from their absence. Men question the disinterestedness of the clergy because they make stipends a necessity, something without which there can be no clergy, something without which they themselves would not be clergy. That is the real difficulty. If once we disabused men's minds of that idea by producing clergy who had no stipends this cause of misunderstanding would be taken away.

(3) Neither would the existence of voluntary clergy undermine the liberality of the laity. Clerics often say that if voluntary clergy were admitted, the laity would cease to support stipendiary clergy, and that they would say, We can get clergy for nothing, why should we pay for them? That argument suggests that the laity do not want stipendiary clergy and must be compelled to have them against their will. Whatever truth there may be in it, and it is a very serious indictment of the present stipendiary clergy as a body, one thing is certain, we cannot make people want what they do not want by compelling them to pay for it.

Suppose that our bishops ordained voluntary clergy. We all know that we must have some men who give up all other means of earning their livelihood: if we do not, we should very quickly find it out. Then we must support them, and, knowing our need of them, we should support them without any entreaty. If all the work which could be done by men earning their own living were done by men earning their own living, much work which now falls upon one man and prevents him from earning his own living could easily be performed by three or four men, all of whom could earn their own living, and all the necessary stipendiary clergy could be easily maintained.

Would that undermine the liberality of the laity? Is there no liberality in service, or is liberality shown only in subscribing money? That is a strange notion of liberality which confines it to the offering of money only.

(4) The distinction between stipendiary and voluntary clergy is not a distinction between men who give their whole time to the service of God and His church and men who give part of their time to that service, but a distinction between one form of service and another. Both stipendiary and voluntary clergy ought to be serving God and the Church all the time in all they do; but the service

which the Church needs that each should do for God and for her is not the same. The voluntary cleric carries the priesthood into the market place and the office. It is his work not only to minister at the altar or to preach, but to show men how the common work of daily life can be done in the spirit of the priest.

In the mission field this want of experience is even more serious than it is at home; because here at home so much of our life is intellectual, whereas there the majority of our converts have very little intellectual experience. Their life is wholly built on practical experience, and what they need in a leader is someone who can understand and appreciate, and speak in terms of that practical experience. All those whom they naturally recognize as leaders are men who have learned wisdom in this school of practical experience. But the church scarcely ordains any who have not been trained from youth in mission schools. Consequently, in the mission field the first converts can have no ministers of their own until boys have been educated in schools. Then these boys are sent as teachers first, then as catechists, and finally as priests, without any real experience of the life of the people whom they are to lead, to guide and direct a congregation composed of mature and experienced men. Thus the organization of the church is delayed in a most unhealthy way, and the clerical order is established on a most unhealthy basis, whilst the natural leaders of the Christian people are suppressed, and put into a very false position.

Among our own people also the church sorely needs clergy in close touch with the ordinary life of the laity, living the life of ordinary men, sharing their difficulties and understanding their trials by close personal experience. Stipendiary clergy cut off by training and life from that common experience are constantly struggling to get close to the laity by wearing lay clothing, sharing in lay amusements, and organizing lay clubs; but they never quite succeed. To get close to men, it is necessary really to share their experience, and to share their experience is to share it by being in it, not merely to come as near to it as possible without being in it. The church needs clerics who really share the life of their people. The life of the voluntary cleric is not divorced from the life of the laity, it is the life of the laity lived as a cleric ought to live it.

(5) That is why I shudder when I hear men talk of voluntary clergy as half-timers. Voluntary clergy are not half-timers. A cleric

can no more be a half-time cleric than a father can be a half-time father, or a baptized Christian a half-time Christian. Our present clerics are not half-time clerics, though a very large part of their time is often spent in social or financial business. Some of them, for instance the clerical secretary of a society like the Society for the Promotion of Christian Knowledge, are engaged all day long in business which might very well be performed by secular officers, but they do not cease to be clerics on that account, nor become half-time clerics. A priest is not a priest only when he is performing strictly priestly offices. We cannot divide life into two compartments, one secular and the other religious, and say that a cleric must only be engaged in those acts which we put outside the secular division. We often talk like that; but in practice it is impossible, and in principle it is false. Such a division is utterly opposed to the teaching of the New Testament. For Christian men all work is Christ's, not part of it; all life is Christ's; He claims the whole of it. Yet the habit of dividing life into sacred and secular compartments is so ingrained in us that Christian priests, who preach the true doctrine and themselves are constantly engaged in what is, in common speech, purely secular work, see nothing inconsistent with their doctrine when they speak of voluntary clergy as half-timers, or oppose their ordination on the ground that they will be too much occupied with secular business.

There can be no such thing as secular business for a Christian man, if by 'secular' is meant 'not religious.' In exactly the same sense there can be no secular work for a man called by God to the sacred ministry of the Church. He has a profession in a very different sense from that in which we commonly speak of the ministerial profession. We speak of the ministerial profession, as men speak of the legal profession, as a means by which a man earns his livelihood. But that is not the true sense in which a priest has a profession. A priest has a profession in the sense in which every baptized person has a profession.

In our Baptismal Service we are told that 'Baptism doth represent unto us our profession, which is to follow our Saviour Christ and to be made like unto him.' That is a purely spiritual conception of profession. It does not depend at all upon the means of livelihood of the baptized. He may be tinker, or tailor, or physician, or lawyer. Whatever his means of livelihood may be, he is bound by that profession. He can follow his Saviour Christ in any walk of life and be made like unto Him. His profession covers all types of work and includes all the acts of life. The whole life is bound up and unified in it. Whatever the baptized may be doing at any time and in any place he is bound by that profession. He cannot be bound by it in one set of circumstances and not bound by it in another set of circumstances.

Just so ordination represents a profession; and I think that it ought to represent a profession always in this sense. It represents a profession of a divine call to minister to Christ's people, a spiritual profession, independent of all material circumstances. The baptized is always baptized: the priest is always a priest. He can never escape from that priesthood, any more than a baptized person can escape from his baptism. The whole life is unified in this profession, as in that. It matters not what the priest may be doing externally at any particular moment. He is not a priest only when he is in church celebrating the holy mysteries: he is a priest always, everywhere, He is not bound by his profession only in one set of circumstances and not bound by it in a different set of circumstances. His profession is independent of the external circumstances, though it may be more apparent to the world in some circumstances than in some others. A minister of Christ is one whom God has called to bear in his person the character of a man called by God to minister always under all circumstances.

(6) The difference voluntary clergy and stipendiary clergy is not the difference between qualified and unqualified men, but between different types of qualification. When men speak of voluntary clergy they often say that they would be unqualified. That is a mistake. They would be fully qualified, as fully qualified as the stipendiary, but differently. It is hard to think that any one who reads the qualifications laid down in the Pastoral Epistles, which I discussed above, could say that the man who possessed them was unqualified: yet that is what we hear today. We are so enamoured of those qualifications which we have added to the apostolic that we deny the qualifications of anyone who possesses only the apostolic, whilst we think a man fully qualified who possesses only ours. A young student fresh from a theological college lacks many of those qualifications which the apostle deemed necessary for a leader in the house of God, the age, the experience, the established position and reputation, even if he possesses all the others. Him we do not think unqualified. The man who possesses all the apostolic qualifications is said to be unqualified, because he cannot go back to school and pass an examination.

(7) Voluntary clergy are not men who simply occupy the position of the present stipendiary without his stipend.

In speaking of voluntary clergy we ought to think more of the church than of the clergy, and we ought to seek not so much for suitable men from the point of view of the clerical order as for suitable groups to be established as churches. We ought to think of the ordination of voluntary clergy as the proper way to establish the group as a church. A suitable group is a group of communicants: the suitable men are the men whose ministrations the group will accept. Such men are suitable ministers for that group, at its present stage of development. The apostolic qualifications then apply. A group which suggested that it should be constituted as a church by the ordination of men who had not the apostolic qualifications would prove that it was not a suitable group; but I think that such a group of Christians would rarely be found. The establishment of churches with voluntary clergy is a very different matter from seeking for individuals to recruit a body of clerics.

Again, I have found men trying to imagine a voluntary cleric in the position of the present stipendiary, and saying that it is impossible. That is because they were thinking of one man in sole charge of a parish, overseas, of an enormous parish. The apostolic voluntary clergy were not isolated individuals in charge of parishes. The apostles always ordained several clergy for each place; and if we returned to their practice today, voluntary clergy would certainly not be put in the position of the present stipendiary. Where there was a stipendiary cleric the voluntary clerics would support him; and sickness, holidays, resignations, removals, of the stipendiary, would cause no interruption of the regular life of the church. Instead of being ruled by one man, every church would be led by a college of priests who between them would be responsible for the due conduct of the services and the proper direction of the church. Where there was no stipendiary cleric, there would still be a sufficient number of voluntary clerics to maintain all the proper services of the church.

It has been said that the appointment of voluntary clergy 'is a question exclusively for the exercise of the episcopal judgment.'[1] I venture to say that is a serious mistake. We must remember that in countless instances the choice is not between stipendiary clergy and voluntary clergy but between voluntary clergy and none at all: we

[1] *World Call*, vol. v., p. 27.

must remember that everywhere it is a question whether the church is to be adequately served. Whether Christian men are or are not to be deprived of their church life and taught to do without it, whether the church is to be adequately supplied with ministers, are questions not only for episcopal judgment, but for the judgment of all good men. The assertion that the ordination of voluntary clergy is a question exclusively for the exercise of the episcopal judgment is a typical example of that terrible division of the Church to which Bishop Mandell Creighton referred when he said: 'The Church is divided into two bodies, one offering, the other accepting Christian privileges.'[1]

[1] *Life and Letters*, vol II, p. 375.

V

Why?

I went one day into a synod office in Canada. I found there two men: the one was a young theological student, the other a man of about fifty years of age who told me that for fifteen years, when he was farming on the prairie, he held services in his own house for his neighbours. At first some six or seven Anglicans came, but later some of the other people came also. They had a celebration of the Holy Communion two or three times a year when a priest passed that way.

I looked at those two men and I could not help asking myself why the bishop was going to ordain the one and why he had not ordained the other. If spiritual experience is desirable for a priest, which of those two men had the largest spiritual experience? If intellectual ability was considered, I had no doubt which of the two was the abler man: if education, a very short conversation revealed which of them was the better educated. If it is important that a parish priest should be able to lead and direct his congregation, who could question for a moment which of those two men most commanded respect? Which of them had the best and strongest social influence? The one was a married man, and his wife and children were respected in the society in which they lived: the other was unmarried and no one could foretell whom he would marry or whether his wife would be a help or a hindrance to him in his work. The diocese was understaffed, and appealing incessantly for aid in money and in men: which of these men would be the greatest burden on its scanty funds? The one was being supported as a student, and must be supported by the diocese as long as he lived, unless he went away or committed some flagrant offence: the other never had, and never would, cost the diocese a halfpenny. The one lived up-country for fifteen years, and during all that time lacked nothing but Orders to be the pastor of his flock: he would undoubtedly have built up the church where he lived. Of the other all that could be said was that he was apparently a very respectable young man; whether he would be a leader of men, or a good parish priest, when he was forty years of age; whether he would stay more than a year or two doing up-country work; whether he would not soon be seeking a town parish, or desiring one, which would equally distract his mind from the work up-country, even if it did not result in his leaving it, who could foretell? Every one hoped for the best, but no one could be certain. All these possibilities made his training and ordination (from the point of view of a diocese which needed above all things the church built up in small scattered groups) a pure gamble with the funds at the disposal of the diocese. No one could be sure how he would turn out. About the elder man there was not a shadow of doubt; he was no novice, he had approved himself.

Why then did the bishop not ordain that man when he was on his farm doing exactly the work which the church needed? Why did he leave him unequipped and hampered by lack of ordination? And why was he determined to ordain only the younger man? It is not as though he said: The diocese needs both, and I shall ordain both. No. He said: I cannot ordain the one whom every group of Christians would naturally think the better and more suitable man; I shall ordain the younger with all the uncertainties which surround him, and I shall ordain the younger only. Why did he do that? I asked men that question, but I got no answer.

If we look at the history of any society which has spread and grown in the world, what do we see? Do we not see that it has grown because members of the society have scattered and have carried with them the ideas and practices which the society was founded to maintain? Do we not see the members creating new branches of the society wherever they go? They think that the society to which they belong is a good society, and they invite others to join it: they band themselves together wherever they find two or three fellow members and strengthen one another. They hold meetings, they practise their doctrine, whatever it may be. They appeal to the parent society for recognition as a true branch of the society: they are enrolled, and their branch is enrolled as a branch of the society.

Is not that the way in which all societies, religious, social, or political, grow? Look at the progress in modern days of Theosophical societies, of Christian Science, of Trade Unionism, of Islam, of Masonry—is it not in that way that they have made progress? Look at the early Church; was it not in that way that it spread all over the Roman Empire, and beyond it?

There was indeed this difference between the expansion of the Church and the expansion of a secular society: that in place of a formal enrolment of a new branch in the archives of a head office, the Church recognized and established new churches by a spiritual act, the solemn ordination of ministers for the new churches, but that did not hinder the expansion; it assisted it.

Suppose we saw a society which insisted that officers must be sent from the head office to direct and manage every new branch: should we not be surprised, and should we not ask how such a society could possibly expand widely? We should probably conclude that the society in question was anxious rather to check than to encourage any rapid advance. We should probably imagine that the society observed some esoteric mystery of so difficult and strange a character that its ordinary members could not be trusted to teach or to practise it, and that the society was far more anxious to preserve the purity of this esoteric mystery than to admit new members. We should conclude that it was not a society designed to admit many, nor anxious to enlarge its borders by the creation of new branches. And if we were told that as a matter of fact the mystery was a very simple rite designed for the use of even illiterate members, and that the society was one which proposed to conquer the whole world, and was eager to see as many branches as possible established, should we not then be utterly nonplussed?

But that is what we see in the church today. We see Christian churchmen who might be, and ought to be, the founders of new churches scattered all over the world, some of them eager to extend the church; but they are carefully taught that they must not practise their religion. If there is anywhere an isolated group of Christians today, they can have no church life, they cannot live as members of a Church in which the rites of Christ are observed, unless they can get one of the ordained class to come to them; for no bishop ordains one or two of them to act for their fellows as the bishops of the early Church did. All natural expansion ceases. The scattered laity are impotent.

Again we ask why is this? It is not a light matter. The scattered members of the church upon whose practice of their religion increase and progress naturally depend are very numerous. The world is sprinkled with such groups. No one who knows anything at all about the facts imagines that we ever have sent, or are now sending, enough clergy to provide for all these groups. Why then do not bishops act now as bishops acted in the years when the church was expanding throughout the Roman Empire? The answer unquestionably is that a long established tradition decrees that the clergy must be an order apart, a professional body of men who engage in no other work than their clerical work, and, unless they have private means, wholly dependent for their livelihood upon their clerical profession. Small groups cannot produce such men and cannot support them: therefore they cannot be established.

The tradition is certainly not primitive; it certainly restricts the expansion of the church; it certainly runs counter to the direct commands of Christ, but it is accepted as gospel by all our bishops and by most of our laity. It has so strong a hold upon the church that it is scarcely ever questioned. Again and again in Canada and in Africa and in India I have seen men taken completely by surprise when I suggested that there was no valid reason why a bishop should not ordain a good Christian to minister to his fellows whilst yet he continued to earn his livelihood by his accustomed trade or profession. They could scarcely believe their ears.

It is this tradition which makes the establishment of the church a matter of finance. This is the difference between the establishment of the church in early days and the establishment of the church now. In those days the establishment of the church was a spiritual operation, today it is a financial operation. That is no hasty exaggerated statement. In those days it was a matter of prayer and laying on of hands: now it is a matter of raising a stipend.

Put in that crude form, which is nevertheless the true form in actual fact, as we see it today, we might even begin to doubt whether such a restraint, a restraint which makes the existence of a church depend upon money, is not farther removed from the truth of the gospel than the practice which insists that the Christians are the Church and must live and act as a church even without episcopally ordained ministers.

There is at least here an equality. Natives of India or of Africa or of China sometimes think that we do not establish the Church among them because we despise them, or think them too ignorant or uncivilized to be ordained. They think sometimes that here is the taint of the colour bar, because we ordain so few nationals. But that is not true. I have said to them: Our bishops treat our own people exactly as they treat you. They say that our own settlers are too ignorant to celebrate the Lord's Supper: they say that they can have no ordered church life unless they can import a young cleric from England to look after them. They treat all alike in this.

All over the world is scattered a multitude of groups of Christians, and a daily increasing number, which depend for any church life upon a foreign source of supply. That is our conception of the way in which the church ought to be established. It is supposed that as the groups grow in wealth they will be able and willing to support a professional minister. That sometimes actually happens; and because it happens in some places, the miserable state of the places in which it does not happen, and the loss which takes place whilst it is coming to pass, is forgotten.

The *World Call*, after speaking of parishes '100 miles from the centre in every direction,' of 'groups never yet visited,' of 'a celebration perhaps once a year,' of 'a week's journey if the settler is to attend a service' and such like cases, with which it says that its 'reports are full,' concludes: 'If no means are found to supply the needs of these impossible parishes, it is inevitable that many people must lapse.'[1]

---

[1] *World Call*, vol. v., p.26.

VI

Appeals

These appeals illustrate that division of the Church into two bodies which Bishop Creighton described as terrible. They treat the church as something distinct from its members, and teach men so to think. The church is constantly spoken of as something remote from its members. Bishops, clergy and laity alike speak of the church as something remote from the small groups of Christians scattered overseas. Members of these groups say: The church did nothing for us, the church neglected us, the church did not minister to us, and we lost touch with the church. And we say the same thing. Our leaders say: The church must follow them, we must send the church after them. It is said of one group that it is beyond the reach of the church, of another that the church came at last, but that it came too late.

In the New Testament the church is never remote from its members. Where the members of the church were, there was the church. In the New Testament there is no hint of the existence of a group of Christians in a place without ministers and without the sacraments which are the proper rites of a Christian church. But with us it is quite common for groups of Christians to exist without any ministers of their own, and consequently without any of the properly ordered life of a Christian church. Their children are not baptized, they cannot observe the Lord's Supper, they are not even married or buried with Christian ceremony as members of a Christian church in the place where they dwell. In such cases there is no local church, and consequently the church becomes remote.

If a small group of Christians appeals to the bishop for clergy and he tells them that he has not got a cleric to send them and that they could not support one if he did send him, might they not naturally conclude that the presence of a cleric is really a spiritual luxury, and that in the opinion of the bishop men can very well lead a Christian life without him? Surely it is not surprising that many men say that: it is rather surprising that more men do not say it. If a small group of Christian churchmen can appeal to a bishop for ordered church life, and appeal in vain, that bishop has proclaimed his conviction that ordered church life is not necessary for Christian men. I myself have said to bishops: If your action is in accordance with the principles of the gospel, and those people do not need clerics, neither do I, nor does anyone else; ordered local church life is a luxury, not a necessity for the souls of men; bishops, clergy, the church are all luxuries, and we can afford to do without them. That argument is not often so baldly stated, but it is the argument upon which many, very many, laymen base their conduct in relation to the church.

If a bishop answered men who asked for ordered church life that he had no cleric to send them, but that, if they would serve, he would ordain, because ordered church life is of vital importance, that argument which I have stated would fall to the ground. It is no answer to say that there are many groups which do not appear to desire any ordered church life. It may be true; but it is no answer to the argument. If there is one group and that one group is refused, the argument holds; and we are constantly told that there are groups, especially of new settlers, who do express a desire for ordered church life. The way in which bishops and clergy overseas talk of the general apathy is most misleading. It is no proof of apathy that men do not appreciate and attend eagerly the services of any priest who may be sent up to hold a service at intervals; it is no proof of apathy that they do not appeal to bishops to give them an ordered church life which they have never even imagined to be possible under their circumstances. How can men ask a bishop to give them resident clergy when they know that stipendiary clergy do not exist in sufficient numbers, and they are convinced that the bishop will refuse to ordain voluntary clergy, even if the possibility of voluntary clergy has ever entered their minds? They have been taught year after year that the only church life that they can have is an occasional visit, and when they grow dull and unready to attend, they are accused of apathy, and their case is used as a proof that properly organized church life is impossible. In my visits to Canada, Africa, and Assam I found again and again that the moment I spoke of the establishment of the Church I met very little apathy. There are men who have been starved almost to death, but there are still everywhere men who are not apathetic, and the fact that they do not attend services held by Mr X, or that they do not make earnest appeals to their bishop

M

for something that the bishop has never offered them, is no proof of apathy.

The lesson which above all our people need to learn at this time is the reality of the church. They cannot learn that by hearing men talk about it. They must learn it by experience, and they cannot learn it by experience unless the church is restored to them with its ordered life, its ministers, and its sacraments, in the place where they live. It is quite clear, and all experience proves it, that small groups cannot support stipendiary clergy. They cannot provide from among themselves young men to be trained and after ordination supported while they do nothing but minister to a handful of people. It is quite clear, and all experience proves it, that appeals to England do not meet the need. The only possible way is to ordain voluntary clergy, and thus to establish the church with all the full life and rites and privileges of a properly constituted church. If we did that we need not talk about the church. One act teaches more than ten thousand words. If we did that, if it were the rule that where there were a few faithful men and women the church was always properly organized with its clergy on a voluntary basis, men would speedily learn what the church is. There would be no groups in which marriages could not be solemnized, children baptized, the dead buried with proper Christian ceremony, and the Lord's Supper duly administered, except in communities which deliberately refused all Christian rites, and they are not so numerous as we sometimes imagine. If we did that the appeals to England would take a very different and a much more healthy form.

VII

Desertion Unnecessary

I suggest that there is only one way in which we can meet this need: I am persuaded that the church could meet the situation if only she would shake herself free from the tradition which may once have been useful in England but is now but a yoke upon our necks, shackles upon our feet. We must distinguish between settled officers of the church, who are necessary for its local organized life, and evangelists or teachers, who wander about from place to place to convert the indifferent or to stir and encourage the members of the settled churches. We must distinguish between those two classes of ministers. It is the duty of the settled local officers to direct the affairs of the local church and to see that her services are regularly and properly conducted: their first care and duty is the local church in which they live. The missionary, on the other hand, is essentially a wandering evangelist or teacher, and therefore he cannot be the pastor of a settled church; because he cannot both move about and be always at hand to serve the church in which he lives. The local clergy of the church must be resident and there must be enough of them in every little local church to make sure that the church is never without its proper ministers. They must have their proper occupation by which they earn their daily bread, and that for two reasons: firstly, that most of these little groups could not afford to pay them, even if they wanted to do so, and, secondly, that if the clergy had nothing but clerical work to do, in little tiny groups they would not have enough to keep them occupied.

Now the moment that we make that distinction, and put the question of pay out of our minds, we can see at once that the church could be established in every little group throughout the whole world. Wherever there were church people who desired to live in an organized church and to enjoy all its privileges and its sacraments, there the church could be at once established. When I suggested that the only possible way of establishing the church in a wide area north of Winnipeg was to send men to seek out the good communicants among the people and then to ordain these as voluntary clergy, so that the lamp of the church would be permanently alight in at least some of the townships, and an example set to every group and a way opened to them by which they obviously could, if they would, secure for themselves a regular church life, the baptism of their children, and the administration of the Holy Communion, I was told at once of men at two places who would be well fitted to serve. Now, if we began with those two places, if voluntary priests were ordained there, the candle of the church would be lighted in the very heart of the great neglected area.

If the missionary had no local church to care for; if it was his business to go up and down the country striving to convert men to Christ and to bring them to realize that they could have the fullest church life the moment that they were willing to receive it; if wherever they heard his message the church was established, two things would inevitably follow: firstly, settlers who desired church life, seeing that it was at hand, seeing that they could enjoy it if they would, and that there was nothing to hinder them if they would serve, would realize their power. There are many, very many, good church people scattered about the world who would respond, and wherever they responded, there the church would be. Secondly, the missionary, being no longer bound to minister to settled groups, would be able to proceed from place to place over a very wide area, and his success would consist not in finding a group which would restrain his further progress, but in establishing a church from which he could make a further advance. If the members of any group over the widest areas had not, in a very short time, a full church life, it would be entirely their own fault, because such a system would supply the need of every group that wanted church life. Working on that apostolic order, every group in the world could have its full church life.

It is no answer to me to say that there are many groups which would not at once respond. My point is that there are some now ready, and that we waste our missionary clergy in taking services for those who could best do without them, to the neglect of those who most need them. If we began to establish churches with voluntary clergy, every church so established would make it more easy for the missionary to extend his labours. When the apostles began their work in Europe they did not find groups of nominal Christians with centuries of Christian life behind them, all able to read, with the whole Bible in their possession. Yet they could so establish churches with their proper ministers that they had no need to remain to hold services for them. We today, starting with that great initial advantage, might surely follow their example. All that is necessary is to break a tradition that Christians must wait for a cleric to come from some distant source to minister to them. If we began at once where men are prepared to welcome the opportunity, we should both set free missionaries for pioneer work and we should have entered upon a path by which every group in the world could be established; and all men would see it. The door would be open for every group of Christian churchmen in the world to enjoy full church life. It is no answer to say that some groups are not ready to respond to an appeal which they have never heard.

VIII

Itinerant Clergy

B ecause we use missionary clergy to do the work of parish priests
we are compelled to spread their services thin. All over the
world I see clergy itinerating over wide areas, ministering to three,
or four, or a dozen, or twenty congregations.

These congregations under one priest and theoretically composing
one parish are distinct congregations often remote from one another.
They do not know one another, they cannot recognize any unity
among themselves as a parish. Consequently the parish has no real,
living unity in itself: it has only a nominal and fictitious unity. No
such parish can act as one unit. The moment that anything is to be
done, such as the erection of a church building, each group in it acts
as a separate unit. Theoretically the bishop deals with the parish as
a unit, but practically the congregations in it are distinct and recog-
nizable units each of which must be treated separately.

Is there to be found in the New Testament, or in early church
history, a church which had not its own proper ministers and its own
proper rites and sacraments within itself? In these groups which we
call churches only too often for three hundred and fifty or more days
in the year there is no minister, no service, no sacrament. When the
priest is urgently needed he is not there; and either he must be sought
with difficulty, or the people must act without him. The members of
such a church do not live in a church which is always present. Can
we call this a church? Is it not rather a parody of a church?

The attitude of our bishops and clergy towards these groups is
certainly in practice the attitude expressed to me by men in Canada,
who told me that it was quite unnecessary that every little local
group should have its own local ministers and its own local church
life. If little groups have occasional services, that is all that they need
and all that they can expect.

If it were true that this is all that they need, it is a great deal more
than many groups can expect, for many lie outside the reach even of
the itinerant clerics. It is notorious that there are many small groups
of church people scattered all over the world which, as a matter of
fact, do not and cannot have even occasional services because there

are not enough itinerant clergy to give them even occasional services. There are large areas into which itinerant clergy have never been with any regularity. There are groups which have had no services for five, ten, or even twenty years. Even if we accept the principle that it is right for a large number of these so-called churches to be under the care of a single priest, we must recognize that the system breaks down most seriously in practice, because there are not sufficient clergy to supply even that. We are told, for instance, that 'consecutive work is difficult even in Khartoum with a British population of about five hundred: elsewhere it is impossible. Even big stations go unvisited for weeks and months. Out-stations can seldom be reached and the more distant ones never.'[1]

Where a cleric is in charge of a large number of these churches, we are constantly told that the people have a service once a month, or something of that sort, and we are constantly deceived. 'Once a month' may mean anything; what it scarcely ever means is perfect regularity for any length of time. The clergy are human beings liable to the infirmities of the flesh, and when they travel about from place to place to hold services, it is quite certain that from time to time they get delayed and the services are not held. When I was in Canada I made it my business to examine carefully into the meaning of this 'once a month' and found, in those cases where I could get exact information, that 'once a month' was anything but a precise statement of the facts. In one case where the bishop told me that a priest went once a month for a certain period, I found that, as a matter of fact, the man had never set foot in the building for the whole of the period. I found that perfect regularity was, as one might expect, impossible. When I say this I am not casting any slur at all upon the devotion and energy of devoted and energetic men: I am simply saying that they are not absolute masters of conditions. They cannot avoid sickness, and they cannot avoid mishaps, and when we are told that people receive services once a month we must take that into account.

A little while ago a bishop in South Africa wrote that he had at last succeeded in securing that all the congregations in his diocese should be visited by a priest to administer the Holy Communion once a quarter. When I went into that diocese the first man to whom I spoke said: 'I will tell you the name of a place where that is cer-

[1] *World Call*, vol. V, p. 112.

tainly not true.' Arrangements of that kind can never be true for any length of time.

Infrequent services, irregular services, teach men to do without any. They grow accustomed to Sundays without services. For three Sundays out of four there is no service. The lesson taught on those three cannot be undone in one. The people forget on which Sunday the cleric is due, and they arrange a picnic or a tennis party. They learn to do without any religious services, and then when they have learnt that lesson the cleric is distressed and troubled, because they do not heed his exhortations and entreaties to attend.

The people learn also another lesson. They learn to think that church life consists in church going. We offer them 'services' instead of the fellowship of the church. The church cannot be a society in which they live all their lives. It has no local existence for them as a village is a local entity for those who live in it. The church seems to appear and disappear with the arrival and departure of the cleric, and church life seems to consist in attending the services, and is, like the services, intermittent. But that is surely not what church life was meant to be. The church was once a society in which men lived, not merely an organization for providing services which they might, or might not, attend. Men lived in the society of the church and enjoyed in the church all the warmth of a society and not merely the advantage of occasional services.

The value of that local union in a local church we have lost because our stipendiary system makes the proper constitution of the church in small groups impossible. Consequently it is not surprising if our people look upon attendance at church as a purely private matter and the baptism of their children as a purely private matter, and then it is not a long step to thinking that, if they turn on the wireless receiver and listen to some hymns and a sermon, it is as good as, if not better than, joining with their fellows in the worship of God in their own church.

Under this system there must be a constant supply of young and vigorous men to take up the work. The itinerant cleric can establish nothing which can abide if he is removed and a successor is not at hand. Everything depends upon him. There can be no sacraments, no church life without him, and he cannot ensure that his successor will be at hand when he retires. If he goes, those people will be left destitute, as destitute as if he had never been. Most men do not seem to realize that at all; but I have seen it happen. I have stood upon the ruins of years of hard work. Some men do realize it, and to them it is a nightmare. It is a grief quite unknown to clergy in large towns where it is certain that another cleric can always be found. In town churches men often fear that their successor may unbuild much that they have tried to build up; but they do not fear that all regular organized church life will come to an end. But in the most needy, the most out-of-the-way places, that is exactly what may happen, and sometimes does happen, because the supply of clergy to take up these tasks of itinerating in the country is not constant.

IX

Lay Readers

Seeing that our clergy cannot possibly do the work, we have adopted the expedient of appointing lay readers. All over the world I see lay readers in charge of congregations. Often this is concealed under the pretence that they are merely assistants of itinerating clergy; but sometimes they are openly and undisguisedly in charge of parishes or missions which would undoubtedly have priests in residence if the people were ready to pay the stipend of a priest, and if priests were sufficiently numerous. In nearly all cases the lay readers are practically in charge for three hundred and forty or three hundred and fifty days in the year. Some of them are voluntary workers unpaid: some of them are paid. They are cheaper than clergy. It is their duty to hold services in the absence of a priest.

This is a new thing in the history of the church. In the Bible we find no churches without proper ministers: in our Prayer Book it is taken for granted that every parish (the reasonable English parish round the parish church, not the 'impossible parishes' of the overseas dioceses) has its parish priest: in our modern practice we find lay readers occupying the place of the parish priest. This change points to a revolution in the church; and it has been wrought silently, and without a word of protest. Men sometimes call the proposal to establish churches properly with voluntary clergy revolutionary: the real revolution took place when bishops began to put laymen instead of priests in charge of church congregations.

It began in the mission field when missionaries appointed catechists or teachers, or, as they are sometimes called, pastor teachers, to take charge of groups of native converts. Then it spread to us, and now it is so familiar that few men realize what it means. It means that the church has subordinated the commands and the ordinances of Christ to the maintenance of a stipendiary clerical order.

Lay readers are set to act in the place of clergy. They take services for people who have no proper resident clergy. To begin with ministers who cannot administer sacraments, but can only read Matins and Evensong and preach, and then to work up to ministers who can administer the rites which Christ ordained: to begin by providing only those services which can be attended by any religious inquirer, and to work up to the services which are peculiar to the faithful: to begin by denying the services which Christ enjoined, and to end by trying to persuade men that the services which Christ enjoined are essential to their soul's health: to begin by creating a church in the place which is marked by the fact that it has no present sacraments, and to end by striving to persuade men that the church is a body which lives by the obedience of Christ: to begin with a ministry which in its very constitution is the denial of sacraments, and to work up from that to a ministry which is sacramental: is not that a strange inversion? We take those things which we call fundamental and make them the coping stones of our building. We work up to our foundations.

When we forsake Christ and his apostles, we naturally fall into absurdities. We say that we appoint men as lay readers because they are not as we think sufficiently educated to be priests, and what do we appoint them to do? To take services of prayer and instruction! Which requires the greater theological education: to preach or to celebrate? to instruct others in the faith or to read devoutly a service carefully prepared and printed? If it is a matter of intellectual education, there is no question which demands the greater education. So we appoint men to do the more difficult whom we declare to be insufficiently educated to perform the simpler act. I remember meeting in Canada a man of position in the State. He said to me: 'I go on Sunday fifty miles to take services, and I said to the bishop one day: "If you send me to take services, why not enable me to do it properly" And he answered: "For that you would have to go to a theological college." ' To publish to the whole world that a man is sufficiently educated and sufficiently godly to preach the faith, and at the same time that he is either not sufficiently educated or not sufficiently godly to perform a very simple rite which Christ told all His disciples to observe, is to insult both the man and those to whom he is sent to minister.

We do not present the truth when we provide congregations with lay readers and say that men who want sacraments can get them by making journeys or waiting for an itinerant cleric to visit them. It is by no means always the case that either of those courses is open. Many groups are never visited by itinerant clergy, and their members cannot travel to places where clergy reside. But the point is not whether men can or cannot 'get the sacraments,' but whether Christian men ought not by Christ's command and apostolic order to live all their lives, every day, in a society in which sacraments are inherently present. The church is more than sacraments only: the sacraments are the rites of the organized society; and the faithful ought to live in that society. It is not the question whether they actually frequent the sacraments daily or weekly or occasionally: the question is whether they ought not to live in a society in which the sacraments are always at hand. That is the truth which we ought to present; and we can only present it by establishing the church in every place where there are faithful church people. If the faithful few were duly constituted as churches with their own ministers, then the others would have something tangible and definite, a real church at hand to which to join themselves, when they were converted and realized their own need. If they saw that wherever there were communicants of the church, there the church was established, two or three of the communicants being ordained to minister regularly and to direct the affairs of the church; if they saw that there was no need to wait for a paid cleric, they would get a new conception of the church and of the ordinances of Christ. They would see the church putting Baptism and the Lord's Supper where Christ put them, and where the Apostles put them, as fundamental rites of the church; they would see them in their simplicity as the bonds of Christian men one with another in Christ. They would see the church as a congregation of Christian people bound together by their observance of Christ's ordinances, not as a vague C of E of which Englishmen are, more or less, members by birth.

If I am told that our people do not want sacraments, I answer that there are many who do; and I ask why they should be deprived because there are others who do not. Our people are accused of vagueness and instability in their religion; and can we cure that disease by pandering to it, and depriving those who are neither vague nor unstable? If men lament that church-people do not want sacraments, it may well be answered that the bishops encourage them in that attitude when they appoint lay readers to have charge of congregations for more than three-quarters, more than nine-tenths, more than eleven-twelfths, of the year.

This use of lay readers is one of the most striking and serious marks of the church today. But everyone knows its cause. It is not due to any real disbelief in Christ's commands or in apostolic order on the part of the bishops: it is due simply to a tradition carried from England that the trained stipendiary priesthood must be retained at all costs as the only priesthood permissible in the church.

X

Teaching

When I have urged the necessity of establishing the local church with its own ministers and its own local observance of Christ's sacraments, I have often met with the response: 'You lay too much stress on the sacraments and you ignore the ministry of teaching; you say that communicants untrained in theological colleges could be ordained priests, and celebrate the Holy Communion, and lead the local church; but you ignore the necessity of teaching. Untrained priests could not teach.' I have heard men talk about the creation of a class of 'masspriests.' I have heard more than one bishop speak as though the ordination of voluntary clergy would be the creation of a body of men ordained to celebrate holy mysteries, but not to teach. The question, then, of the teaching of the church in dioceses overseas is one of great importance to our present discussion.

Let us begin by considering the present position in the scattered groups overseas. Let us first look at those groups which no priest ever visits regularly. What teaching do they now receive? None at all. Now suppose that a bishop visited such a group, and, finding there one or two faithful men, ordained them to minister to themselves and their neighbours. The argument before us maintains that those men are not sufficiently trained to preach the Faith or to teach one another; but that they are sufficiently godly and sufficiently well educated to celebrate. The bishop who uses it is taking it for granted that he would license men to celebrate, but not to preach or to teach. These men, then, would celebrate: the little congregation would enjoy the sacraments of Christ; they would live in an organized church where services were duly held; but no one would be licensed to preach.

I ask, then, would they not be better off, even in the matter of teaching, under those circumstances than they are now, when they have nothing at all? Putting the preaching of sermons on one side, it is impossible to imagine that these priests would not read the services of Matins and Evensong as well as celebrate: for no bishop would license a man to celebrate and not to read Matins and Evensong. Is there, then, no teaching in our services of Morning and Evening

Prayer apart from the sermon? Is there no teaching in our Office of Holy Communion apart from the sermon? I cannot conceive any man maintain that argument. Whatever one may say of a Mass celebrated in a language which the people do not understand, or of Offices repeated in a language which the people do not understand, I think that it is quite impossible to maintain that the reading of our services of Morning and Evening Prayer, with their regular Biblical lessons, are not full of teaching of the very highest order, or that the celebration of the Holy Communion according to our Liturgy is not teaching of the very highest order.

Again, would these priests of whom the bishop is thinking not prepare their children and the children of members of their congregation for Confirmation, and, in preparing them, would they not teach them the Church Catechism? I can scarcely imagine a bishop ordaining a priest and refusing to allow him to prepare children for Confirmation by teaching them the Catechism. But is not that teaching, and teaching of a very high order? I know that someone may be found to say that such men could teach the Church Catechism, but could not teach it intelligently because they have not been to a theological college; but the objection seems to me simply absurd. Children are extremely well prepared for Confirmation by people who have not been to a theological college. The Church Catechism is not unintelligible to people of ordinary intelligence.

Putting the case, then, at its very worst, it seems to me that the gain is wholly on one side; but, as a matter of fact, that extreme statement of the case is exaggerated. If we look at the expansion of some of those strange sects which are spreading overseas, we see that their local leaders are not men trained in special colleges, yet we cannot possibly say that men who join those sects receive no instruction. The members of them are often well instructed in their religion, and they nearly all get their instruction for themselves. We may say that the teaching is erroneous, but that is not to the point. The point is that, where people join these sects, they do not remain ignorant of the teaching of the sect. They do not remain ignorant, largely because it is impossible for them to rely on a teacher who turns up once a month or once a quarter, but are compelled to hold their own services and instruct themselves and one another from literature provided at their own expense. Why should we imagine that church people alone, when put into a position to hold their own proper services, would learn nothing and teach one another nothing, or, if they learnt anything, would learn only heresy? Is there any reason whatsoever for that assumption? As a matter of fact, a large number would be men of good education, and the most ignorant could read, and there are excellent manuals which the bishops could recommend. Why should churchmen alone be so utterly obtuse that they can learn nothing for themselves, and must depend entirely upon the sermons of a man who has had a year or two's training in a theological college? Would ordination incline them to wish to know nothing? On the contrary, the position of authority and responsibility would certainly move them to inquire and to learn more than they have ever known before. No one can doubt it.

I suggest that the Bible itself is a book of teaching for the church, and might be read as such, not in snippets, but in large complete passages. One priest in Canada told me that he read to his people the lives of the patriarchs and the prophets and the life of our Lord as complete biographies, and that years afterwards he had been told that more profit had been derived from those readings than from any sermons that he had preached. I suggest that bishops might send books of instruction in the Faith, sound theological writings, to voluntary clergy, who, like my friends, did not feel able to preach, and that from such connected reading the whole congregation would derive immense benefit.

The question of teaching is really not the difficulty. The difficulty is that church people are taught to rely entirely upon somebody else to provide everything for them. The ordination of voluntary clergy would break down that deplorable habit in the local churches. And many more men than we imagine, not only could, but would, read and prepare and preach very good sermons if they felt themselves responsible for the religious life of their local church. The sermons might not indeed be the type of theological sermon with which we are familiar, but they would be extremely practical and closely related to the life of the little community from which they sprang. They would be far more intelligible to their hearers than many of the sermons preached by the clergy trained in the theological schools.

When it is a question of ordaining voluntary clergy untrained in theological colleges, this question of preaching is always thrust into the foreground as an objection; but when it is a question of appointing lay readers, the very men who say that they could not trust a voluntary cleric to teach because he has not been to a theological college, appoint a lay reader to do that very thing, in spite of the fact that he has not been to a theological college. They attempt to establish the church on the basis of lay preachers, while they argue that they cannot establish the church with the proper ministers because there are no men capable of preaching.

N

XI

Domination[1]

The foreign domination which we maintain and approve in the mission field is not a personal domination of individual missionaries, but a system which we deliberately uphold. We keep all spiritual authority in our hands. In the last resort the episcopate holds the keys; and we are determined not to establish any native episcopate until such time as we think fit. Foreign bishop succeeds foreign bishop in our missions with painful regularity. In the last few years a few native bishops have been consecrated, but these are nearly all assistant bishops, and all sit in a house of bishops in which foreigners are in a large majority. And nearly all, if not all, the native clergy depend for their livelihood, directly or indirectly, upon foreigners. We have made our position as secure as we possibly can. In the last resort, we are supreme.[2]

That domination is a domination which holds fast all spiritual authority. We defend it as good for the church. We hold it on the ground that we believe and maintain that the native Christians are not fit to be trusted with it, and that we are. It is a fact of history, and ought to be treated as a fact, and as a very unpleasant fact.

It is not as though such a domination had any warrant in Holy Scripture, or in the early history of the Church, or even in the history of the conversion of our own country. No such evidence can be produced. The Bible teaching is plain: the apostles established, not mis-

[1] [It will be remembered that Allen was writing in 1929-30. There has been much progress since then. It is unlikely that Allen would have assessed this progress as warmly as we often do ourselves; he might draw attention to the fact that in 1960 if there are African diocesan bishops in West Africa, in East Africa there are only assistants and in South Africa no African bishops at all. Ed.]

[2] I hope that no one will imagine that I am advocating the consecration of native bishops to hold such sees as our bishops now occupy in the mission field. Seeing that I have argued that those vast areas which we call 'sees' and 'parishes' overseas, and in the mission field, are gigantic absurdities, I certainly do not suggest that natives should be consecrated, or ordained, to occupy them. Of course, I am speaking only of local bishops and local clergy with small dioceses and small parishes, where the bishop can be in the very closest relationship with *all* his clergy and their people, and the priests the familiar pastors of *all* their flock, known intimately by every one of them.

sions, but churches fully equipped for growth and expansion. In the history of the first six centuries it is rare to find an example of a foreign missionary bishop succeeded in his see by another foreigner. In our own history, St Augustine was consecrated bishop, not of England, but of Canterbury. He was consecrated in AD 597; seven years later there were two other bishops, in Rochester and London. Forty years later (AD 644) a native was consecrated to Rochester, and he by himself consecrated the first native bishop of Canterbury in AD 654, and at that time all the bishops derived from Augustine were natives; that is within sixty years of St Augustine's landing. Of course, nearly all the clergy were natives.

If we examine Bishop Stubb's *Registrum Sacrum Anglicanum*, we find that the last of the Augustinian mission to be consecrated was Honorius (AD 627) to Canterbury. In that year Felix, a Burgundian, was consecrated to Dunwich. After that the only foreign bishops were Theodore of Tarsus (AD 668) to Canterbury, Agilbert (AD 650) to Dorchester, and Leutherius (AD 670) to Winchester. Both these last were from Paris, which was much nearer in every respect to the south of England than Canton or Shanghai to Peking. Between the years AD 669 and AD 687 Theodore consecrated twenty bishops, of whom only one was not a native of this island.

If we look at the sees established—Lichfield was founded in AD 656, and all the names of its bishops are native; Lindsey was founded in AD 678, and the names of all its bishops are native; at Dunwich, after Felix the Burgundian, all the names are native; at Elmham (AD 673 —AD 1055) they are all native; at Worcester (AD 680—AD 1095) they are all native; at Hereford (AD 676—AD 1079) they are all native. In fact, see after see was established, and see after see was established with a native bishop.

It is as though we had sent a small mission to North China, one member of it had been Bishop of Peking, one of Tientsin, and one of Yung Ching; and that within sixty years of their arrival all those sees and any others that had been established were all occupied by natives; and, if we consider Peking as the metropolitan see, its occupant had himself been consecrated by a native. If men speak of civilization as they do, China is a far more civilized land than was England in those days. I ought to have chosen my comparison rather in Africa than in China, if I had designed to make the comparison close in the matter of civilization.

Still, it is not the mere fact that we are foreigners which gives to the outcry its bitterness. Many churches have deliberately chosen a foreigner to be their bishop; many congregations prefer a foreign pastor to be in charge. The cause lies deeper even than that. To find out its secret we must go back to the beginnings of the missionary activity of the church, against which educated young natives now kick.

In the beginning the foreign missionaries felt it to be their duty to guide and direct the lives of their first converts; they settled down as pastors and teachers: they let it be felt that any religious activity on the part of their converts must be exercised only under their authority. That was a severe check upon any spontaneous activity. The missionaries were influenced by kindly motives, they were devoted to the welfare of their flock, but the flock was in their care; and they taught by word and deed that all expression must be directed by them. No one foresaw the consequences. For a long time the converts were glad that it should be so; as many of them still are. They reaped many advantages: they did not know that they were bound; they did not feel any chain. But as time went on the younger and abler men began to grow restless, as we see today in India. They did not know what was the matter with them, but they began to feel tied up. They were really tied up by their own incapacity to express themselves, an incapacity induced by the surrender of their fathers' powers and by their own early education. They felt bound, and they began to seek, as they are now seeking, for some explanation of their uneasy restlessness. Naturally they turned upon their foreign teachers. 'It is you who hold us down: it is your insistence upon your Western creeds which has crippled our thought: it is you who will not put us into positions of authority: it is you who will not trust us with the money which you have taught us is necessary for any religious expansion.' The missionaries had believed that they were training these men for freedom: they found that they had only exasperated them, and driven them into revolt; and that they were not prepared for freedom, nor had the self-discipline which would enable them to use it well: they saw that those who cried out most loudly against their domination had little idea what they would do with liberty, because they did not know how to express themselves. When, by way of experiment and to assuage the rising tide of fury, they devolved responsibility upon Indians, nothing great was done. The men who thirsted for liberty did not know how

to use it. They could only follow, still doing as well as they could precisely what their foreign leaders had done. And they could still only
cry out that they were in chains, and that they wanted more authority.
They had learnt from their foreign teachers that money was all important, and so control of finance was their chief desire: of true spiritual self-expression they were ignorant: they had nothing to express:
their souls were full of the teachings and examples of the foreign missionaries and nothing else could come out of them.

That is, I believe, the true domination of the foreign missionaries,
not so much a lust to keep power in their own hands, as an incapacity
to see that to nurse converts in the beginning, and to act as their pastors, is to become lords over them; and that to stifle their first unrecognized, unspoken instinct for self-expression, is to make certain
first of sterility and then of sterile revolt. The problem for us now is
not so much how to yield to the clamour of discontent, as to know
how to escape from repeating the same mistake again. We are making
the same mistake in every mission where we are making new converts.
We are still becoming pastors and lords. We still tacitly but effect-
ually check any spontaneous expression on their part; we still bind
catechists, teachers, evangelists, the whole church, in the bonds of
our salaries; we are still planting elsewhere the seeds of the same
difficulty which we experience in India today. It is only a question
of time and education when those seeds will produce the same fruit
everywhere. But there is still space for amendment. The discontent
of which we hear so much is at present the discontent of a very small
minority. The fear is lest it may become, as it must become, unless
we amend, the discontent of a majority.

We must face the truth that to allow our fear lest natives should
misuse spiritual liberty and authority to prevent us from giving them
authority is to suppress the instinct for self-expression, the desire to
propagate, and that is to do a very serious wrong to our converts, in
spite of the fact that in the beginning it looks like kindness and reasonable care for their well-being. In the later stages what they think that
they need is authority to control finance and policy, what they really
need is power born of the exercise of authority to govern themselves
in the earliest stages, and to expand without any question of stipends.
That is the reason why it is desperately important to establish the
first converts in any new place with full spiritual authority whilst yet
they have no irrational eagerness to reject the creeds and all things

Western simply because they are associated in their minds with a foreign domination.

That sterility should follow the observance of such doctrines is only what we ought to expect. And it does follow. We are tied by the numbers of our trained and paid workers. We can never train and pay enough. One of the most pitiable sights that I ever saw in my life was an archdeacon from Africa lamenting that he had seen open doors unentered because he had no recruits to send in; one of the most pitiable letters that I have ever read was a letter from Bishop Weston of Zanzibar, bewailing the falling off of a fund by a few thousand pounds because it would stop all advance. Of course all advance depends upon money, when we depend upon paid workers for any advance. Teach men as one of their first lessons in the gospel that pastoral work and evangelistic work ought to be paid, and will they not believe that? They would all believe it if the Holy Ghost did not dispute our teaching. It is a powerful proof of the presence and grace of the Holy Ghost that they do not all believe it and act accordingly.

When we enter a new field there is often a rapid advance, and great numbers are converted to Christ. That goes on until the people have grasped the meaning and force of our teaching about stipends, and our insistence upon keeping spiritual authority in our own hands. Then the movement towards the church gradually dies down, and the ground is spoiled. Opposition to foreign domination takes the place of eager interest in the teaching of Christ, and thereafter the work is left to paid mission agents.

XII

The Lesson to be Learnt

If we are to maintain the stipendiary system as the one and only system permissible in England today, we must do so, not on the negative ground that to ordain voluntary clergy would be to break a church tradition, but on the positive ground that its maintenance is obedience to the mind of Christ, is in harmony with the Spirit of Christ when He ordained His sacraments for His people.

The question before us is not whether we are being driven by a shortage of clergy to make up the deficiency with a miserable 'second best', but whether the shortage of clergy is leading us to a larger truth. The question before us is not whether it is lawful to ordain men who earn their living by some other means than their clerical profession, but whether the restriction of ordination to men who live solely by their clerical profession is the best way in which we can fulfil Christ's word here today.

We have seen that overseas the tradition manifestly hinders men from living in the full life of the Church as Christ ordained. There it manifestly robs them of His grace. We must inquire now whether the same consequences follow its strict maintenance at home. Here as overseas we may be on the eve of a new and fuller conception of the life of the church and the relation which ought to exist between the clergy and the laity.

My readers must have observed throughout this book how I have been constantly struggling against a division within the church itself, a division between those who offer and those who accept spiritual privileges, protesting against such expressions as: 'the church must send,' 'the church must provide services for' groups of Christian people overseas, who really ought to be the church in the places where they live; protesting against that conception which represents a body of Christian people in a place waiting for some other body to send a man to minister to them, helpless unless such a man is sent. Again and again I have insisted that in the beginning the local church was a society of men bound together by their faith in Christ and their communion with Him and with one another in the observance of the sacred rites which He ordained for them. It was an organized society with its own officers chosen from its own members. It was a unity.

But now the church is divided. By slow degrees the clerics organized themselves as a distinct body within the church. For centuries no apparent harm resulted. The laity were almost wholly uneducated, and their clergy were for the most part their sons or their brothers, educated in a monastic school, or members of an order established in their midst. But as time went on the professional spirit grew in the clerical order and the division became dangerous.

Not priesthood, but clericalism was the danger. It was not a lofty conception of priesthood, but a strictly professional maintenance of a closed order with its own privileges which emphasized the division. As a separate body within the church the clergy aimed at making that division between themselves and the laity sharp and clear. It was their part to rule in the church; it was their part to minister in holy things; it was the duty of the laity to hearken and to receive.

So long as the laity were wholly uneducated this was no doubt the best way in which the church could observe the Lord's commands; but as education grew in these modern days there appeared a certain strangeness. The church had really returned to the condition of the first century, with this difference: then the clergy were of the church, and were no better educated than many members of their congregations; now the clergy are no better educated than many members of their congregations, but they are not of the church which they serve: they are members of a distinct body within the church and they are sent to minister to a church which does not know them intimately.

There is today a strangeness in this which often escapes our notice; though I think we are nearly all dimly conscious of it. When a good cleric is sent to a new parish he begins by trying to make friends with the people. But is it not strange that a society should have as its officer a man whom its members do not know, a man who must begin by making their acquaintance? Societies do not naturally first appoint a man, and then find out by experience whether he is their friend, and whether they can trust him. Naturally their minister should be a man well known among them before he becomes their minister: he becomes their minister because he is known and trusted by them. But the local church today is like a school for which masters and teachers are chosen from a professional body; only that the local church today is no longer in the position of the uneducated

child; and the division between the local congregation and the pastor
so sent is the division between master and boys with this difference,
that the boys know that they are grown up, and that many of them
are better educated than the master.

In a dim way the clergy have for many years past recognized this,
and they have sought to give some place to the laity, almost any place
which did not seem to touch their own peculiar function. They established church and diocesan conferences, they established paro-
chial church councils on which the laity might express themselves.
They did everything except recognize that the church is one body
and not two.

A severe lesson was necessary to teach us that the church is one
body and that the church cannot be divided between those who offer
and those who receive without disaster. So long as every congregation in England had its ministers we deceived ourselves with a fiction
of unity. We admitted that the church was the laity with its clergy;
we preached that in our pulpits and we said in every case: here is the
church, here is the laity with its clergy. Thus we concealed the fundamental division, and stopped the mouths of any who might have
said: These are not *our* clergy: they are men sent to look after us, with
or without our will; they are not *of* us. That was possible only so long
as every congregation had proper ministers in charge. But the shortage of clergy has already driven us from that position: there are today congregations which have not clergy, in that proper sense.

We have multiplied all over the country mission rooms where services are held. These mission rooms imply distinct congregations.
When an altar is set up in an outlying district of a parish it proves
that a new congregation has come into existence. The parish priest
goes there when he can and celebrates the Holy Communion for the
people who attend that hall as a separate congregation. A single
priest is, in fact, in charge of two, or three, or more separate congregations, which he visits as best he can. Churches are being established
without priests of their own: they have a third or fourth of a priest.
In the absence of the priest in charge, whilst he is attending the other
congregations, either a lay reader conducts the services, or no services are held.

What I suppose that we ought to look for if we ordain voluntary
clergy is that every congregation would have its local voluntary
clergy in itself and of itself. Stipendiaries would be in the position of

rural deans looking after the conduct of a group of country churches, or of a small town parish with some neighbouring country churches, or of a large town parish with its local churches (the present mission rooms, or mission churches); and these stipendiaries would have at their own parish churches a body of voluntary clergy to assist them, so that they would be at liberty to go round to visit the local churches frequently.

Congregations of Christians deprived of their proper church organization naturally seek some other bond of union, some other means of expressing their common life. Though many seem to think it quite normal and encourage it, yet I have heard some good clerics and laymen lament that the congregations of mission halls tend to use them as social centres rather than as places in which the religious life of the people finds its proper expression in common worship. They organize whist drives and concerts rather than religious services. That is inevitable. The congregation must have some common life, some common expression of its life, and the proper expression of that life is denied to it. The hall was not built, the foundations of the congregation were not laid, on the foundation of Christ. The first members could not organize their own religious life as the life of a community bound together as a body in the faith of Christ, to live under Christ's direction a life in hope of the glory of God. All such idea of the church is separated from them by the fact that they have no proper ministers. For any such conception of their life as members of a church they are entirely dependent upon a cleric who comes when he can to visit them. In themselves, if they are to find any common bond, that bond must be found elsewhere, in something which they can provide themselves. Teas and whist drives and concerts take the place of the Holy Communion and services of instruction in the faith. What else can they do? All religious life is dependent upon a cleric who has others to care for. A gulf is then created between the life of the congregation as a religious body and the life of the congregation as a social body. Many people enter into its life as a social body who do not enter into its life as a religious body. Confusion reigns. There is no unity binding together the members as members of a religious body, with definite aims and objects and hopes and laws of conduct unknown to the world outside. There is no church organization in the true sense.

We cannot answer that by saying that the members of the church which meet in the mission room are all members of the church in the parish, and can attend the central parish church. It is true in a sense. It is true in the sense that all members of the church in a parish are members of the church in a diocese, and can attend the cathedral services if they like. The parishes were organized as parishes with their own proper clergy, because there was some local reason sufficient to make the organization of the parish with its own ministers desirable or necessary. But precisely the same local considerations led to the establishment of the mission room as a centre at which the faithful who lived near it might meet to unite in the rites and services which are the proper rites and services of Christian folk. They were not in sufficiently close touch with the parish church for that church to be their proper centre. If, then, the mission hall was established at all as the home of a faithful congregation it ought to have been established properly, so that it might be the religious home of the faithful. Then there could have been true church life for the congregation which met in it.

Neither in grouped parishes nor in mission halls can there be the church life which Christ ordained when He instituted His sacraments as rites for His church. This is more than a question of the frequency of celebrations: it touches the conception of life in the church which the observance of the rites ordained by Christ imply and the apostles set forth in their teaching. Life in the church is more than attendance at services. It is life in an organized society which knows itself as a society set in the world to live the life which Christ designed for it; it means life in a body in which the sacraments are inherent, organized so that the sacraments may be ever present in it; and that ought to be as true of the local as it is true of the universal church. The universal Church must be represented in the local church. Wherever then an altar is set up, wherever a congregation is gathered together, there the Church should be in its fullness, that its members may live in the life of the Church, not in a maimed and partial form, but in its fullness. The division of the church into those who offer and those who receive spiritual privileges denied that, and the consequences are growing increasingly serious every day.

Today the fact is plain for all who will choose to see it. The stipendiary system sets the clergy over against the laity. The church is torn asunder. Christians are as lost sheep, utterly helpless, unless a stipendiary can be found to go to them, to look after them; they are babies incapable of looking after themselves; they are spiritual paupers here in our own land. They are not really such; but the stipendiary system insists that they shall be treated as such; and under that treatment they appear to be such. I went to one of the new districts in the London area and I asked my hosts how they liked it. The moment that I spoke they responded. But what could they do?

It is this tradition, which spiritually pauperizes our people, divides the church, compels us to bow down to Mammon, and makes void the word of Christ, which we must cast aside today; for we can no longer pretend that it assists us to keep the word of Christ even at home.

We cannot go back and break down the division between the professional clergy and the laity, but we can build a bridge between the two. That bridge voluntary clergy would form. The conception of the church as one must be recovered by the faithful, nor merely by accepting a cleric sent to them, but by recognizing themselves as the body of Christ, and finding amongst themselves the best men among them to be their ministers. Then they would know their unity with the clergy, and all men would know it.

This reform could be brought to pass without interfering with the elaborate legal system of titles and endowments and advowsons and presentations and institutions. The bishop has only to ordain voluntary clergy, who are outside all that system, and the thing is done. The legal stipendiary must then work with his fellow clergy, and working with his fellow clergy, who are really of the laity in a sense in which he can never be, he must inevitably share some of the advantages which they bring, whilst they inevitably share some of the advantages which his special education and training bring. So the division of the church would be healed, not by going back and trying to undo the past, which is always vain, but by going forward.

We should not have perceived the evil of this division of the church had there been no shortage of stipendiary clergy. It is the shortage which is compelling us to see it. By the mercy of God we are finding it difficult to maintain the stipendiary system, which is the key which locks the door of that division: and we are being slowly forced to see the division which Bishop Creighton saw as a 'terrible' thing.

For years we have prayed for clergy and laboured to get sufficient money to maintain the division of the church. All the recommendations of the Archbishops' Committees were based on the assumption that the division was divinely right. They took it for granted that the provision of clergy for the church must be in the form with which they were familiar. They looked for causes which might explain the falling off of the supply of young men in the hope that by removing the apparent obstacle the difficulty might be overcome, and things continue as they were in the church. But that there was anything fundamentally wrong, that the old order was passing away because it had served it purpose and that a new order was at hand, that never entered their minds. The whole purpose and intention of all the efforts that have been made to provide a sufficiency of stipendiary clergy has been based upon this initial assumption that the stipendiary system and the ordination of youth has been established on a divine foundation; that it expresses the mind and will of God for the organization and establishment of His Church.

All our prayers and all their labours have been answered by an increasing shortage. We must learn the lesson which God is plainly teaching us. We have prayed and laboured for clergy, hoping that God would fill our theological colleges with young men and inspire the laity to provide for them; but that would have taught us nothing. God's answers to our prayers are often greater than we expect; for He gives more than we desire, and often in a form which we do not like. If He had given us what we asked as we asked, we should not have seen that we cannot establish the Church throughout the world as we have been trying to do in the past. The denial of our requests in the form in which we hoped must open our eyes. God is plainly teaching us how we can establish the Church throughout the world, by showing us that our familiar type of cleric cannot by itself suffice for us at home.

7

*To the Parishioners of
Chalfont St Peter*

Editorial Note
This letter explains itself. It is included not only for its biographical interest, but also because the issues which Allen raised are now, more than fifty years later, very much alive, not least under the form of 'baptismal rigorism.'

My Friends,

I am very anxious that you should all understand the reason why I am resigning my work here.

From the earliest times the Church has always asserted her right to ordain the conditions on which she admits people to her privileges and to reject those who deliberately and persistently break her laws, which are the laws of God. This principle is definitely asserted in several places (see the rubrics before the Holy Communion and the Burial Offices) and tacitly implied everywhere in our own Prayer Book. But in process of time it has come to pass in England that on the one hand nearly everybody in the country is, at least in name, Christian, and on the other hand the machinery by which the law of the Church was intended to be made effective has fallen into disuse, and in practice it is now almost impossible to enforce it. Thus the widest inclusion of every kind and class of man has been accompanied with a relaxation of the means by which the morality of the society was maintained. The result is that it has become customary for people who make no profession of believing the doctrines of the Church, or who make no profession of keeping the laws of the Church, to demand and use her offices as if they were theirs by natural inheritance.

In consequence we see the strange and painful sight of men and women who habitually neglect their religious duties, or who openly deny the truth of the Creeds, or who by the immorality of their lives openly defy the laws of God, standing up as sponsors in a Christian church, before a Christian minister, in the presence of a Christian congregation and as representatives of the Church on behalf of a new-born child solemnly professing their desire for Holy Baptism, their determination to renounce the world, the flesh and the devil, their stedfast faith in the Creed and their willingness to obey God's holy will, whilst they know, and everyone in the church knows, that they themselves neither do, nor intend to do, any of these things. Then they are solemnly directed to see that the child is taught the faith and practice which they set at nought. Or again, we see that sad sight of the dead body of a man who all his life denied the claim of Jesus

Christ, or who set at nought the moral laws of God, brought into Christ's church in order that a service may be read over his body which, whilst alive, he utterly scorned.

I am, of course, aware that no priest is legally bound to admit any but communicants as sponsors, but immorality of life is no bar to the legal use of the Burial or Marriage Services. In the one case the law, in the other custom (more powerful often than law) compels the acquiescence of a priest in a practice which he cannot justify.

For no one can justify these things. They undermine the fundamental principle that the Church stands for morality of life; they suggest the horrible doctrine that the Church does not regard morality as an essential part of religion. They embolden men to go on living in sin in the hope that they will not be rejected at the last. Ignorant men speak as if Christ and His Church had nothing to offer which is not the natural inheritance of every Englishman, nor any right to lay down rules and conditions on which those gifts may be obtained; because they see every man, whatever his belief or his character, admitted without question to the highest privileges which the Church can bestow.

They bring the services of the Church into disrepute and make them an open scorn. There is a horrible danger in using holy services in the case of people who deny by word or deed all that is implied in them. People think and speak as if the services of the Church were 'mere forms.' God is not mocked. Services used in the name of God are high and holy things, sources of real blessing, and to degrade them into 'mere forms' is a serious offence, of which the consequences are terribly real.

Now, as parish priest, it is my duty to uphold morality and to defend religion, and I feel that in acquiescing in these customs I am neither upholding morality nor defending religion. I cannot satisfy my conscience by exhorting people to refrain from doing what is wrong, and then in the last resort, if they will not listen to me, giving way to them. I have done that, I fear, too often. I have carried my exhortations to the point of seriously annoying some of you. I have entreated and advised till we both were weary, but you knew and I knew that in the end I could not absolutely refuse. In one or two cases I regret that I did not refuse; but my mind was not clear as to the right course, and I preferred to obey the law. Now I am clear: I cannot and will not do these things any longer.

I am well aware of the serious character of my decision. I am not ignorant that I cannot act as I am determined to act, and yet hold any benefice in England. It has indeed been urged upon me by some that I might retain my position and wait until some serious case arose and I was forced by law to resign. I feel sure that I could, if I would, do that. I believe that so long as I acted wisely and discreetly, I should enjoy again, as I have enjoyed in the past, the sympathy and support of every communicant in this church. But that would not be right. Legal processes are not easily understood by the poor and ignorant, and some of those who would most bitterly resent my refusal to obey the law are very poor. I will not do in the case of a poor man an action for which he cannot force me to pay the legal penalty. I think the poor man would feel a just resentment if he were treated in spiritual matters in a way which a rich man could resist by process of law. And more than that, it seems to me scarcely honest to hold and enjoy the emoluments of an office of which I deliberately refuse to perform the legal obligations.

If that were not enough I should be compelled to resign by my sense of the very serious nature of resistance to law. I believe that passive resistance to law is sometimes a duty, but I do not believe that it is a light matter or one to be undertaken without the most serious consideration and the most deliberate determination to bear cheerfully the penalty whatever the penalty may be. A passive resistance which costs little or nothing is a passive resistance which I despise and dread. It tends to undermine an authority which the Bible tells us proceeds from God, and it is only justified by the strongest moral obligations and the most complete self-surrender to serious consequences. For me to resist the law whilst I enjoyed my office, trusting to your sympathy and support to save me from the consequences, would be, in my opinion, to commit that offence.

One form of protest, and only one, remains open to me, and that is to decline to hold an office in which I am liable to be called upon to do what I feel to be wrong. I have chosen that. I have resigned.

There remains one serious objection to all that I have said and it is an objection of which I am profoundly sensible. You are all well aware that a great many good and thoughtful men hold these positions and perform these offices without reproach, and you know that one will be found to take my place when I am gone. I am very anxious to explain this so far as I can. For the past three years I have been restrained from taking any action solely by the feeling that I must be wrong in refusing to do what so many good men can conscientiously do. I felt that I could not face the charge that I was setting myself up to be better and wiser than these men when in very truth I knew that I was not. They argue, if I understand them rightly, that they can do more good by continuing in their cures to perform these offices than by any other course. They hope to raise the standard of public opinion in these matters by continual teaching, and they can point to many signs that the standard of opinion is being so raised. They believe that it is their duty in a world of imperfection, to tolerate the imperfection which they cannot remove whilst they strive after the perfection which they desire. They think that refusal to perform these services is contrary to law, and that to resign rather than to obey is a counsel of despair which would reduce all church work in England to chaos. They plead that acts done by the ministers of the Church are done in the name and with the authority of the whole Church, and that therefore no individual priest can be held individually responsible for acts so done. They say that the Church as a matter of history has never been free from these difficulties; that we must look forward to the quiet growth of an enlightened public opinion, and that meanwhile it is the duty of a good minister to do his best under the conditions in which he now finds himself.

These arguments are sufficient to satisfy the minds of many good men: I can only say that they do not satisfy me. I have repeatedly told you from this pulpit that I believe we ought always at all costs to act according to the dictates of our conscience—that when our conscience tells us that a thing is wrong we ought not to do it whatever the consequences may be. When a difficult question arises, when our conscience protests against some action which is commonly done by a great many good men, I think we ought carefully to inquire whether our conscience is well informed (for a conscience may be morbid or misinformed), we ought to take time and pains to make sure that we are not suffering from a delusion; but if after all that careful examination our conscience still persists in forbidding us to do it, we must obey. It is better to do anything, to suffer anything, rather than to live under the condemnation of that voice which speaks to us with the authority of God.

And I believe further that in the end it will be found that no man can better fulfil his duty to others than by strictly observing that rule. It may appear now as if obedience to conscience and the service of the church in this place were in opposition, that to obey conscience in resigning is to abandon all hope of useful work. But I am persuaded that in the end it will be made plain that these two things which now appear to be in opposition are really one, and that I can do no service to you so true as to refuse to serve you in this. I believe that Christ's teaching about simplicity of aim, singleness of eye, is directed to just such difficulties as these; that He meant to teach us to refuse to be blinded by doctrines of expediency, by side issues; to do simply and obediently what He tells us, and that if we do that we shall find that in the end we have not missed the other. I believe that in resigning I am seeking not merely my own salvation, but your best interests and the interests of the church of which I am a minister.

I resign with very deep regret. I have valued most highly your sympathy, your forbearance, your ungrudging help, and as time goes on, I shall more and more feel the loss of it.

I have asked the Bishop to declare the vacancy at Christmas, and I have asked the patrons, S. John's College in Oxford, to use all possible urgency that is agreeable with care in seeking the right man to supply my place.

Till Christmas I shall continue my work here. Then I must seek work where it may please God to call me.

Meanwhile, I commend myself, the Bishop, the patrons and the parish to your earnest prayers. You will pray, I am sure, for me, that I may be guided aright. You will pray that it may please God to send to this parish a faithful and true pastor.

And this may He do for His mercy's sake.

Believe me,

Your sincere friend,

ROLAND ALLEN

Bibliography

Bibliography

I. BOOKS BY ROLAND ALLEN

1. *The Siege of the Peking Legations.* London: Smith, Elder. 1901. pp. xi+304.

2. *Missionary Methods: St Paul's or Ours?* London: Robert Scott, 1912. Re-issued, London: World Dominion Press, 1930, 1949, 1956. pp. xxiv+230. Re-set, and with a memoir by Alexander McLeish, London: World Dominion Press, 1960; pp. 192.

3. *Missionary Principles.* London: Robert Scott, 1913; New York: Fleming H. Revell, 1913, under title *Essential Missionary Principles.* pp. 168.

4. *Pentecost and the World: The Revelation of the Holy Spirit in 'The Acts of the Apostles.'* London: Oxford University Press, 1917. pp. 91.

5. *Educational Principles and Missionary Methods: The Application of Educational Principles to Missionary Evangelism.* London: Robert Scott, 1919. pp. xxii+138.

6. *Missionary Survey as an Aid to Intelligent Co-operation in Foreign Missions.* (Written in collaboration with Thomas Cochrane.) London: Longmans, Green, 1920. pp. xxii+183.

7. *Voluntary Clergy.* London: S.P.C.K., 1923. pp. vii+87.

8. *The Spontaneous Expansion of the Church and the Causes which Hinder It.* London: World Dominion Press, 1927. Re-issued, 1949 and 1956. pp. xii+212. Re-set, and with a memoir by Alexander McLeish. London: World Dominion Press, 1960. pp. 180.

9. *Voluntary Clergy Overseas: An Answer to the Fifth World Call.* Privately printed at Beaconsfield, 1928. pp. viii+143.

10. *The Case for Voluntary Clergy.* London: Eyre & Spottiswoode, 1940. pp. 315.

11. *S. J. W. Clark: A Vision of Foreign Missions.* London: World Dominion Press, 1937. pp. xxii+170.

2. PAMPHLETS BY ROLAND ALLEN

12. *Education in the Native Church.* London: World Dominion Press, 1926. Reprinted 1928. p. 26. (Reprinted from *World Dominion*, III, 3; III, 4; IV, 1.)

13. *Devolution and its Real Significance.* London: World Dominion

Press, 1927. pp. 30. (Chapter I, 'Devolution,' reprinted from *World Dominion*, V, 3; Chapter II, 'The Real Significance of "Devolution",' by Alexander McLeish, reprinted from *World Dominion*, V, 4.)

14. *Le Zoute: A Critical Review of 'The Christian Mission in Africa.'* London: World Dominion Press, 1927. pp. 39.

15. *The Establishment of the Church in the Mission Field: A Critical Dialogue.* London: World Dominion Press, 1927. pp. 31.

16. *Jerusalem: A Critical Review of 'The World Mission of Christianity.'* London: World Dominion Press, 1928. pp. 38.

17. *Non-Professional Missionaries.* Privately printed at Beaconsfield, 1929. pp. 31.

18. *The 'Nevius Method' in Korea.* London: World Dominion Press, 1930. pp. 16. (Chapter I, 'The Self-Support System in Korea', by Floyd E. Hamilton; Chapter II, 'The "Nevius Method" in Korea'; both reprinted from *World Dominion*, IX, 3.)

19. *Mission Activities Considered in Relation to the Manifestation of the Spirit.* First edition of uncertain date and publisher; second edition, World Dominion Press, 1930. pp. 33.

20. *The Place of 'Faith' in Missionary Evangelism.* London: World Dominion Press, 1930. pp. 23. (Reprinted from *World Dominion*, VIII, 3.)

21. *Discussion on Mission Education.* London: World Dominion Press, 1931. pp. 26. (Chapter I, 'A Crisis in Mission Work,' by H. Bunce; Chapter II, 'The Chinese Government and Mission Schools,' by Roland Allen; Chapter III, 'Education and the Missionary Task,' by a Mission Secretary—all reprinted from *World Dominion*, IX, 1; Chapter IV, 'Discussion—Mission Education,' being correspondence from H. F. Wallace, Roland Allen, S. Chen and Roland Allen—reprinted from *World Dominion*, IX, 2.)

3. ARTICLES BY ROLAND ALLEN

(a) In *World Dominion*

22. I, 3. June 1923. 'Brotherhood: A Contrast between Moslem Practice and Christian Ideals.' (A review of a pamphlet, *Brotherhood: Islam's and Christ's* by W. H. T. Gairdner.) pp. 92–4.

23. III, 2. March 1925. 'A Constitution for the Indian Church.' pp. 64–8.

24. III, 3. June 1925. 'The Essentials of an Indigenous Church.' pp. 110–17. (See No. 12.)

25. III, 4 September 1925. 'The Native Church and Mission Education.' pp. 153–60. (See No. 12.)

26. IV, 1. December 1925. 'Education in the Native Church.' pp. 37–44. (See No. 12.)

27. IV, 2. March 1926. 'The Maintenance of the Ministry in the Early Ages of the Church.' pp. 107–14.

28. IV, 3. June 1926. 'The Influence of Mission "Activities".' pp. 172–83.

29. IV, 4. September 1926. 'Spontaneous Expansion: The Terror of Missionaries.' pp. 218–24.

30. V, 2. April 1927. 'Voluntary Service in the Mission Field.' pp. 135–43.

31. V, 3. July 1927. 'Devolution—The Question of the Hour.' pp. 274–87. (See No. 13.)

32. VI, 2. April 1928. 'The Need for Non-Professional Missionaries.' pp. 195–201.

33. VI, 3. July 1928. 'The Work of Non-Professional Missionaries.' pp. 298–304.

34. VII, 1. January 1929. 'Business Man and Missionary Statesman: Sidney James Wells Clark: An Appreciation.' pp. 16–22.

35. VIII, 1. January 1930. 'The Place of Medical Missions.' pp. 34–42. (A review of *A Survey of Medical Missions in India*, published by the National Christian Council of India, Poona.)

36. VIII, 3. July 1930. 'The Place of "Faith" in Missionary Evangelism.' pp. 234–41. (See No. 20.)

37. IX, 1. January 1931. 'The Chinese Government and Mission Schools.' pp. 25–30. (See No. 21.)

38. IX, 3. July 1931. 'The "Nevius Method" in Korea.' pp. 252–8. (A review of *The Korean Church and the Nevius Method* by Charles Allen Clark, 1930.) (See No. 18.)

39. XI, 4. October 1933. 'The Application of Pauline Principles to Modern Missions.' pp. 352–7.

(*b*) In the *Chinese Recorder*

40. August 1925. 'The Essentials of an Indigenous Church.' pp. 491–6.

(c) In the *International Review of Missions*

41. October 1920. 'Islam and Christianity in the Sudan.' pp. 531–43.
42. April 1927. 'The Use of the Term "Indigenous".' pp. 262–70.

(d) In the *Church Missionary Review*

43. December 1918. 'The Christian Education of Native Churches.' pp. 398–405.
44. March 1920. 'The Relation between Medical, Educational and Evangelistic Work in Foreign Missions.' pp. 54–62.
45. December 1920. 'The Whole and the Parts in Foreign Missionary Administration.' pp. 329–37.

(e) In *The Cornhill*

46. December 1900. 'Of some of the Causes which led to the Preservation of the Foreign Legations in Peking.' pp. 754–76.
47. February 1901. 'Of some of the Conclusions which may be drawn from the Siege of the Foreign Legations in Peking.' pp. 202–12.

(f) In *The Church Quarterly Review*

48. January 1933. 'The Priesthood of the Church.' pp. 234–44.

(g) In *The Church Overseas*

49. April 1931. 'Voluntary Clergy and the Lambeth Conference.' pp. 145–53.

(h) Translations from the Swahili

50. 'The Story of Mbega' by Abdallah bin Hemedi bin Ali Liajjemi. Translated by Roland Allen. (A translation of Part I of *Habari zu Wakalindi*, published by U.M.C.A. Press, Msalabani, about 1900.)
    In *Tanganyika Notes and Records*, vol. 1 (1936), pp. 38–51; vol. 2 (1936), pp. 80–91; vol. 3 (1937), pp. 87–98.
51. 'Utenzi wa Kiyama': Special Supplement to *Tanganyika Notes and Records*, n.d. (about 1946?)
52. 'Utenzi wa Kiyama: The Release of the Prophet.' Supplement to the East African Swahili Committee's *Journal*, No. 26. Kampala 1956. pp. 72.
53. 'Utenzi wa Abdur Rahman' (probably to be published in 1960). 'Inkishafi.' *African Studies*, December 1946. pp. 243–9.

Index of Bible References

Index of Bible References